PREJUDICES IN DISGUISE

PREJU
IN DIS

ROBERT CRAFT

PREJUDICES IN DISGUISE

ARTICLES, ESSAYS, REVIEWS

ALFRED A. KNOPF NEW YORK 1974

THIS IS A BORZOI BOOK
PUBLISHED BY ALFRED A. KNOPF, INC.

Published in the United States by Alfred A. Knopf, Inc.,
New York, and simultaneously in Canada
by Random House of Canada Limited, Toronto.
Distributed by Random House, Inc., New York.

"Toward the Flame" and "The New Music: Sound and Sense" (*The New York Times*, April 5, 1970, and March 7, 1971) are published with the permission of *The New York Times*. Copyright © 1970/1971 by The New York Times Company.

The following appeared originally in the *New York Review of Books*: "*Moses and Aaron* at the Paris Opéra"; "Mahler the Modern"; "Letter from Nohant"; "Stravinsky's *Svadebka*: An Introduction"; "Stravinsky: Relevance and Problems of Biography"; "*Non Credo*: *Mass* by Leonard Bernstein"; and "Pay Dirt: Notes on the New Nudity." One part of "Elegy and Iambus" appeared in the *New York Review of Books*, the other in *Encounter*.

"Diaghilev and the Ballets Russes" originally appeared in *Dance* Magazine; "Vera Stravinsky: Painter" in *Saturday Review;* and "*Virgil Thomson* by Virgil Thomson" in *Harper's*.

With the exception of "A Bell for Adorno," which is published here for the first time, all of the remaining pieces first appeared in *World* Magazine.

All of the previously published articles appear here in a slightly revised form.

Library of Congress Cataloging in Publication Data:

Craft, Robert, date.
Prejudices in disguise.

1. Music—Addresses, essays, lectures.
I. Title.
ML60.C9 780'.8 73–20095
ISBN 0–394–48935–7

Manufactured in the United States of America
First Edition

FOR MY MOTHER AND FATHER
ON THEIR FIFTY-FIFTH
WEDDING ANNIVERSARY

CONTENTS

PREJUDICES IN DISGUISE

PROLEGOMENON—
In Which I Paint Myself into a Corner

Before attempting to practice music criticism I should try to describe what I think it is and to define what I think it should be. I should also try to identify the species of critic to which I belong, since at least two exist. All of which, by the sound of it, promises to be about as entertaining as a College Entrance Exam. Except that no one could be further from academe than a musician-critic (as distinguished from a music critic), which is what I am, being a musician first. Not that I wish to belittle either academe or music critics. I am, on the contrary, admitting that the musician-critic reasons from his musical emotions, and that therefore his principles are prejudices in disguise. Of the two species, the principles-first and the disguised-prejudices, the former is perhaps more independent, the latter closer to music.

My first subject, however, is the usefulness and effectiveness of music criticism. Ineffectiveness, rather, for in the sense of changing the quality of musical life, its results are modest indeed. It reacts but seems powerless to initiate, neither the established institutions nor the more sporadic musical activities appearing to be much concerned with its commentary. To give one example, criticism has generally concurred on certain failings of the Metropolitan Opera: the repertory, the star system, the often slovenly musical standards. Yet the Metropolitan responded to these criticisms with regard only to the neglect of new operas—a disastrous response (*Cleopatra*), if that is what it was.

Nor does music criticism exercise much influence on standards of performance—as the word "notices" to describe the reviews of round-the-calendar recitals and concerts seems to concede. Technical standards improve as a result of conditions within the profession, including the challenge of increasingly difficult new music and new sources of competition such as Korea and Japan. Then, too, the failure of criticism to interest musicians themselves is well known. They respect it as no more than a necessary evil (although it seems to many a largely unnecessary one). For whom, then, *does* it have any import? For the talent industry, first of all, the agents, managers, impresarios, the concert and recital mail-order houses, in whose eyes "criticism" is of two kinds: favorable and unfavorable. It is, in other words, synonymous with publicity, that wheel of Ixion to which all contemporary artists are bound. Second, it is for the "general" audience, precisely those who suspect, and rightly, that most of it is obfuscation.

As for what I think music criticism should do and be, I agree with Shaw that all professionalisms are conspiracies against the public. Yet this particular "ism" hardly exists in music, and the few who qualify as professionals are too few to "conspire."

The critic's "absolute" values are the masterpieces of the art. All criticism is correction, or compromise, in the direction of those values (or masterpieces). If other ends exist, which they do (in its time a sacred cantata by Bach was only indirectly a musical end), I am indifferent to them.

In music—unlike philosophy, in which one cannot hold contradictory views—it is possible and desirable to love and enjoy a variety of music of disparate tendencies. This is not the official, progressive view, yet it ought to be that of the layman, and of all musicians except path-breaking composers. We must choose between one thing and another, of course, but should endeavor to widen, not narrow, the field of choice.

Music criticism directs a larger part of its attention to performance than to the music performed. Thus, the "great" violinist who offers Wieniawski (and the "greatest" of them, when he plays at all, still does) should be ignored in favor of the merely very good player who offers the Schoenberg Concerto.

In a living musical culture, the new music must have primacy over the old, if only because the new obliges us continually to revise our relationships with the old. This has become a tiresome argument, particularly in New York City, but it is nevertheless true even though most new music is bad—as it always has been. It follows that the composer is the center of musical culture and that a new work, such as Wuorinen's Concerto for Amplified Violin, is of far greater consequence than the most publicized antics of Big Personality Conductors. By "new," incidentally, I do not necessarily mean New Look. Nor do I exclude it, in spite of the high incidence of impostures.

The reasons for at least some of our musical backwardness are not strictly musical but rather the fault of the cultural economy. Stockhausen's *Gruppen* and *Carrée*, for instance, acknowledged classics of postwar "advanced" music, have yet to be performed in New York City. The causes are neither political (Establishment opposition) nor musical (technical difficulties), but social and economic. Apart from requiring listeners conditioned by other new music, both pieces need more rehearsal time than the present system is able to justify, as well as more stage space than is available in any hall except Madison Square Garden—not the most suitable venue for a composer, even a bellicose one. The problem is related to such questions as government support for the arts and the maintenance of symphony orchestras as civic adornments, to name only two of the unprogressive facts of American cultural life. (Since the state of the arts more and more reflects the state of the government, one is tempted to say that we have pretty much what we deserve in both.) But these are matters for futurological, sociological, and what-not committees rather than for a mere horse-and-buggy musician-critic.

New York City is the largest part of Musical America. But in at least two domains, opera and contemporary music, it does not make a showing commensurate with its size as a world capital of music, at least by my criteria, and is in danger of being limited to the Philharmonic and the Met, both heavily dependent on artistic foreign aid.

Music journalism still tends to dismiss pre-Bach as archaic and not worth general notice. (Discussing repertory in *The New York Times* recently, Harold Schonberg complained that "great music of the Renaissance is ignored by the major symphony orchestras." And by the minor ones, too, I might add, since symphonic music did not yet exist in the Renaissance.) But music before Bach, though smaller in scale than painting and architecture, should take its place with the other arts. Its purposes and effects are radically different from those of the music which comprises the basic training of the general public. They are effects of a high order, moreover, and it is an inestimable loss that Machaut and Josquin, Monteverdi and Schütz, are not among the so-called options of our everyday musical life. The blame is no one's in particular, the textual and interpretive problems being formidable, and the music all but unknown in performances that give it anything like its due; a truly vast amount of work is necessary before the man who appreciates Chaucer can learn to enjoy the *Roman de Fauvel*. Yet the main difficulty is not technical but the one unwittingly exposed by Mr. Schonberg. In the simplest terms, the reason that entire musical eras are mute is the lack of means of performance. Nor is the loss confined to pre-Bach, for who can pretend that the Haydn quartets are as vital in our everyday lives as they should be (or will be until string quartets are as numerous in New York as they were in Beethoven's Vienna)? Or that Bach cantatas can become as popular as they deserve, until performing organizations exist of the right size, kind, and training? Lost performance practices can be recovered to some extent by a combination of conjecture, musical instinct, book learning, studies of instruments (such as the effect of different bows on phrasing and articulation). But a good deal *is* known: what we need are people who know how to put it to use.

Recordings are often of greater importance than events in the world of live music, partly because they are shared by more people and last longer. (The record catalog offers an infinitely larger repertory, of course, than a dozen seasons of live music.) Thus the Solti recording of *Parsifal,* following so soon after the Boulez, is an ideal opportunity not merely to compare conductors but to attempt to see the work anew as it emerges from two different readings. Few of us will ever hear a live performance by either conductor, let alone both in juxtaposition.

Books about music and musicians—musical "appreciations," that is, and the lives of the composer-saints—are of little value to the general public since the clues that can be gleaned from them are so general as to be meaningless. This is not to say that the life of a composer has no bearing on his work, but only that it does not necessarily elucidate or explain it. The life, in my view, is a subject for culture historians, students of abnormal psychology, biographical statisticians. Musicology, as distinguished from this, is valuable to the extent that it makes more music available, helps the listener to derive more from it, and is directed toward performance.

Apart from correcting facts, negative criticism is worth

the time only if it questions false and inflated values, and only when these are in danger of usurping higher ones. The critic should delegate someone better qualified than himself to review music with which he is out of sympathy, but which others, whose judgment he respects, consider to be valuable, or music with which he feels sympathy but about which he lacks knowledge.

Finally, it must be admitted that criticism of music *itself* is an impossibility. Musical ideas cannot be communicated, or even described, in words. At best, they can be pointed to by means of an exiguous vocabulary. We read words, hear music, look at "art" (recently "de-defined" by Harold Rosenberg), and talk about all three. But so far as the experience of music is concerned, the talk is illusionistic and nonsensical—an admission that almost paints me into my corner.

As for the chief failing of practically all critics, this, I think, is that they do not know when to retire. The mortal kind grows stale very quickly, after a year or so at the most,[1] for the same reason, in part, that the immortals, like Berlioz, are forever fresh, namely because the critic confines his subject more and more to himself. Instead of trying to give us the autotelic masterpiece of music, he falls back on "the autobiography of my concert life." He tells us that he never enjoyed the Bruckner Ninth more. In short, not what makes the Bruckner Ninth tick, or fail to tick, but what happened in the critic's sensory system. Another danger is that instead of being a guide who helps the reader make his own discoveries, the critic becomes a provider of opinions. And, worst of all, these opinions are soon predictable—as they should be if he stands for anything. By that time, when his readers

1. Of the thirty-seven pieces in this book, all but five were written within a year.

are able to say, "R.C. would have said this or that," R.C. himself is superfluous.

Now in my corner, however, all that I can do is to offer one simple test of progress. If at the end of a reasonable time together you still like what you like, but nothing of what I like and have tried to interest you in, even that is not total failure, for your tastes and prejudices will have been examined and confirmed.

LETTER FROM NOHANT—

Thoughts, Out of Season, on Chopin

At first glance the demand for a George Sand "revival" in her country would seem to be about as pressing as one for a J. Fenimore Cooper revival in his. The recent Garnier edition of her correspondence has provoked interest, nevertheless; some of her other works have been reissued; and, as I write, the lady herself—in photographs and in a new Pléiade picture book, *Album Sand*—is the subject of a display in Gallimard's boulevard Raspail window. Special attention is also being given to an intimate of Sand's Nohant circle, Eugène Delacroix, in books (T. J. Clark's *The Absolute Bourgeois*, for one) as well as in exhibitions. The Musée Delacroix, in the artist's former studio on the Place Furstenberg, is currently featuring several of his drawings of Liberty (in "Liberty Guiding the People"), surely one of the most famous "top-less" females ever to appear in public.

As an observer of a third frequenter of Nohant, Frédéric

Chopin, himself well beyond any effect of revivals, vogues, critical reappraisals, Delacroix seems to me a more valuable witness than Sand. His testimony obviously lacks the varieties of perspective provided by Sand's ten-year liaison, yet he had a rare appreciation of both the man—*"C'est le plus vrai artiste que j'aie rencontré"*—and of his music, the latter on a level Sand could not reach. But, as a "way" to Chopin's artistic world, the novelist reminds me of a street in Vierzon, on the route to Nohant, called *Impasse George Sand.*

In truth, Sand differed so profoundly in mind and sensibilities from her paramour—"he was always foreign to my ideas," she wrote—that one seeks to explain their relationship in terms of such psychological mechanisms as role-reversal. To read her today is to conclude that she should have lived in the *nineteen*-seventies. Her independence, activist zeal, and especially her thesis that social equality may be attainable through equality between the sexes (an idea that intrigued another of Sand's Nohant friends, Matthew Arnold) are more appropriate to this decade than to the century before. On second glance, therefore, the Sand "revival" is not really mysterious. Madame George could be a Charter Sister of NOW.

Shortly before eloping with Chopin, Sand wrote to his friend Grzymala, whom she looked upon as the composer's guardian and *her* judge; and rightly: Grzymala later blamed her for Chopin's death. A snippet from this letter, in so far as rhetoric of the sort *can* be snipped, gives a fair example of her style:

> . . . for certain minds the whole question of fidelity is inseparable from possession; this, I believe, is a mistaken idea: one may be more or less unfaithful, but when one has allowed one's soul to be invaded . . . the infidelity has already been committed and what follows is less serious . . . [Chopin] seemed to fear to soil our

love . . . [but if] this last embrace is not something as holy, as pure and as sacrificial as the rest, no virtue lies in abstaining from it . . . A result of this separation of the spirit and the flesh is that we need to have convents and brothels . . .

If Sand dominated her Nohant soirées with similar proclamations and polemics, and she did sometimes give readings from novels-in-progress, Chopin must have felt the threat of suffocation from his "angel," as he called her, as well as from his disease. They were incompatible by temperament, in any case, and it is clear that Sand had little sympathy for Chopin's. "So many things alarm him," she wrote before one of his concerts, "that I told him he should play without candles or audience and on a dumb keyboard."

In her *Lucrezia Floriani,* Sand is said to have endowed the character Prince Karol with Chopin's traits, and Heine, recognizing the transposition, said that she had perfidiously maligned "*mon ami Chopin.*" Not surprisingly, Karol is "unworldly," and so, no doubt, was Chopin, at least compared to Sand—the Beatrice of the same book, described therein as "a nature rich in exuberance," in contrast to Karol's "nature rich by exclusiveness." But, in actuality, Chopin in his letters is far from lacking in worldly sophistication. He writes of his hosts in the British Isles: "Conversation is always genealogical, like the Gospels, who begat whom, and he begat, and he begat, and he begat, and so on until you arrive at Jesus . . . They are stifling me out of courtesy, and out of the same courtesy I don't refuse them." Nonfictionally Sand remarked that Chopin did not "understand human nature in any detail." Yet he understood hers in at least two, as an entry in Delacroix's *Journal,* January 29, 1849, shows:

With reference to [Sand's] *Memoirs,* [Chopin] told me that it would be impossible for her to write them. She has forgotten all that: she has flights of sensibility and then quickly forgets. I told him that I saw an unhappy old age for her. He does not think so. Her conscience does not reproach her with any of the things with which her friends reproach her.

Chopin was right about her memory but wrong in assuming that it would constitute an obstacle. He was also right about her conscience; preoccupation with her own feelings evidently overrode even the most bothersome considerations for anyone else. How, otherwise, could she have written of Chopin, "*J'avais la sensation de coucher avec un cadavre*"?

Yet Chopin, not Sand, was the jealous partner. And, Grzymala to the contrary, without her solicitude the composer probably would not have lived even as long as he did. When she finally understood the seriousness of his illness, in that nearly fatal winter in Majorca, the *Bohémienne* became the devoted nurse (though whether to the extent of cutting down on her cigars I am unable to say!). Moreover, from the beginning of his affair with her, new powers entered his music. He may have preferred Paris to his mistress's Nohant homestead, where in fact he was a somewhat reluctant guest, but his seven summers there were the most productive of his life.

"*Nohant n'a plus changé que La Vulgate*," a guidebook says. But its next edition must acknowledge an inn, restaurant, parking lot, George Sand bookstall. Nor can the site now be described as a retreat. During my visit several presumed pianists, to judge by their hand spreads and keyboard postures, alighted in front of the château, posed for publicity photographs (of such is the contemporary pilgrimage!), swept on. Queues will soon have to form before the shaded walks, gardens, pastures with period-piece—Mademoiselle Bonheur—cows. Of the main attractions, the château and the cemetery, the latter is the more congenial. But then, waxworks—tables set for dinners in 1840, "everything as it was"—strike me as morbid. Nor do Sand's quill, Delacroix's umbrella, Chopin's white gloves do much to replicate the past. The château is haunted not by the great spirits who once inhabited it but by a theater of leering puppets, once the pride of Sand's children.

—

"How he adores Mozart," Delacroix noted of Chopin, "and how little he resembles him." The same could be said of Chopin's reactions to, and negligible influence from, the biggest of the musical Big Bosses, Beethoven. Therefore, the first phenomenon of Chopin would seem to be simply that a Pole, bred on the outer periphery of Viennese classicism, could succeed in slipping through the German monopoly on musical genius.

In fact Chopin's musical origins are remarkably obscure. Polish scholars have unearthed the likely Polish precursors, and as much as possible has been made of debts to Italian opera and to John Field. But this adds up to very little. Furthermore, Chopin seems to have been less impressed by the music in the Rossini and other operas[1] than he was by the attractions of the prima donnas—eyes and teeth as well

1. But compare Chopin's Nocturne in A Flat,

with "*Sevra il sen*" from *La Sonnambula:*

as techniques of vocal embellishment. (It was a flash of exceptional musical insight on the part of the author of *Trilby* to have seen that the Impromptu in A Flat is coloratura in style from the first warble, no matter how superhuman in range and speed.) As for Chopin's indebtedness to Field, this is beyond question. But to my mind the Nocturne in E Minor, written when Chopin was seventeen, already surpasses the dozen best efforts in that form by the nomadic Irish composer.

Thus the second Chopin phenomenon: the musical personality—harmonic predilections, keyboard style, melodic tournure (the greater frequency of the ascending interval at the beginning of the phrase, the dallying and indirectness)—is already unmistakable in this youthful Nocturne, as well as in the A-Minor Mazurka of the same year. Models were at hand for these pieces, as they were for the still earlier but less readily identifiable Rondos, Variations, Polonaises. But these models cannot have been of much consequence, and in any case do not account for the originality of the Nocturne and Mazurka. Only talent, not teachers and schools, can explain Chopin's sudden development. The phenomenology of genius has yet to be written, yet it seems safe to say that the crucial factor will prove to be unique gifts for self-learning.

The third phenomenon of Chopin is that he achieves universality in the simplest of dances and wordless songs—forms, in other words, highly limited both structurally and by conventions. Thus his early Mazurkas observe the traditional repeats, whereas the later ones avoid them or disguise them with ornaments; yet the classical mazurka form is never drastically altered. So, too, the conventional left-hand accompaniments—undulations, bass notes on strong beats and chords on weak ones—are scarcely modified in the early music, but are varied and transformed in the later, or, in the case of linear and polyphonic passages, dispensed with entirely. Yet the conventional style is nonetheless essential to the music as a whole.

Chopin's balance between convention and invention is attained largely by confining the two to different spheres. Thus the radical innovator in harmony and rhythm will resort to the tritest formula in ending a piece. In fact, "A finish worthy of the start" is surprisingly rare in his music, and even a masterpiece such as the Nocturne in D Flat is to some extent diminished by its unnecessary and perfunctory final chords, which sound like nothing so much as *A-men.*

"Chopin would not admit sonority as a legitimate source of sensation," according to Delacroix, and was "indignant against those who attribute part of the charm of music to sonority." As the supreme musical charmer the composer must be heeded, even if only to "do as I say"—for sonorities *are* subordinate to musical ideas, and colors, ranges, volumes, dynamic shadings *are* secondary—and "not as I do," Chopin himself having drawn upon a larger spectrum of sonorities than any other composer for the piano. He uses the pedal to create a Niagara out of the sixteenth notes in the final Etude, for one instance, and, for another, by means of tinkling effects in the treble and a mechanical ostinato in the bass, makes a Berceuse sound like a music box. But, ironically, though his music suggests the orchestra—from symphonic Beethoven in the transition to *tempo primo* in the twenty-second Etude, to Iberian Debussy in the middle section of the Nocturne in F Sharp—Chopin defies orchestral translation. *Les Sylphides* is a misunderstanding, in this respect, while, conversely, *Dances at a Gathering* owes a large share of its success to its fidelity to the piano as the musical medium.

"With Mozart, science is always on the level of inspiration," Chopin observed to Delacroix. But Chopin's own inspired science, though constantly renewed, is seldom of long duration. If he could not sustain large forms, however, the F-Minor Ballade proves that he could successfully expand small ones. (But not always; the loud is too often also the pompous in Chopin and length often leads to grandiosity, a quality not to be confused with exaltation, the mood of the G-Minor Ballade.) Chopin was not a "sonata composer," and for all the good music in the one in B minor, its development sections are foreign to his music as a whole. His formal innovations are in other directions, in the new dimensions of some of the Preludes, for example, one of whose heirs, particularly of the elliptical second, is Anton Webern. To measure him by Viennese classicism, or to evaluate the longer and the larger as the innately superior, is absurd.

Apart from the huge commerce in the "Chopinesque," the composer's direct lines of descent are rather narrowly Russian and French. The effects of the Preludes on Moussorgsky, and of Chopin in general on Scriabin, are well known; a less familiar influence on another Russian is that of the end of the C-Sharp Minor Nocturne on the *Pas de Deux* in *Apollo*. But Debussy and Ravel are closer to Chopin than that. The Prelude, Opus 45, with its chromatic parallel chords, might have been by Debussy, while a considerable part of Ravel's idiom is there for the asking in Chopin's Etude in E Major, Opus 10 (*cf.* the sequences of major thirds in the fifth measure).

The meter of Chopin's music, like its dimensions and exclusivity of instrument, is another seeming, but not actual, limitation. By definition the Mazurkas, Polonaises, Scherzos, Waltzes, Boleros are in the constricting triple time of dance music. Several Nocturnes, Preludes, Etudes, concerto and sonata movements are also in that meter, while still more music *feels* as if it might be: sections of the Nocturne in B, Opus 9, for example, despite the written six-eight; of the G-Minor Ballade, despite the six-four; and of the Nocturne in A Flat, despite the four-four, since each quarter-beat of the first theme could be construed as a measure of three.

But Chopin transcends this sameness by a rhythmic vocabulary enlarged with quintolets, septolets, and still smaller subdivisions; by combining these with other rhythmic patterns, regular and irregular (such as the seven-against-three in the Opus 34 Waltzes); by breaking the symmetries of phrase, pattern, accent (*cf.* the cross-rhythm of the tenth Etude); by distorting both rhythm and tempo with *rubato* and with embellishments—for Chopin's luxuriant ornamentation is a rhythmic element as well as a melodic and harmonic one. Paradoxically, the rhythmic complexities in some of these tiny triple-meter dances are comparable to the intrications of contemporary music—except that the textures of Chopin's rhythms are always transparent.

What astonishes with its newness is Chopin's harmony. Above and beyond prodigious skills in modulation, chromatic movement, the handling of remote keys, Chopin had the richest harmonic imagination and the most "modern" harmonic ear of his time—which may help to account for some of his curious aloofness from his contemporaries. Delacroix quotes a remark of Grzymala to the effect that Chopin's improvisations were "bolder than his written music." To have heard them, therefore, might have been to fore-audition some very modern music indeed, to judge by the "boldness" of the written ones. Chopin uses dissonances not merely in passing, but for their own sake, and in isolation, to sharpen an accent or rhythm—as in the percussive sixteenths in measures 37 and 39 of the "*Notre Temps*" Mazurka. Further, most of his embellishments—trills, acciaccaturas, appoggiaturas—are a source of dissonance, since they begin, or should begin, *on* the beat. Harmonic constructions as ingenious and as beautiful as Chopin's do not appear until much later in the century, with Wagner, whose own might not have been written but for

Chopin's example. Certain progressions in the Mazurkas, Opus 56, No. 3, and Opus 59, No. 2, however, are startling even today.

According to Delacroix, Chopin believed that Beethoven was "tormented" by Bach, but the thought may be a projection. In spite of aesthetic dissimilarities, Bach, of all composers, made the most profound impression on Chopin. He planned at one time to make an edition of Bach, and while in Majorca set about expunging another editor's markings. That *The Well-Tempered Clavier* was to Chopin what the Bible is to a fundamentalist is evident schematically in Chopin's use of the gambit of keys in his Preludes and Etudes. More important, much of Chopin's music is in two voices, and though these are not in the same contrapuntal relationship as they would be in Bach, Bach was undoubtedly Chopin's inspiration.

Chopin's use of strict contrapuntal devices is rare—the two-part imitation near the end of the F-Sharp Minor Mazurka, the three-part imitation in the F-Minor Ballade—but the later music shows an increasing concern with polyphonic design. Occasionally, too, Bach's direct imprint *does* appear: in the figuration of some of the Etudes, in the recitative ending of the Nocturne, Opus 32, No. 1, in the "hymn" sections in the C-Minor and two G-Minor Nocturnes. Finally, at least one entire piece, the Mazurka, Opus 59, No. 3, is inconceivable without Bach.

"What constitutes logic in music?" Delacroix asked one day, an impossibly large question that Chopin answered by naming Bach's fugues. Though Chopin had composed no inconsiderable amount of "logical" music himself, the remark confirms his ideal. What surprises is that he failed to recognize the unsuitability of his own talents for the composition of fugues, the solitary example that he did write being certifiably his only because of the existence of the manuscript and of his corrections on it. Nevertheless, like Schubert toward the end of *his* life, Chopin aspired to master the academic forms of contrapuntal art and actually labored over Cherubini's exercises in counterpoint—a spectacle as ludicrous as it is pathetic.

—

Maurice Brown's *Chopin* has recently been revised and republished.[1] This useful index gives the thematic *incipit* of every piece, the order of composition, the location of manuscripts (including fragments in autograph albums discovered as recently as 1970), and much information concerning early editions. The importance of this last, in Chopin's case, is difficult to exaggerate since no thoroughly reliable edition exists. The one published by the Chopin Institute in Warsaw, although its volumes are something of a national monument, does not include all variant readings, and it offers the final Mazurka only in the version by Chopin's pupil, Franchomme, who, no doubt disbelieving his ears, omitted one of its most amazing passages.

Chronology is important. Shortly after the composer's death, the highest opus numbers were assigned to the posthumous juvenilia, with the result that even today—in Rubinstein's incomparable recordings of the Mazurkas, for instance—the latest and the earliest are senselessly juxtaposed. The difficulty in establishing chronology on internal grounds is exemplified in the Waltz in D Flat—Opus 70, but a product of Chopin's nineteenth year!—which anyone with tendentious notions of a "progressive" chromaticism could easily mistake for a product of the composer's extreme old age (*i.e.*, midthirties). Chopin's own grouping together of the compositions of different periods is not always successful, and if the second and third Nocturnes of Opus 15 clearly do not belong side

1. Da Capo Press, New York, 1972.

by side, the reason may be that he gave birth to forty-two pieces between. Chopin has traditionally been performed and recorded by category: *all* of the Waltzes, Scherzos, Mazurkas, Polonaises, Nocturnes, Impromptus, Ballades, Sonatas. But it would be enlightening to hear the compositions of certain years seriatim, even breaking the cycles of Preludes and Etudes to do so.

Mr. Brown's researches have added to our knowledge of the malpractices of Chopin's first English publishers, who not only attached spurious French and German titles to his works—the Nocturnes, Opus 9, for instance, were called *Murmures de la Seine*, and the B-Minor Scherzo, *Le Banquet Infernal*—and falsely advertised a Rondo as having been based on the Cavatina in *L'Italiana in Algeri.*

—

Delacroix, writing from Nohant, sets the scene for a friend in Paris: "Chopin is at work in his room and every now and then a breath of his music blows through the window, which opens onto the garden, mingling with the song of the nightingales . . ." Was Delacroix aware, one wonders, that Chopin may have been thinking as much about death as about music? He had written from Majorca three years before, mocking the verdicts of three doctors: "The first said I was dead, the second that I was dying, and the third that I am going to die . . ." adding, however, in another tone: "I can only cough and, covered with poultices, await the spring or something else." A pupil later describes him as "feeble, coughing much," and taking "drops of opium in sugar and gum water." He was to write from Nohant that he had dreamed of death, picturing himself dead. The "something else" had been recognized, a reality ever-present, within himself.

The sense of timelessness in Chopin's music (the Nohant sky: did any cloud ever wander lonelier than Frédéric Chopin?) may be due in part to isolation, both historical—

Chopin's music is not a "step" in a "development" but comes from and goes nowhere—and emotional, an intensity of feeling that may be more competently explained by a respiratory pathologist than by a musician. Whatever the reasons, we do not think of these Mazurkas and Preludes and Nocturnes as having been fabricated but as always existing. Which is a way of saying that a world without them is difficult to imagine, and that a measure of eternity must be in them.

MAHLER THE MODERN

The two books entitled *Mahler,* by Henry-Louis de La Grange[1] and Kurt Blaukopf[2] respectively, represent decades of research. One question, then, in the minds of those who read both, is how it can be possible for so much dedicated scholarship to yield so many conflicting facts. According to Blaukopf, the composer was one of twelve children, five of whom died in infancy, while a sixth committed suicide at the age of twenty-five. But La Grange provides vital statistics for fourteen children, showing that seven of them died in infancy and that the suicide was in his twenty-first year. Blaukopf further states that the *Lieder eines fahrenden Gesellen* were inspired by "an actress," although La Grange

1. Translated from the French by Herbert Weinstock, Mrs. Rudolf Bunzl, and the author; Doubleday, New York, 1973.

2. Translated from the German (not without solecisms: "In 1897 the journalists were not on the ball") by Inge Goodwin; Allen Lane, London, 1973.

positively identifies the woman as the singer Johanna Richter. And where Blaukopf accepts a merely approximate dating for Mahler's discovery of the *Knaben Wunderhorn* anthology, La Grange verifies both the year, 1887, and the circumstances, the home of Carl Maria von Weber's grandson, during the period of Mahler's infatuation with that gentleman's wife.

But these discrepancies are too numerous to tabulate here. Sufficient to say that La Grange's sources are more abundant, that he has read deeply in them, that his documentation and detail are encyclopedic, and that, thanks to him, a full image of Mahler's personality has been drawn for the first time. On the strength of this mammoth volume one—the second is promised in two years, the time most readers will need to finish the first—the completed work is assured a place on the small shelf of permanently valuable biographies of composers.

All the same, it is unfair to compare the two books. Blaukopf's is a brief survey of the whole life and works; La Grange's, what we now have of it—and this first installment takes the story only as far as Mahler's marriage—is a very long one, primarily of the life. An introduction by Karlheinz Stockhausen tells the reader that La Grange "has refrained from interpreting Mahler's music." Unless technical analysis is meant, however, this is misleading. La Grange offers valuable musical insights in passing but relegates his program-note musical discussions to an appendix, as if to emphasize that the symphonies and songs should be allowed to play and sing for themselves. As for the book's length, this is due in part to extensive quotations of correspondence of a nearly extinct species—and a greatly-to-be-regretted one, for biography in the electronic age, compiled from tape-recorded and eye-witnessed "recollections," will be a lot less literate, whatever else.

Blaukopf, for his part, bravely tries to meet the music head on, and with such novel suggestions as that the architecture of the concert halls of the 1870s and 1880s "demanded" blendings of sound in space on the Mahler scale; that the differences in texture and orchestral style between the first four symphonies and the later ones are attributable in some degree to Mahler's renunciation of his habit of composing at the piano. "Rid yourself of the pianist," he advised another composer in 1896; "[your orchestral music] is conceived for the keyboard." Mahler later maintained that certain "bold passages and figures" in his own Fifth Symphony had come to him "just because I do know the orchestra and its instruments so well." Blaukopf's or anyone else's "new approaches" are welcome, it should be said; despite popularity polls, certain passages in the Sixth and Seventh symphonies are still formidably difficult for even the most acute ear to grasp and retain.

Since Mahler gave far more of his time to conducting than to composing, his career as a conductor inevitably occupies the larger part of both books. But this disproportion is frustrating, his place in today's pantheon resting on his compositions, not at all on his concert life. Furthermore, since no written account can conjure more than an illusion of his performances (one of the better attempts, surprisingly enough, is by Mallarmé's friend Catulle Mendès), the biographer is obliged to devote a great deal of space to such peripheral subjects as the conductor's repertory. Fortunately in Mahler's case this brims with curiosities. He was inordinately fond of *Rienzi* (twenty-seven performances during his reign at the Vienna Opera!) and of Cornelius's *Barber* and Humperdinck's *Hansel*, while at one time his admiration for *L'Amico Fritz* (". . . there are many affinities between Mascagni and myself") was practically boundless.

Mahler's philosophy and technique of conducting are

analyzed, his rehearsals and performances are described, the curtain calls counted and durations and decibels of applause measured. But as one concert or opera follows another, the story becomes repetitious. What does stand out is the contrast between the vast amount of experience and the slow recognition of a conductor in Mahler's time and ours, when it is not unusual for a "music director" still in his twenties to have at least two major orchestras a continent or ocean apart, and to lead his first performance of a Mozart opera in Salzburg, his first of a Wagner in Bayreuth. Before attaining a fraction of such eminence, Mahler, in his mid-thirties, conducted 54 different operas in a single season, 135 opera performances in a year, and 21 in a single month, all of these in addition to his concerts.

Throughout his book La Grange compares reviews of Mahler's performances with the composer's own reports of them in letters and in conversations. Condemned at first for his "exterior show of passion," Mahler is criticized first to last for his exaggerated nuances and eccentric and unsteady tempi. (That his tempi would have been highly flexible is obvious from the frequency of the verbal directions in his own music and the infrequency of metronome markings—nonexistent after the earliest works.) In *Leonore* No. 3, for instance, "Mahler always stated the first theme of the Allegro slowly and did not reach the main tempo until the forte repetition." (That even so specific a comment as this fails to evoke a concrete impression of what the actual effect may have been proves that no performance can be truly "described." Therefore, the wisest explanation for Mahler's phenomenal success as a conductor may be that of his last great witness, Otto Klemperer: "You felt it couldn't be otherwise."[3])

3. *Conversations with Klemperer*, edited by Peter Heyworth, Gollancz, London, 1973.

One thing seems certain, however: Mahler's own conducting would probably have displeased today's audiences, and this notwithstanding the vogue for many of his interpretative licenses. To mention only one objection, he totally disregarded the historically correct. Treating the classics as sacred but far from sacrosanct, he had no qualms about revising their instrumentation according to "the intention of the composer as revealed by the score [allowing] not only for the changed construction and techniques of certain instruments but also for the historical growth of the orchestra" (Blaukopf).

In practice this meant that he would arrange Mozart's *secco*-recitatives for strings and add a piccolo clarinet to the woodwinds in Beethoven's Fifth Symphony—to strengthen a line rather than to change the sonority, except that the one result is inseparable from the other. But the argument is weak, the "intentions of the composer as revealed by the score" being sufficiently difficult to determine in the written notes, to say nothing of the unwritten. (*Viz.* the dotted rhythms in the Andante of Beethoven's First Symphony: these should be played neither "as written," nor mechanically double-dotted, nor exactly between the two, nor even in the same way in all sections of the movement; they *are* played according to some vaguely "instinctive" criteria of rhythmic feeling.)

Like Wagner, Mahler used chromatic brass in Beethoven's Ninth Symphony because "the . . . brass instruments in [Beethoven's] time precluded certain tone sequences necessary to the melody. This very shortcoming ultimately led to the perfecting of these instruments, and it would seem outrageous not to use them now." But this is dubious logic, and again, in practice, the losses often outweigh the gains. (Thus, in an ascending line of the same Andante, the flute doubles the violins until they go beyond its register, rejoining them on their descent. Some new editions continue the doubling on the grounds that Beethoven would have done so too if he had had the larger-range modern flute. But this obliterates an antiphonal effect from the change in color, for Beethoven used the instrument that he *did* have with unimprovable art, being unaware of its limitations as such.) The Mahler thesis, tenable for him, perhaps, because he was a composer himself, has been partly responsible for many latter-day abominations in the name of Bach. (Whether Bach would have "used the resources of the symphony orchestra" is irrelevant since he would have done so in his own way.) So far from "keeping up" with the "historical growth of the orchestra" by renovations of the Mahler-type, we should cultivate the varieties of ensembles from all periods.

How much more engrossing is Mahler's biography when it turns from the conductor to the composer! Here, first of all, we feel a power of self-analysis rare if not unparalleled among musicians. Mahler observes, for instance, that "the artist represents the feminine element opposing the genius that fertilizes him"—which sounds like Tantrism and at the same time makes one regret that Mahler's August 1910 meeting with Freud was not "taped," in the lamentable manner of contemporary election politics.

As in the case of other composers, Mahler sometimes had ideas for music that could not be used in the opus on which he was then engaged. Thus, "instead of ideas in quadruple time, which I need for my finale, I now have only ideas in triple time." He also speaks of having composed a sketch that would not "fit in," then of recognizing it as the "most important passage of all." Once "a voice in the night," thought to be that of Beethoven (!) or Wagner (!), advises him to "bring the horns in three bars later," which, the next day, he sees as the right solution. Statements such as these bring the reader close to the working composer. For anyone seeking to understand the processes of the creative musical imagination, few sources are as rich as Mahler.

—

"Mahler, with his genius for parody and the grotesque, is already a modern as compared with Wolf." "Modern," in Mahler's case, must be defined by its qualities, which, in addition to these two that La Grange names, include several noted by the composer himself: "the farcical and tragic at the same time," for one, and "humor that inspires fear rather than laughter." In a more comprehensive sense, a "modern" is almost automatically an explorer, innovator, expander-of-means. And of course Mahler qualifies here, too, having discarded all conventional concepts of symphonic structures, materials, lengths, while at the same time enlarging the dimensions of his art—increasing volumes as well as intensifying colors and stretching tessituras. (He raised the ceiling of the orchestra in pitch, a probable consequence of having raised the roof.)

But Mahler considered himself a "modern." In a letter that reads like a manifesto, he declares that "we moderns are in need of a large musical system to express our thoughts"; that a "modern" must possess not only as much art as an "ancient," but "even finer, more subtle senses," since his "eyes are learning to discover . . . an increasing number of colors and more and more beautiful and delicate modulations"; that the "modern" composer's instrument is the orchestra. Furthermore, "modern" composers "are obliged to make a louder noise in order to make themselves heard by larger audiences"—*i.e.*, his "Symphony of a Thousand" played for Woodstock–Watkins Glen multitudes—a statement that reveals some of the composer's social as well as musical philosophy. Finally, implying that "the whole spiritual history of humanity" stands behind him, he reminds his correspondent: "We are what we are, we 'moderns.' "

So much for Mahler's professed modernism. That it involves more than this and is not confined to "pure music" should be evident. One of its features, in fact, is a mystical, supradenominational religiosity, expressed in the life no less than in the music and its texts. While composing the *Resurrection* Symphony he had searched "through the whole of world literature, including the Bible, in order to find the liberating word." (Compare that to Hugo Wolf!) But, with or without words, all of Mahler's music has a "message," to communicate being one of his highest aspirations. A prophet of the reach-out-and-touch generation, he deplored the "self-tormenting egotism which makes all men wretched; always I, I, never you, you my brother." His nature-worshipping *Weltanschauung* is also close to that of today's youth, however different the roots—for those of Mahler include Hölderlin, Jean Paul, E. T. A. Hoffmann, and the make-believe medievalism of Brentano and Von Arnim. It follows that Mahler identified himself with his music: "To anyone who knows how to listen, my whole life will become clear, for my creative works and my existence are interwoven." Which is a long way from the indifference of the artist to his "handiwork" expressed in Stephen Dedalus's manicuring image.

Mahler's modernism is evident from the beginning, as he himself recognized on discovering the manuscript of *Das klagende Lied* thirteen years after composing it:

> The essentials, all the "Mahler" whom you know was revealed at a single stroke . . . [E]ven in the instrumentation nothing has to be altered. . . . I see that the only progress I have made since then is technical. . . . *Das klagende Lied* is already "Mahlerian."

These reflections are echoed by Pierre Boulez in a preface to the pocket score, reprinted as an album note for his CBS recording.[4] But Boulez, going on to stress Mahler's rejection of "formal frames in which, architectonically, one is obliged to repeat oneself,"[5] arrives at this premise:

> . . . if it is true . . . that musical form since Wagner has chosen an impulse toward the future . . . and if it is then true that a return backward, or confrontation with the past . . . has been abolished, Mahler has immediately faced up to this new historical situation, straining all his forces toward a musical continuum. The recall of a theme is not, properly speaking, a repeat, but a landmark dramatically placed at the important junction: it allows us to follow the work, as in a novel.

Apart from the analogy with the novel, purloined from Adorno, and the detour on the deterministic hobbyhorse, it is incontestable that Mahler's "impulse toward the future" is more important than his traditionalism, and no less incontestable that he created new continuums by new means. The great opening movement of the Ninth Symphony, an extended song in three perfectly proportioned parts, does not even take sonata form into account. No "architectonic" obligations to the past here, certainly, however numerous the other kinds. Boulez's argument is erroneous, therefore, only in suggesting that "impulses toward the future" and "confrontation[s] with the past" are mutually exclusive.

In fact, the case for Mahler as a sometime neo-classicist is surprisingly strong. "I am quite content to pour my message into traditional molds," he remarked of his Fourth Symphony, adding that the first movement is constructed "in accordance with the academic rules of form." But Mahler's countless "confrontations with the past" resemble those of

4. M2 30061. La Grange, incidentally, defends Mahler's decision to exclude the *Waldmärchen* movement that Boulez includes.

5. Mahler had said this also, claiming that one of his "essential principles" was "the desire to compose without literal reprises."

other great composers; the repeats in the Scherzo of the Ninth Symphony, for example, so far from being "landmarks dramatically placed," are functionally the same as their models in Mozart and Beethoven. Finally, too, Mahler's awareness of his "new historical situation" is manifest no less in his ironic use of the past (the double fughettas in the same symphony) than in his rejection of "formal frames" in *Das klagende Lied*.

Of the "familiar" Mahler in the latter opus, Boulez singles out an "assured instrumental sense." (The "orchestration," however, he qualifies as "naturally, a tributary of the models achieved by his precursors." Tributary of? Or outlet from? Something seems to be flowing in the wrong direction.) But among the many unmistakable features of the mature composer in this early work are marches (where would Mahler be without them?); fanfares; organ points and ostinati; the surprise noise (at [29]); the numerous changes and modifications of tempo; the almost motionless string music near the end (anticipating the Adagietto and even the late Adagios); the constant shifting between major and minor; the prevalence of the interval of the fourth; the successions of thirds in the horns—these, together with the parallel sixths in the same instrument, being so common in Mahler's music that they almost turn the Nietzsche movement of the Third, and the first movement of the Ninth, into "Alpine" symphonies. Yet listeners hearing *Das klagende Lied* for the first time have identified not Mahler but Bartók as the composer of its most dramatic moment (at [26]).

The superior *role* of the orchestra, however, a characteristic of Mahler's *Lieder* in general, is at least as significant in this early work as his "assured instrumental sense," being central to his musical personality. He once admitted that "it was both difficult and strange for him to conduct any opera in which the voice predominates throughout while the orchestra merely accompanies," and his comment on Melba was that he "would have preferred to listen to a clarinet." On the other hand, he maintained that "each orchestral part should sound as though written for a human voice" and that "even the bass tuba and the kettledrum should sing." He was concerned, too, as no composer before him had been, with color and other relationships between voices and instruments, and "the degree to which the word sustains the sound . . . when you pass from wordless music to text." Mahler was a song composer in everything that he wrote. Add to this that two of his ideals were "power" and "grandeur" and it should surprise no one that the orchestra plays so large a part in his vocal music, or that the orchestra so often lifts the song from the singer's throat, as it does in the dirge of "*Der Abschied*," to continue the music in a more profound and powerful voice.

Mahler was obsessed with the pursuit of clarity. "Everything must be heard, everything must sound," he said, and he boasted that "the aspect of instrumentation in which I consider myself ahead of past and present composers can be summed up in a single word: clarity." As we learn from the testimony of musicians, as well as from the composer's letters, he was constantly revising his scores to correct instrumental balances and otherwise achieve the greatest possible precision. But Mahler meant more by the word than adjustments toward orchestral perfection. His deepest quest was for purification of the idea and its expression, a goal he attains to an unprecedented degree in the Eighth and Ninth symphonies, as well as in "*Der Abschied*." In this last, in fact, his "ends" may even have diverted him from his normal "means" since he actually seems to have accepted the principle of economy. (Or was this composer of extremes simply on the rebound from the colossal expenditures in the Eighth Symphony?) For whatever reasons, not clarity alone but a unique simplicity enters his music in "*Der Abschied*" and the Ninth Symphony.

Yet it is the great density of Mahler's music that counts as one of the most apparent elements of its modernism—as well as a chief reason behind his search for lucidity. The mélange of noise and music at a country fair provoked him to say that *that* was true polyphony and "anything else . . . mere part-writing and disguised homophony. . . . Themes must come from a lot of different sources and differ from each other in rhythm and melody." Mahler did not go as far as Charles Ives in this direction, yet the statement helps to explain those great climaxes of the principal melodies and motives together in the late symphonies. And also to explain the deliberate harmonic clashes ("We are what we are, we 'moderns' ") that led to Mahler's "emancipation of the dissonance"—to borrow Schoenberg's words but not his sense, for, unlike Schoenberg, Mahler never attempted to "free" himself from tonality but, rather, increased its importance as one of his principal construction tools.

The sense of contrasting key relationships in Mahler's music is unerring, though not necessarily unusual: *viz.* the conventional use of the key of B flat in relation to the home key in the first movement of the Symphony in D Major. Mahler: "One is always building a new edifice with the same stones." A further and favorite device, the contrasting of a tonality in its purest and most polluted forms, is another expression of that taste for freakish juxtapositions evident from the first piece he ever wrote, "Polka with Introductory Funeral March." Thus a passage in the first movement of the Ninth Symphony lilts along between tonic and dominant, then suddenly explodes into harmonic combinations resembling that country fair.

Mahler exulted in the creation of his Eighth Symphony. And at least one of the reasons was that the man who had spent his life conducting other people's operas had found an opportunity to compose "operatically" himself, at least to the very limited extent that he wished to go; the Faust movement of the Eighth displays an absolute mastery of operatic scene-setting. But the clarity of the music is even more astonishing: of form, above all, no doubt because of the text that imposes it; of thematic and tonal structure, these being simple and clear in inverse proportion to the complexity of vocal and instrumental timbres; and of the orchestration, for nothing is lost in this immense apparatus, and even the thunderous organ does not blur. The vocal and instrumental music are very different in kind, and the latter, especially in the purely orchestral passages, is the newer. The first instrumental interlude in Part One contains the most modern rhythms that Mahler ever wrote, the last interlude in Part Two some of the most modern sonorities and spacings of sound.

The transparency and radiance of sound in "*Der Abschied*," Mahler's supreme song as well as his "*Abschied*" to Song, are unique. Here even the kettledrum—and every other instrument—*does* sing as Mahler said it should. He had predicted that "the future of music resides . . . in untried combinations of color . . . leading to unknown combinations of sound." One such combination, in this song, is composed of a melody played by flutes in a low range (doubled by clarinets and supported by mandolin, harps, strings) and of another melody played by violins in a high one. The sound of the flutes, as a rule scarcely audible in this register, is here extraordinarily translucent, partly because of careful dynamic shadings but largely because of the great space between the two principal lines. When other instruments and the solo voice join in, and the motives interweave (in a double canon), the clarity of the individual lines is reinforced by rhythmic means, groups of fours in three-meters, and of threes in the fours giving the maximum relief to each part.

Mahler knew that he was serving the future in other ways besides composing for it—and not only that special future once thought to be attainable strictly through his direct heirs, Schoenberg and Berg. True, Mahler, after Berg, can sound like a compendium of sources: the music at [11] in the first movement of the Ninth Symphony, for instance, would have been suitable for one of Wozzeck's psychotic tailspins. Nor are Mahler's Schoenbergian moments less abundant. (The flute part at [95] in the second movement of the Seventh Symphony is well within the world of *Pierrot lunaire.*) Schoenberg's relationship with Mahler's music is more elusive than Berg's, however, and it is to be hoped that La Grange's second volume will throw light on whether, for example, Schoenberg had seen the score of Part Two of the Eighth Symphony before composing *Die glückliche Hand.*

But Mahler's universality has now transcended his family heirs. And Mahler's standards, Mahler's struggle, Mahler's whole uncompromising existence in and out of music have helped to form the conscience of a younger generation. It is in this sense that his life may have had almost as much bearing as his work on the future of music, even if, as he believed, the two were inseparable.

NON CREDO—

Mass by Leonard Bernstein

John F. Kennedy Center for the Performing Arts
Washington, D.C., September 8, 1971

Mr. Bernstein's latest musical is his weakest to date. But the title and the mixing of texts "from the Roman Liturgy and by the composer," in a proportion of about one line of the former to fifty of the latter, do not amount to the monstrous impertinence one might reasonably, if prejudicially, expect. The work is too insubstantial to wreak any harm more lasting than embarrassment. The Jewish Defense League can call off its picket line, and RCs may go back to boycotting either the Tridentine vernacular or the Ordo Missae.

Mass is a musical message-drama, a sentimental expression of Mr. Bernstein's sympathy for good causes. It is a Mass, therefore, in spite of the Church, for his version is "liberal," inclusive, and (absurdly) protean. But the implied criticism of the Church is specious and fails to cut, giving the impression not so much of spite as of spate. Nor does Mr. Bernstein succeed in making his sympathy theatrically incarnate. *Mass* is hardly invested with enough dramaturgical necessity, in fact, to justify the staged format. And so far from abetting any real causes (which it is only doubtfully within the power of art to do), *Mass* may have set some of them back.

That, at any rate, was the view of the Vietnam Veterans

Against the War, who distributed leaflets reminding the gilded ticket holders that while they were callously "celebrating" in "marble edifices" and indulging in "splendor" and "illusions [*sic*] of grandeur," people were still dying in Indochina. This, however, was not a very effective indictment of the facile liberalism that was the unwitting subject of the entertainment on sale inside. Yet the damage to real causes was also not serious. What concerns me here, however, are not Mr. Bernstein's feelings about them but his art.

And little need be said about that. Mr. Harold Schonberg, for one, has already given reasons enough why the piece does not work. Oddly, though, his main musical criticism was the opposite of the one that actually fits the case—which is not to say that the piece would have succeeded if this objection were untrue. *Mass* is a "very chic affair," he writes, poaching a bit on the notorious Mr. Wolfe. It "uses fashionable techniques." But it doesn't. It uses very unfashionable ones that the thickest application of fashionable make-up cannot conceal. Even the sociopolitical subject matter is no longer timely, though it *could* not be unless it were in some measure time*less;* and, for that, art must be not merely up-to-date but some distance ahead. Only once, at the very beginning, which sounded like *Les Noces* as it might have been recomposed by Berio, did the music threaten to become fashionable.

After that, when the curtain rises on a Parsifal in denims strumming a guitar, Mr. Bernstein quickly settles into a Broadway arranger's chord chart of many seasons ago. In fact, the mystery of this score, as well as of Mr. Bernstein as a composer in general, is how he could be in the spotlight of musical life for so long and still register so little effect from developments since mid-Copland, on which *Mass* displays not a whit of progress. The truth is that while Mr. Bernstein has a certain personality as a composer—albeit difficult to uncover, his need to be all things to all people keeping him in a perpetual identity crisis—his creative resources are meager. Thus far, at any rate, he has not shown a large command of a maker's musical language.

Mr. Schonberg rates "the jazzy, super-rhythmic sections" as "by far the best," adding that "Bernstein at his best has always been a sophisticate." But those super-rhythms are no more than accented syncopations repeated in crescendo over triadic ostinati. Sophisticated or otherwise, most musicians today regard them as corn. And even in this outworn idiom Mr. Bernstein does not know where to go, which is the underlying reason why his two-hour *Mass* is musically so static. Being unable to develop, Mr. Bernstein is forced to rely on contrasts—of dynamics, speed, color—along with innumerable extramusical diversions. But none of these substitutes is helpful in slow and quiet sections, the two being virtually synonymous here, I might add, as fast is with loud. I think that what Mr. Schonberg is really saying about the jazzy, super etcetera is that the slow music is so motionless and lacking in event that he prefers the simulated movement of the fast.

The music, especially the repetitions, fade-outs, responses, quickly becomes predictable. Mr. Bernstein cannot resist the temptation to add an echo or comment, usually in the chorus or the percussion. "Let us pray," cries the Celebrant after his iconoclastic tantrum—a bad scene in the straight sense—and "thud" goes the drum. "You cannot imprison the word of the Lord," someone sings, evidently not a student of history, and the band promptly replies with a *fa-sol-do*, which is one of the "catchier" motives, but then, after some forty opportunities, who could fumble it? In fact the only expectation ever denied is the ending. This is cruelly protracted through a hymn, an "Amen," a "voice" saying "Go in peace," an orgy of embracing (part of the script), and an explosion of mutual congratulating (possibly the same). Mr. Bernstein is never elliptical, but, in his reluctance to let the audience go, his timing is intolerably slack.

Greatly to the surprise of the musical reader, Mr. Schonberg's other "fashionable elements" include "orchestrations by Hershey Kay." For while Mr. Kay's techniques have postponed the extinction of many an incompetent composer, they could hardly be called fashionable, besides which, one wonders if he should be "credited" with those overworked timpani, woodblocks, bongos, xylophone-doublings-of-violins. And what about the old-fashionables? The choirboys, for instance, even if nowadays they not only sing sweetly but do cartwheels and handstands? And the incense, if disintoxicated? And the marching high-school band, and the J. Arthur Rank gong?

And what about the props? That staircase to the stars, for instance, struck one as *déjà vu.* And the choreography, which is *Fiddler*-like now and then, and in which the dancers alternately crouch beneath the Almighty and exhort Him, like Disney's Sorcerer invoking the elements: Is this really still "in"? Finally, what of the fashionableness of the lyrics, a better than average example of which is in this couplet of the wrong Joyce—Kilmer, that is—mixed with *Prufrock*?

I might have been a simple tree
Or a barnacle in the silent sea.

On the great day itself, a *New York Times* editorial congratulated the Center on its opening, partly, I suspect, to offset the evaluation of the paper's architecture department—overcomplimentary, as it seemed to me, although the Center is inevitably an improvement on Unconstitutional Hall. The editorial went on to say that "the schedule of events is extremely promising," and another writer in the same issue described it as a "cornucopia," listing Mr. Rod McKuen as one of the juicier fruits. A fear was expressed, however, that the economics of the Center would "dictate a quick and drastic lowering of the sights"—an impossibility, if opening night is meant as the starting point—and a fear that the Center might "go down the drain of shoddy commercialism"—although back up the drain is the only direction open. Which raises the questions of what makes one kind of commercialism shoddy and another respectable, and which kind was opening night? If not to commercialism, moreover, where would the Center go? Do noncommercial performing arts exist? And what, by the way, is the purpose of a performing arts center?

The *ignis fatuus* of art centerers, apart from the assumption that the arts should be centered in the first place, is the belief that buildings themselves somehow hatch new art, that the "marble edifices" of a "$70-million-dollar" investment are bound to provide the manure. But the ingredients of the manure are far more important, as well as more elusive, than the physical plant. (Will craftsmanship again become one of them? An expertise of the kind that formerly enabled a composer to dedicate a new hall with a decently made if dull *Ode to St. Cecilia*, and at the drop of a hat? Or, on three days' notice, and at the drop of a patron, supply a *Trauer-Ode*?)

For the creative arts, as distinguished from the performing, may suffer intimidation rather than derive incentive from a Kennedy Arts Center. If the truly new continues to come out of the experimental underground, assuming that it comes at all, one can hardly imagine it growing up on this stage and satisfying the only kind of audience that could support it. The artist in the egalitarian society is every man, according to Tocqueville's prediction, but the only step in the prophecy that has so far come to pass is the disastrous one of the elimination of the cultural elite. The custodians of the culture centers are moneymen, real estate brokers. And that is why they understand Mr. Bernstein. He is hot property. He can be publicized, merchandised, sold. In these terms the custodians got value for their money, precisely the value they deserved. The only victim, apart from the public, is Mr. Bernstein, our Number One musical success figure.

Which is also why our sympathies are with him, together with the reason that at the end, after all, he is spreading "love." The "cast of over two hundred" hugs and kisses each other, the lights go up in the bordello-red hall, and the choirboys walk through the audience squeezing hands and bidding everyone to "pass it on." At length, or soon, Mr. Bernstein himself appears, and although nearly overcome, looks as if he means to embrace everyone in the house. Does he just possibly protest too much? And do you ever suspect that what he is really saying is "I loveyouloveme"? But we do, Lennie, we do!

PAY DIRT—

Notes on the New Nudity

I—HOLLYWOOD

A copy of Michelangelo's "David" is being displayed
at Forest Lawn Memorial Park here without a fig leaf.
"We thought the time had come to try it,"
said Charles Pink, manager.
—The New York Times, 7/20/69

Lunch at The Telephone Booth is no ordinary feed. Except that the point is not food but the topless and bottomless waitresses—"only the salad comes with dressing"—who serve it and take turns "dancing" on a dais. The ringside seats for these ballets are at the bar, but the performers' charms, fore and aft, are in direct or mirror view of every table. The room is dark, the more fulgently to set off spotlighted and powdered epidermises and at the same time to shield the viewers, some of whom, as if expecting a televised police raid, hide behind smoked glasses as well.

Who are the audience? Leering lechers? Inveterate voyeurs? Not all of them, at any rate. One bashful gastronome, in the booth next to mine, hardly bothers to glance in the direction of the dancers, or, for that matter, away from his plate. Most of the more overt and steady watchers seem to share a predilection for bosoms, seldom lowering their sights from that level. But then, if more bizarre penchants existed, would they be detectable in the circumstances?

Despite the salad-only advertisement, the girls wear short black jackets during their stints of waiting on table (pushing drinks). These garments are shed on the dais, toward which, incidentally, each dancer is cued by a recorded tune (a favorite? the only one she recognizes?), but they conceal so little in the first place that the strip is teaseless. All the same, the first disrobing provokes a "Get a load of that!" from an ogler newly installed at the bar. "That" is a case of bouncy overendowment which the girl seems to defy the customers to notice, looking them straight in the eyes, if that is where *they* are looking. But her ballet is a dilly, indescribable in fact, unless it could be called pussyfooting.

A platinum *Playboy*-cartoon blonde appears next. Apart from the moues, she is wearing pasted-on fluorescent nipples and very sheer panty-hose—against the chill? not enough time for body make-up? She is half bombed, I suspect, but her dance, so far from a bacchanal, might have been copied from a circus pooch. Though no more than twenty-three, which is middle-aged in this profession, she is obviously repelled by sex and contemptuous of men. One wonders at what more halcyon time of life she discovered that her virtue was irretrievable, and how many more years as an itinerant go-go stripper graduating to call girl she will be able to take.

The next "waitress," at the other extreme, is tough and able to take care not only of herself but of every man in the room—some of whom, to judge by her claque, may have been taken care of already. She inspires no lewd ambition in me—apart from a Theseus-like wish concerning the hidden portion of her gold-chain G-string—but this could merely be a sign of Craft ebbing. She would not have fetched the top price in a seraglio, being too angular for Ingres ("*Le Bain Turc*"), despite a localized tendency, perhaps from usage, to pleat and sag. But whereas her colleagues do no more than go through their paces barely, she puts soul into hers, simulating the throes of denouements with clenchings and unclenchings, excruciating thrusts and gyrations. "Hey, that hurts," a castration-threatened spectator cries out, while another, apparently even more worried, rounds on him with: "It would break it off." At this point a dirty old man at the bar chimes in with "How'd ya like to take *her* home?"; and the answer this time comes from someone obviously married: "Yeah, only anywhere but *there*." Strutting off after her number, the nymph remarks out loud that "these Monday mornings are really getting to me." But a suggestion from the floor is offered for this, too: "Why don't you go and entertain our troops in Sweden?"

The next girl, tall, Junoesque, a brunette postiche down her back, is the beauty of the bevy, at least as an example of theater in the round. Her movements are muzzy, however, perhaps from "grass" or oncoming menses, yet she alone—that cadent, if rented, hair—could raise my libidinal temperature a therm. (Only a necrophiliac could be bothered by the other exposures.) After her act I tell her that of all the girls, she would look best in clothes (see-through clothes, anyway), but she is uncertain whether the remark is a compliment, and what started as a smile turns to a "level-with-me-Mister" expression. She is the least at home here, at any rate, and that in itself goes some way toward making her the most attractive.

—

The male spectator's kicks from the sexual object under a glass bell depend in part on aesthetic gratifications governed by his psychological make-up as a whole. (The girls' kicks, apart from money, seem to be similar to those of the child discarding its clothes in order to gain attention.) Experiments have now been carried out to isolate and measure the susceptibility of the male to the female form, *qua* form. This is done by projecting adjustable outlines of female shapes on a screen and then enlarging, shrinking, and otherwise modifying them to the subject's desiderations. The latter are not simply avowed but, owing to the unreliability of the subject in imputing the tendency of the attraction to his own impulses, determined by electrical sensing devices. The findings thus far, after comparison with personality data, indicate that the breast-fixated American male is better adjusted than the bottom-fixated one. Furthermore, options for comparatively large amplitudes, a rise in the graph, earn correspondingly higher marks in psychosocial stability.

In the absence of any "meaningful" coordination between the natural and the social sciences, this cannot be accepted as a pragmatically conclusive fact—or even as a fact at all, in view of the present low repute of this kind of psychological testing. (Until recently, the retardation of the heartbeats of submerging crocodiles was thought to be one of all-wise Nature's protective devices for the conservation of oxygen. It has now been discovered, however, that the slow-downs were caused entirely by fear of the scientific experimenters. In *crocodiles*?) Further research along these adjustable lines will undoubtedly continue as sex is further removed and eventually separated entirely from procreation.

Meanwhile, it is obviously better to "make love, not war," and no matter that the biological overlove in lovemaking is as wasteful as overkill. (A mere seventeen nuclear missiles are said to be enough to destroy human life on the planet, yet thousands of these missiles exist; so, too, though a single sperm cell is enough to create human life, every ejaculation of male seed contains at least two hundred and fifty millions.) Necessary as it may have been, and whatever if anything it may have to do with "love," the sex explosion, as distinguished from a long-awaited and more profoundly subversive Revolution of Eros, has become a bore. One already looks forward to a time beyond when it will be possible to do it and forget about it and even to go on to other things. "We liberate sexuality not in order that man may be dominated by [it]," Freud wrote (in 1908!), "but in order to make a suppression possible." *Voilà!* Temptation exists to be resisted.

II—NEW YORK

Bless thee, Bottom.
—A Midsummer Night's Dream

The first half hour of *Skin,* said to be representative of the new sex flicks, takes place at the Botanical Gardens. One supposes that this is in order to compare phalli to flora, except that no human ever appears and the audience soon begins to suspect that the title refers to lemons and oranges. The dermatological mystery deepens in the second scene, a drama about the Bay Area needle set, but in the scene after that a blotched and mottled female rump (rondures only, no connecting anatomy!) canters about the screen in time with the

D-Minor Fugue from *Fantasia.* What was it Plato said about "the desire and pursuit of the whole"?

Television commercials are well into the exploitation of the third-sex market. "For women only" proclaims the husky contralto on behalf of Virginia Slims, which have been promoted as a Sapphic cigarette. And an advertiser for an electric lawnmower, after demonstrating the superiority of the machine over a grazing sheep, considers whether the animal might be roasted for dinner but concludes that "that would be like eating the gardener." The advertiser, moreover, identifies himself as one "Dick Palmer."

Oh! Calcutta!, on the other hand, is for regular guys. Or is it? Are the men the real attraction, perhaps, and the women merely decoys? Men in pairs, fissiparous sex, make up a large part of the audience, in any case, although most of the episodes deal with country matters and none can be construed, except wholly transposed, as a form of gaiety. But whatever the audience's sectarian proclivities—and its other conspicuous feature is the absence of the young and freaked-out—it inhibits as an entity. Communality on so large a scale at a peep show contradicts long-ingrained notions of privacy. (But see Roheim on group onanism in the Intichiuma ceremony of Australia.) Nor does one's awareness of the collective ever let up, thanks to the univocal laughter, embarrassed at first, but first, last, and at all other times, embarrassing. Spasms of it afflict my neighbor at the drop of a trouser.

Until now, the limitation of pornography to male fantasies has been explained as a consequence of the involvement of "more extensive higher cortical control" (Lionel Tiger) in male sexual activity than in female. Whatever the truth of that, the decline of the mystery of sexuality has challenged both the taken-for-granted supremacy of the female nude and the bartered-bride system which encourages women to think of their bodies, and men to think of women's bodies, as their most valuable possession. Which cannot be a welcome development to the woman of the streets.

So far as the stage is concerned, male nudes are still handicapped, if that is the word, by the ban on virile members—not, perhaps, in dramas involving urological examinations but certainly in amorous action pieces such as *Calcutta.* A young man in the buff, approaching a young and reasonably comely woman in the same, is expected to register a visible physical reaction. But the young men thus engaged in *Calcutta* are sapless. And whatever the reasons—saltpeter, pederasty, androgen deficiency, sexual shell-shock, the milking of the actors like vipers before each performance—their failure to become potent does not meet the minimum realistic requirement of the circumstances. In sum, while no holds are barred on stage, tumescence is permitted only in films, a double standard that denies the stage actor the opportunity to perform at the top of his bent. And this, of course, exposes him to prejudicial reflections on his manhood and character, for the audience is left to deduce that if he rises to the occasion at all, he must do so like a thief in the night and is thus relegated to the same class of invertebrates, morally speaking, as Blake's worm. The double standard is tripled and quadrupled when compounded with bookselling laws, actual sex laws (different in every state), and the Blue Laws of the Independent Government of Television, whose theater critics would be unable even to describe *Calcutta* with apt and ultimate brevity, that particular tetragram still being outlawed on the medium.

Nudity wears off quickly. In fact clothes are not long off in *Calcutta*—but long enough for the observation of details reassuring on the whole to the male ego—before the audience is ready for an entirely new cast of bodies. (You could hardly call it a *dramatis personae.*) The interchangeability of anatomies, and the greater uniformity in nude than in clothed ones, are premises of the depersonalized presentation of sex—the only possible presentation, obviously, if the third-party role of the audience is not to be intolerable.

A further premise is that to start over again fully clothed can reinvigorate. It does, to some extent, in the sadomasochist fantasy scene. A fully dressed girl carrying a rod kneels head to floor, bottom high and audienceward, and one by one, but forestalling the final one, upraises her numerous petticoats. The ultimate revelation, abetted by good countdown technique, is a comparatively *foudroyant* effect, the sheer effrontery (or backery) of it holding the audience in a trance until dissipated by overexposure. But an unrelated-to-other-features derrière loses its identity. And *we* lose our bearing, forgetting what it is—an enlarged peach? an *idée fixe?*—and why we are basking in it.

On balance, and for purely negative reasons, *Calcutta* is worth the while of anyone concerned with improving the prevailing standards of "erotic culture." First, it obviates further demonstration of the dullness of sex as a subject for a full evening in the theater. Second, *Calcutta* neglects variety. The bedwork scenes should have been interspersed with illustrations of the polymorphous perverse—with peeks at selected fetishisms, especially bestiality, for at least that would allow for a bit of horseplay.

Calcutta also shows the undesirableness of puerility in pornography (as in everything else), particularly in the two episodes that had starting possibilities as social satire, the takeoff on swinging *via* the sexual want-ad columns, and the send-up of Masters and Johnson. The latter is the most nearly successful caper of the evening, partly because its clinicalism fits the genre. Furthermore, it turns the tables to show that the "sexual response" of the volunteer lovers, who are attached with electrodes and wired to a computerlike console that lights up when copulation begins, is far less remarkable than that of the kinky institute staff.

What, I wonder, not breathlessly, will be the use of the

artistic-merit and redeeming-social-value clauses when our moribund living theaters move on from group therapy to the theater of intercourse? At the present rate of escalation, by which onstage erections may well be *de rigueur* in another six months, and *Calcutta* making a comeback as camp in a year, the likelihood is not far away. Does anyone still recall that only two years ago the Mayor of New York City had to overrule a ban on a troupe of bare-breasted African *danseuses,* and that he could do so, after all, only because they were "savages"? Meanwhile, *Calcutta* is a stage in the betrayal of the sexual revolution by conformism.

Finally, I wonder whether *Calcutta* celebrates sexual freedom as much as it does its frustration. Catharsis, in any sense at all—well, what *was* that function old Reich once made so much of?—has never seemed more remote. "I want it now," a singer moans at the end, but *does* anyone, do even sexual have-nots as a result of incitement by these exhibitions? Or are the latter something of an antiarouser, in the sense that while substitute performances may nourish the imagination, they can also reduce it.

Speaking for myself, I am beginning to think that the unclothed state may have been intended only for the gods, and the gods at home, moreover, for sea-changed Venus had to be draped before entering the mortal sphere. Or intended for those who, like the Doukhobors and the Digambora, practice it in the names of gods. But that is to overlook two other passages well suited for the condition: Naked I came into the world, naked I shall go.

CELESTIAL MOTIONS—
The City Ballet

Which composers since Beethoven can survive the exposure of seven one-man exhibitions seven days in a row? Schumann and Brahms would be among the contenders, of course, if *Lieder* and piano recitals were included along with the chamber and orchestra repertory; and Chopin and Tchaikovsky. But seven nights of unmitigated Brahms might be more of a test of our endurance than of his, while a Mahler cycle of that length, whether or not it would kill off the composer, could prove to be lethal (in the effects of so much *Weltschmerz*) to the audience. Richard Strauss, on the other hand, a more prolific composer than Stravinsky, would as surely not withstand so large a display without the help of his operas, while more than three programs of any kind by Debussy, for whom less-is-more, would all but deplete him, or, if not him, us. Yet Stravinsky survives and would have been in still better health if the exhibits had lasted a fortnight. Some of his most popular music, after all, including actual ballets such as *Petrushka, The Rite of Spring, Les Noces, Jeu de Cartes*, was ignored.

Would even Stravinsky have come through unscathed, however, without the choreographic superstructure? The performances were not concerts but theatrical spectacles, and watching was at least as important as listening—in many cases more important, the music being subliminal, to judge by the musically deaf applause. (This is also a feature of opera, the prima donna's claques often being vociferously indifferent not only to the continuity of the score but also to the work as a whole.) But what *is* this superstructure, choreography being an independent art with its own techniques? And what is the relationship of choreography to music? My answers, limited to examples from the City Ballet's Stravinsky Festival, are that choreography ranges from distractions that impinge on the music (in which event one closes one's eyes) to aesthetic constructions that are justifiable in their own right. And at best, as in the best of Balanchine, choreography can provide equivalences to music, and illuminate and mirror music. Essentially, however, choreography is irrelevant, ballet being one thing, music quite another.

Stravinsky won the seven-day marathon partly because his music inspired delectable visual entertainment, that being due, in turn, to the music's diversity and wit, and to the composer's miraculous power to "make it new." It is almost incomprehensible that masterpieces so different as *Histoire du Soldat*, *Pulcinella*, and the *Symphonies of Wind Instruments* could have been created within two years—not the quantity of the music, of course, but the abundance of the new. Stravinsky's art continued to mature with each opus, and to grow in spirit as well as in mastery, yet *Agon*, composed at seventy-five, is the music of a young man, a younger one, first-time listeners might reasonably suppose, than the sixty-five-year-old (official retirement age!) composer of *Orpheus*. Nor does the power of newness diminish in the *Requiem Canticles*, written at eighty-four, but in which age is betrayed only by the intensity of focus. Stravinsky came fresh to everything, in life as in art and as a listener as well as a composer, being able to hear the Beethoven quartets again and again, for instance, but always for the first time. Whatever his other powers in comparison to those of the great composers, no one has equaled him in his capacity for rejuvenation.

One might adduce from this year's City Ballet Festival that not all of Stravinsky's music lends itself to choreography: the Octet, for example, the Concerto for Two Solo Pianos, and the Serenade in A, though one of the problems in this last was that the volume of the offstage piano was unable to compete with the thunder of the onstage hoofs. Yet it could be the choreographers who lacked the skill to borrow from Stravinsky, which is to say that the same scores might have stirred other imaginations to better effect. *Duo Concertant,* one of Balanchine's new marvels, was no more promising as raw material than these other three concert pieces.

Clearly not all Stravinsky *should* be choreographed, however, including the early, and fitfully bombastic, Symphony in E Flat, which is not remarkably prophetic, and is too long for a mere lesson in origins. Few or none of the composer's characteristics (except one foiled sequence) are discernible in it, nor is it redeemed by his orchestral skill, in spite of Miaskovsky's remark after the first performance: "More instrumentation than music." Neither did *The Faun and the Shepherdess* add much. The performance was provided with scenery—a backdrop of Central Park in the still further polluted future (down to eleven trees), with the soprano pitched like a pup tent in the foreground. But if a concert piece, why not one containing more Stravinsky than Tchaikovsky? And when the verse is Pushkin's, why not sing it in Russian? One may as well not understand Russian as not understand English, and the first English word that I "understood" was "candidity."

The festival being homage to a composer, the role of music in ballet was recognized before all else. But no musician, no conductor, followed Stravinsky *all* the way as did George Balanchine. When *Agon* and the *Movements* were new, and *Variations* was the piece that passeth all understanding, it was New York's resident dance company, not the Philharmonic or the visiting orchestras, which gave us the opportunity to hear them. Moreover, the ballet orchestra plays the music very capably even though it performs under great handicaps. The acoustics of the pit are an unbreakable sound barrier, isolating one section from another with deleterious effects on ensemble, balance, intonation. (The basses in the *Exaudi* of the *Canticles* could have played the A-sharp in tune only by marking the string with chalk.) The orchestra is further hampered by an insufficiency of strings, especially violins, which can scarcely be heard in many *tutti* passages and which, even when playing alone, in *Apollo* and *The Cage,* sound as if they could be in a cistern. Contrast this with the percussion, every utility of which from knocked-over music stand to dropped trombone-mute resounds in the outer lobby.

It would be an impertinence to extol the dancers, whose *esprit de corps* (*de ballet*) explains why, in a sense, the week was no seven-day wonder. One observation that could be risked is that the balance of power between the sexes is shifting, that either the company's long tradition of female supremacy is being challenged or Balanchine is giving the male dancers greater participation. In any case, dancers, by themselves, are no more than intelligent acrobatic anatomies. Ballets are made by choreographers, and of these the City Ballet has all but cornered the market. Balanchine classicism is still the company's only style, despite strong offshoots by Robbins. All of the successes were products of one or the other, as well as triumphs of dancing over storytelling. But the failures (*The Firebird,* in this version, and *The Song of the Nightingale*) and the mixed bags (*Pulcinella* and *Orpheus*) prove the same: plot pieces, pageants, the world of make-believe are not the City Ballet's forte. It follows, too, that costumes and decor are not only inessential but a liability. (In *The Firebird* they are a disaster.)

The Nightingale should be given in the complete 1914

score, with the singers in the pit. Stravinsky was right in insisting that *The Song of the Nightingale* is not a ballet, but it could have been a better one on this occasion if the Nightingale herself had been more active and the Emperor rather less, for, near death though he is, he still fights several rounds of a wrestling match. Purely as music, however, the piece promises more than it delivers. As for *Pulcinella,* Eugene Berman's combinations of rags and riches, Piranesi and Callot, filled the stage and the eye, but play-acting is not for the City Ballet.

The difficulties with *Orpheus* may have begun with the casting of the title part. M. Bonnefous is a natural comic, darting here and there like Buster Keaton, then rapidly looking about to see if he is in the right place. Once he was not, having miscalculated his distance from Green Mountain, which he backed into instead of vaulting but which a hand with "the power to move mountains" quickly uprighted. The hard-laboring damned on the rock piles in Hades looked like weight lifters in a gym, while the stones themselves would have been more useful on Earth, replacing the attic staircase from which the god takes off for Parnassus in *Apollo.*

Not all of the successes and failures can be attributed to a position on one side or the other of the categorical fence between storytelling and classic dance. *The Cage,* for one exception, is a prime example of a mistaken tendency of choreographers to "orchestrate" rather than to come in from an angle. And whatever the reasons for the failure of the Concerto for Piano and Winds, the ballet could have been improved only if the musicians had been on the stage and the dancers in the pit. The festival's biggest hit, for its length, was the *Circus Polka,* with Robbins as ringmaster and the Ballet School's little girls as powder puffs, that being what they looked like in their tutus. But its companion piece for grown-up little girls, *Scherzo à la Russe,* failed to hatch. The accordion-style music seemed to require at least one male, the stage full of hens at least one rooster.

Next year's Stravinsky week should open with that perfect program, untried even by Diaghilev: the complete *Firebird, Petrushka, The Rite of Spring*. Mr. Balanchine does not believe that *The Rite* can be danced, but he has not yet seen the recently recovered score of the Stravinsky-Nijinsky choreography. This outlines a strictly musical approach to the ballet, contrapuntal in movement and phrasing and with no attempt to imitate or match the images of the orchestra. The year 1973 is *The Rite*'s sixtieth anniversary. If only to render historical service, the City Ballet should produce this greatest of all ballets in the version in which it was conceived, Mr. Robbins choreographing the groups, Mr. Balanchine the *élue* and the other solo parts. *Renard, Histoire du Soldat,* and *Les Noces* comprise a second natural, sequential program, and *Les Noces* still awaits a performance based on Stravinsky's own stage directions. A complete *Le Baiser de la Fée* is also overdue. The *Divertimento* that Stravinsky excerpted from it has strong symphonic form but is ruined by the peremptory ending. Balanchine's excerpts, though weak in musical shape, were one of the festival's peaks, nevertheless, which indicates that the whole would be a supersuccess. *Le Baiser* belongs on a program with revivals of that first Stravinsky-Balanchine-Kirstein collaboration, *Jeu de Cartes,* and the last, *Variations,* amnesty being granted Suzanne Farrell to dance the latter. Room could be found on other evenings for *Perséphone,* not yet staged in New York (or anywhere, properly), and *The Flood,* which should appeal to Mr. Robbins's genius as well as to his showmanship.

The Violin Concerto, *Duo Concertant, Requiem Canticles, Dumbarton Oaks, Circus Polka* must be repeated, of course, along with *Capriccio, Movements,* and the Trilogy, this last in the achronological order *Orpheus, Agon, Apollo,* as Stravinsky and Balanchine did it in Hamburg in 1962. (The birth of *Apollo* was more beautiful in the original choreography, incidentally, with the unswaddling of the god like the unwinding of a geisha from her obi.) Thus an even more dazzling celebration would be assured for next June. I can hardly wait for that mock-Bayreuth fanfare in the foyer, the entry into the arena, and the thumbs-up for the company that is America's greatest artistic pride.

THE THEATER—

Venice and London

What with interregnums at La Scala, the Paris Opéra, and Sadler's Wells, the opera lover in me was less well served, on a recent trip, than the balletomane and the theater buff. Not that the Royal Ballet's Diaghilev centenary at Covent Garden was a second choice; on the contrary, the opportunity to see Diaghilev ballets in their original choreography and decor is unavailable in America. My theater-addict side fared somewhat less well, however, although the production I have chosen to discuss won an international prize in Belgrade and provoked critical storms in Italy and France.

This was Luca Ronconi's staging of the *Oresteia* in Venice, where it was overpublicized and oversouled. The city is a European New Haven, theatrically speaking, except that it specializes not only in tryouts ("We Bombed in Venice") but also in revivals. Verdi's *Giovanna d'Arco,* for example, received a fair trial there during my last visit—and a unanimous recondemnation to the shelf. Venice is famous, of course, as a host to experiments in the visual arts. But this year the Biennale had bequeathed an aftermath of "art objects" to the streets and *campi* even more ominous as portents of the approaching end than the plank-and-sawhorse bridges stacked all over the city in expectation of the floods. Santa Maria del Giglio was imperiled by a huge metal "construction," a battered harvester perhaps, and by what appeared to be a bronze outhouse—so used, at any rate—while the hotel Bauer was faced by something resembling a mammoth tuning fork, a threat in the Jericho sense, one would hope, to its Fascist-mausoleum architecture. But the most bizarre of these alfresco ornaments were the bread statues by Enrico Job. Featureless except for heads, arms, legs, they made one think of thalidomide children or partly baked bodies recovered from the oven of a concentration camp. Ten of them were exposed on the Academy side of the bridge, where they were warily pecked at by pigeons—long accustomed not to "bite the hand that feeds you"?—though small birds crawled over them like maggots.

Theater has not heretofore shared so important a part in the Biennale as what, if only for purposes of classification, are still referred to as music and the visual arts. But after Ronconi's *Oresteia* this will no longer be true. Known to New York for his production of *Orlando Furioso* in a tent in Bryant Park, Ronconi has earned a reputation for exploiting audience involvement to an unprecedented degree. In *Oresteia,* by contrast, the audience is totally uninvolved. This time the center of attraction was the stage itself, a more compelling performer than any of those who appeared on it, although limited to acrobatics and squeaks. A badminton court in size, it would have been a more suitable arena for a cockfight than for Aeschylus' trilogy. Yet no cockfight either, since its forty-five-degree roll obliged the actors to spend the evening ascending or descending hills, an activity one would have thought more appropriate to a play about Sisyphus. This seesawing incidentally exposed the "backstage" under the stage: workmen reading newspapers and eating sandwiches, a prompter following the text, actors preparing to go on—all of which competed very favorably for audience attention with the tragedy unfolding just above their heads. The stage was evenly divided as well, each half periodically departing for the ceiling or basement, like a freight elevator or *deus ex machina*.

Ronconi's most successful novelty was in the treatment of the chorus, especially in the polyphonic distribution of the long prologue. At times the actors spoke in unison; at others they entered and exited in canon or shared lines in overlapping hockets while always rotating the part of the leader. For action they writhed on the ground as if suffering seizures; stuffed cotton into their mouths; flung "ordure" about, some of it landing in my row, which was as close to "direct audience participation" as the production came. Apart from the chorus, the performance depended heavily on howling and screaming, especially when the principals stood at opposite ends of the small and resonant hall. It was no less dependent on props. These included a phantom staircase, three armillary spheres with fire at the cores, and one of Signor Job's bread people (a groan from the audience), this one representing the corpse of Iphigenia, whose limbs the Elders of Argos broke off and munched with more evident appetite than that of the pigeons. But the most dramatic moment was also the most repugnant—an ax falling on a sacrificial lamb that may or may not have already been dead and from which a haruspex withdrew a handful of entrails.

The performance was unbearably slow, partly because of too deliberate enunciation; "significant" words such as "justice" were dissected ("*gee-ewe-steet-tsee-ah*"), as if the theater were a speech-therapy clinic. No one can have survived the whole of the six-and-a-half-hour ordeal. The physical deterrents alone were too great—the airless, claustrophobic room; the backless benches; the vertigo and *mal de mer* brought on by the tilting stage—to say nothing of the mental obstacles, for the staging constantly drew attention to itself and away from the play.

—

The theater of Serge de Diaghilev is a garden of delights not only by comparison. Neither before nor since have musicians, dancers, scenic designers so perfectly complemented and integrated their arts, for it was Diaghilev's unique gift to recognize and marry the talents of others. The choreography and decor of the Royal Ballet's triple bill—*The Firebird*, *The Rite of Spring*, and *Les Noces*—were only two-thirds Diaghilev, however, *The Rite of Spring* being unrelated visually to his productions of the ballet. The following discussion is confined to *The Firebird*, therefore, a faithful re-creation of the original Fokine choreography (1910) and Goncharova decor (1926); and to *Les Noces*, Bronislava Nijinska's re-creation (1966) of her own choreography for the original production (1923), also with decor by Goncharova.

Yet Mlle Nijinska has changed two sections, the scene of the weeping mothers and the ending, seriously damaging both. The former, almost static in the original, was played in front of the curtain, whereas the re-created version employs the full stage and a style of dancing not unlike that of Martha Graham, a peculiar solecism in this otherwise angular and impersonal choreography. As for the ending, the new one contradicts not only the musical content but the instructions in the libretto. After forty-three years, the motionless coda must have struck Mlle Nijinska as too bleak.

Her revision temporizes, extending the entrance of the Bride and Groom into the nuptial chamber during most of the music. At the point where the Groom is heard alone, a point at which all movement should cease, the dancers in this re-created staging have only just begun to form their concluding frieze. The set, too, though apparently the same as the original—Stravinsky used to say that the single window was too high, more appropriate to a prison than to an *izba*—employs two stage levels. This allowed for Mlle Nijinska's protracted choreographic ending but was definitely not part of the composer's plan.

The choreography as a whole is one of the century's greatest dance achievements. Like the music, it unwinds as mechanically as a clock, but with no appearance of winding down, then stops suddenly. The stage action, whose high point is the rowdiness and boisterousness of the Fourth Tableau, matches the simplicity of Stravinsky's conception; in comparison to which the version by Béjart needs the Winter Palace. But every other staging is most solemn precisely where Stravinsky is most ironical. Dance critics regularly note a quality of modernity in *Les Noces* missing even in *The Rite of Spring*, but they do not account for it. Surely the explanation, so far as Mlle Nijinska's choreography is concerned, is in the disjunct groupings, which correspond to the fragmentation in the text and music.

The Royal Ballet's *Firebird* is now regarded in London as a seedy spectacle, and the performances I attended were the company's hundred-and-third and hundred-and-fourth. The ballet has become almost as routine as *Swan Lake.* The monsters, the bolibotchki and kikimoras, are more funny than fierce, the enchanted princesses and their golden apples (only a juggler could save this scene) are merely insipid, and Kastchei's beckoning Fu Manchu fingernail is yesteryear matinee kitsch. Yet the score should not be cut by so much as a measure, nor should any deviation be permitted from the original choreography. New York ought to see the ballet this way, I might add, rather than chopped into dance movements, which eliminate the drama, for the episodic sections, the recitatives between, tell the story. Moreover, their musical quality is as high as that of such set pieces as "The Golden Apples," and in some cases higher, as in the passage after the *Pas de Deux* which points to *Petrushka* and *The Nightingale*.

The Covent Garden *Firebird* offers the quintessence of the first and greatest years of the Diaghilev Ballet, as near to it, at any rate, as we are likely to experience. Nor is it in need of updating. The arabesque, which expresses the captured Firebird's struggle for release, no longer excites any *frisson*, but that hardly justifies the substitution of something that will. In fact, every musical event was planned so literally for choreographic action that to tamper with the latter is in some degree to misconstrue Stravinsky's intentions. (What *could* be tolerated are a few orchestra rehearsals—a more ragged and dragged reading scarcely being imaginable—and at least one adjustment of a costume: that of the Tsarevitch should be returned to Santa Claus.) In short, just as it is, "sumptuous," "old-fashioned," "romantic," the Covent Garden *Firebird* is pure delight.

Diaghilev himself remains something of an enigma, and a comprehensive biography is long overdue. It is clear from recently uncovered materials that his portrait cannot simply be retouched but will have to be painted anew. The aesthete, the drawing-room charmer, was also a man of tyrannical action, which was not unknown except in extent. His correspondence with Stravinsky, for instance, often borders on the bellicose. "*Il faut attendre conditions qui seront certainement pas les tiennes*," Diaghilev telegraphed from Paris to the composer in Clarens, April 14, 1913, and from Rome,

January 16, 1915: "*Suis revolté sans limites.*" Stravinsky was capable of an equally hard line: "*Accepte aucune condition ni termes payement . . .*" (Morges, October 13, 1919), and even when the two compatriots made up, it was transparently for ulterior motives. Thus the pretended purpose of a letter of Stravinsky's dated August 15, 1928, is a request for his old friend and collaborator to purchase books for him in Russian and Slavonic, but its real one is to win an argument concerning a rival ballet company's right to perform *Apollo.*

The inauguration of a Diaghilev museum, if it comes to pass, should include the Royal Ballet's *Firebird* and *Les Noces.* The museum, if it is not to be simply a well-furnished but unoccupied house, must exhibit the living creations for which the world celebrates Diaghilev.

DIAGHILEV AND THE BALLETS RUSSES

If by virtue of its pictures this book is a product for the coffee table, then the text might be described as a demitasse of very weak Sanka. Yet the product is worth having no matter how ersatz and insubstantial the reading matter. Many of the photographs are unknown, and most of them are appealing. Nor will devotees be deterred by the price—$35.00, but only $29.50 if you go now and pay later[1]—despite the

1. *Diaghilev and the Ballets Russes,* by Boris Kochno, Harper and Row, New York, 1970.

glut of similar publications all militating against that one much-needed good book.

The title leads the reader to expect a fuller history than the book provides. M. Kochno has already given us some of this in his yet-to-be translated *Le Ballet* (1954). Instead of taking the story on from there, however, and publishing letters and other documents in full, the present volume consists mainly of a recompilation, ballet by ballet, of elementary plot descriptions, most of which could have been put together by anyone from two or three standard ballet books. Much of the other material could also have been compounded in the same way, from a few volumes of the memoirs of ex-dancers.

But whereas the photographs contribute to scholarship, the text contradicts or ignores it at several points. After finding one of Cocteau's best-known drawings attributed to Picasso (p. 147), the reader begins to wonder whether the book was even proofread. Furthermore, the drawing is not dated, but, then, scarcely a dozen illustrations, out of some four hundred in the book, *are* dated. Nor does M. Kochno's chronology inspire confidence. We read (p. 17) that Diaghilev "resolved to present *The Sleeping Beauty* in London" in 1922, though that presentation had taken place the year before. And we are told (p. 190) that "In Paris, *Les Noces* was a triumphant success"—all of the Ballets's successes were triumphant, just as the "ovations" it was given were invariably "thunderous"—"but in London, three years later, the work was coolly received. Among its few English admirers was H. G. Wells, who went on record with a statement published in June 1923." But this is the date of the Paris premiere. In fact the reader doubts that the author has gotten his own birthday right. Can it be 1904? But look at him together with Stravinsky in 1922 (p. 255). Is he really only eighteen? He did, of course, have a reputation for precocity and promise as a poet during the Revolution when, shades of Rimbaud, he would have been about fifteen.

And "on record" where? Few sources are cited, no bibliography is included, letters are quoted only in bits and always in translation, and even the photographs are not credited. I have already complained that the captions are incomplete. In addition to some notion of when and where, the reader would like an adequate description of the contents. Only one line of Diaghilev's note reproduced on the flyleaf is translated, yet all of it is of interest. And what does Stravinsky's inscription on M. Kochno's copy of the *Mavra* score (or program?) actually say? This is important both because M. Kochno's name survives as the librettist of that opus and because the composer can be revealing even in a few words of dedication. Certainly he is that in the more legible dedication to Kochno on the photograph on page 190, the year after *Mavra,* where the tone is about as cordial as it might have been to any autograph collector.

The Introduction by Alexandre Benois, dated 1944, purports to describe "The Origins of the Ballets Russes," but is largely confined to Benois's own, surprisingly large role: "I can consider myself the instigator and originator of the whole enterprise." Whereas on some points his account is so obviously, hence harmlessly, incorrect—the poses of the dancers in *The Rite* were "intended to represent the condition of slaves in antiquity"—the distortion of emphasis in others requires comment. Was *Pavillon d'Armide* (Benois-Tcherepnine) more "crucial" than *Petrushka,* as Benois claims, let alone *The Rite of Spring*? I am aware that Haskell and Grigoriev support Benois's claims, and I am prepared to believe that, as he says, "my theme interested and touched [the audience]; my sets and costumes evoked thunderous applause." Yet Benois's perspective often fails to give due importance to the integration of music and spectacle, and time has endorsed not *Pavillon* but *Petrushka,* Benois's most famous collaboration, about which he refuses to talk, for the reason, I suspect, that he had had a spat with the composer.

Lacking the space and the inclination to contest M. Kochno's emphases and to correct his errors both of commission and omission (which would require a companion volume the size of his), I will confine myself to a gloss on his version of the most important moment in his life. He titles it "My First Meeting with Diaghilev." It was, I am convinced, the second. Kochno says that:

> It was while I was posing for my portrait that my friend Soudeikine spoke to me about the Ballets Russes and asked me to see Diaghilev on his behalf to discuss various questions concerning an eventual revival of [Florent Schmitt's] *Salomé* at the Paris Opéra.

But is it likely that Sudeikine would entrust such an ambassadorship to a boy of seventeen who, moreover, had not even met the none-too-approachable impresario? Sudeikine himself had known Diaghilev intimately for many years, having accompanied him on his strange voyeurist expeditions in Paris in 1909 (pairs of young girls and very close up!). All the same, M. Kochno relates how Sudeikine prepared him for his mission and he goes on to describe the meeting:

> On February 27, 1921, at ten in the morning, I arrived at the hôtel Scribe, which was the address Soudeikine had given me, and asked to see M. de Diaghilev. The concierge replied that Diaghilev had not lived at the hotel for years but that most likely I would find him at the Continental . . .

It seems no less unlikely that Sudeikine, who was on close terms with many of the Ballets' personnel, would have been unaware that Diaghilev had moved from a well-known hotel *years* previously. But never mind. The truth is that M. Kochno had already met Diaghilev a day or two before. All that winter he had been importuning Madame Sudeikine to arrange an introduction. When Diaghilev telephoned her one afternoon to say that he was coming to tea, she therefore obligingly invited the young poet to drop by "unexpectedly." He did, of course, and the concierge announced a "Monsieur Coquenault," a name that seems to have stuck. According to the then Madame Sudeikine, Diaghilev did all of the talking and departed first, but not before he had invited "Monsieur Coquenault" to lunch at the hôtel Scribe. As it happened, this rendezvous fell on a Sunday, and M. Kochno found himself razorless and all barbershops closed. A slave to the fashion begun by Scipio Aemilianus, M. Kochno called on the Sudeikines again, to borrow the necessary implement, all of which may or may not have some connection with the shaving scene in *Mavra.* On this second visit, too, Sudeikine may very well have asked him to mention *Salomé* to Diaghilev. And at this point the reader may safely resume M. Kochno (p. 154).

That none of this is of the slightest consequence is precisely my point in telling it, for I offer it as an all too typical specimen of the Diaghilev literature—*versus* the literature that is needed nowadays, a critical evaluation by someone with no claims to have known Diaghilev. In the absence of films, this is a difficult undertaking. For though the great impresario conceived, planned, produced, and participated in the execution of ballets, he did not actually compose, costume, or choreograph them. His only tangible is his repertory. Yet that can be studied in untried ways, and the achievement separated from the legend. Until someone performs that task for us, I recommend this book for the photographs.

VERA STRAVINSKY— Painter

"Where's Vera? Is she painting?" This used to be Igor Stravinsky's first question as he emerged from his workroom, and the answer, that Vera was indeed painting, assured him that in the center of his world all was well.

For nearly twenty years composer and painter unveiled their work to each other first, before anyone else heard or saw it. And for twenty years the composer was the painter's most helpful critic. Stravinsky had an unerring eye for composition in painting, as well as the eye of a cartoonist for the characteristic feature, the essential detail. He so cherished his wife's pictures that to exhibit them for him was to risk having one or more impounded in the already overcrowded gallery, museum, flea market of his studio. As for the painter's criticisms of the composer, I have never heard of any. But I can testify that he wrote all of his music for her first, that the first sharing of his discoveries with her was sacred to him, that her response was more important than "the world's."

Vera de Bosset was born on Christmas Day 1892 in her parents' St. Petersburg home, near the ice-bound and snow-covered Neva, at Pesochnaya Ulitsa, 4. (She counts herself a Capricorn, using the Old Style Russian calendar, and is a devout believer in her horoscope.) Half a century later, Thomas Mann described her as a "specifically Russian beauty," but she has no Russian blood (which does not invalidate Mann's description). Her mother, Henriette Malmgreen (also born on Christmas, 1870), was Swedish; her father, Artur de Bosset (born 1867), French. One of his ancestors was the Monsieur de Beausset, Prefect of Paris, who brought the portrait of L'Aiglon from the Empress to Napoleon before the Battle of Borodino.

Vera did not grow up in St. Petersburg, and in fact visited the city only once in her childhood, to see one of her grandmothers. She lived in Gorky, which means "little hills" or "bluffs," the De Bosset country estate in Novgorodskaya Province, midway between St. Petersburg and Moscow. The De Bosset home was surrounded by forests, fields, and lakes, a landscape that entered profoundly into the child's feelings, for it is still evident in the paintings. Her education at Gorky was entrusted to governesses, Fräulein Erna in the winter, a Parisienne in the summer. Vera was fond of Fräulein Erna —"Except when she threatened me: she would say that unless my manners improved I would end up marrying Aneesim, the old peasant who carried logs to the hearths and lighted the fires." Fräulein Erna was a competent pianist, and under her instruction young Vera became one too. The pupil had an excellent ear, and she can still repeat the intervals of the Kaiser's automobile horn, which she heard frequently while living as a student in Berlin. Also thanks to Fräulein Erna, the painter's second language, like the composer's, was German. (It is franglais now.) Still another teacher, though hardly thought of as such, was her father's gardener, Alexander Kalistratovich. Vera's love of flowers antedates his service with the De Bossets, but she says that most of her practical knowledge of plants and flowers comes from—I almost said stems from—him.

Vera's closest companion in the country was her mother. The two rode horseback together, gathered mushrooms together (for stomach, not soul food in those days), and joined in pampering Vera's pets: Mashka the cat, Kashtanka the dog, Mishka the baby bear, Schwetka the horse, Cheezhik the young bull, *La Générale* the cow, and Murzilka the goose who honked after Madame de Bosset wherever she went. Mother and daughter even danced together. When Vera was a student in Moscow, she saw Isadora Duncan perform, and, coming home afterward, Vera removed her shoes, induced her mother to do the same, and cavorted with her parent *à la* Duncan. In the 1920s, in Paris, Vera and Isadora Duncan were neighbors and glancing acquaintances, sometimes dining together.

Artur de Bosset owned an electrical-equipment factory in Kudinova, a village some forty-five minutes from Moscow on the Nizhni-Novgorod line. Vera remembers that when the Tsar's train passed Kudinova, soldiers stood on either side of the tracks and pointed their guns toward the houses, the windows of which had to be curtained. Artur de Bosset was a liberal. He refused the Order of St. Stanislas, and named his daughter for the leftist Vera in Goncharov's *The Precipice.* The Marquis Theodore de Bosset, however, Artur's cousin, was one of the Tsar's naval advisers, owing to which the De Bosset relatives fled to South America after the Peace of Brest Litovsk—Theodore to Lima (where he is buried), Artur to Santiago (ditto, August 1937). On the way, Artur resided for a time in Berlin, where he divorced Vera's mother. His second wife, Irena Mella, moved from Santiago to Buenos Aires after his death; in August 1960, she met her stepdaughter there for the first time. Vera saw her own mother for the last time in 1925, in Paris, after which Madame de Bosset returned to Moscow, where she died during the war.

In her thirteenth year, Vera entered a boarding school in Moscow, remaining there for the next four years with the exception of weekends at home and vacations there and in Switzerland. School was a trial, except for a *nanya* who called her "Bossic," and Vera was soon leading a hunger strike to protest the rations. "Shall I send to Tiestov's for lobsters?" the headmistress asked her rebellious boarder, who replied that this seemed a capital idea. Vera kept up her musical studies under David Shor, of the Shor, Krein, and Ehrlich Moscow Trio, and created a stir at school by including an Etude by Scriabin in her recital.

Vera's greatest delight in Moscow was the theater. She would pawn her most prized possessions to buy tickets. It was the heyday of the ballet, of Russian opera—Tchaikovsky's *The Little Slippers* was the first opera she ever saw—of Stanislavsky. She had the astronomical luck, in the first two plays she attended, to see Eleonora Duse and Sarah Bernhardt. Duly imitating the great actresses in drama classes at school, Vera made a hit by fainting in the Bernhardt manner: "I went down like *that*,"—she gestures—"and there I was, *par terre*."

Graduated *cum laude*, gold-medaled, and certified to teach mathematics and French, Mademoiselle de Bosset hoped to continue her studies in Paris. But the young ladies of her father's acquaintance who had been finished at Parisian schools were distinguished more by their affectations and wanton ways than by their intellectual accomplishments. Vera's father considered the German capital safer and more serious, and, accordingly, she was enrolled in the University of Berlin and sent to a *pension* "kept by a pair of despotic old maids." She studied philosophy and science (anatomy, physics, chemistry) in her first year, but switched to an art curriculum in her second, attending the lectures of Heinrich Wölfflin—who, she says, "opened my eyes." After the second year, her formal education was cut short by World War One. She returned to Russia intellectually improved and without affectations, remaining free of them all her life, being immune to the fault.

In Moscow, she entered the Nelidova Ballet School, "not

to become a ballerina," she says, performing a mock *arabesque penchée*. "I was too tall and too late-starting. But I wanted to acquire poise, be able to move less brusquely, and learn something about bodily expression. The ballet was the ideal basic training for an actress, so I thought, and that is what I had determined to become." At the Nelidova she first heard of Diaghilev and Stravinsky.

After appearing in the Kamerny Theater as a dancer, she was discovered by movie scouts, or whatever the Russians called them. A screen test was arranged and as a result she played in a dozen film comedies in the next two years, some of them with Marius Petipa, the actor son of the choreographer of *Swan Lake*. But the high point of her cinema career came later, in the part of Helen in *War and Peace*.

While still at the Nelidova, she married a Mr. Schilling—"*niet kopeki* and now a Schilling," her poorer friends commented. But Schilling was a compulsive gambler and the newlyweds were constantly in hock. In 1916 she finally left Schilling and eloped to St. Petersburg with the painter Serge Sudeikine. The couple resided in an apartment on the Ekaterinsky Canal, and were living there when Rasputin was murdered, as well as during the Revolution of March 1917. As a result of being forced to lie in the snow in a bullet-raked street, she became very ill and, as soon as she was able to travel, returned to Moscow. Then, reunited with Sudeikine, she joined the exodus of practically everyone who could afford it to the Crimea. There she began to paint. Her first works, silhouettes on glass, were exhibited in Yalta in 1918, where, on February 11, she married Sudeikine.[1]

1. The marriage was dissolved by a Boston court, March 5, 1940, by which date the Sudeikines had not seen each other for more than fifteen years. On August 15, 1945, to satisfy a Los Angeles court, ruling on the Stravinskys' application for citizenship, the composer fabricated a statement saying that his wife's marriage to Sudeikine had been terminated on February 20, 1920, in Tiflis.

With the approach of the Red Army in the spring of 1919, Vera and Sudeikine sailed for Constantinople. Vera Stravinsky recalls that Vladimir Nabokov's father was on the same Yalta pier, and that so was the dowager Empress, who was rescued by an English cruiser. The Sudeikines' ark was more modest, a mere thirty-footer, loaded with oil drums. A heavy storm came up and, many queasy hours later, the boat docked at Batum at the wrong end of the Black Sea. From there they journeyed to Tiflis, where camels were still the main means of transportation in the bazaar, and to Baku, where women still wore veils. Tiflis was their home for the next year, a happy one, despite the Revolution, to judge from Vera's diaries.

In May 1920 Vera sold her diamond-with-pearl earrings for 3,000 rubles ("the Kerensky ruble was as worthless as the dollar will soon be") to buy passage for herself and Sudeikine on the *S.S. Souhira*, a French steamer bound for Marseilles. They encountered many adventures on the voyage, before reaching Paris during the city's celebrations of the canonization of Jeanne d'Arc, May 20, 1920. After finding an apartment in the rue de la Boétie, they met former friends among the large population of Russian refugees, including dancers and decorators of the Diaghilev ballet. Before long, however, Sudeikine went to America to fulfill commissions as a designer for the Metropolitan Opera, and for more than a year Vera shared an apartment with Gabrielle Picabia. At this time Vera became a close friend of Picasso, Cocteau, Tzara, Chanel. Even before this, and not long after her arrival in Paris, Diaghilev, calling on Sudeikine, met and was captivated by his wife. (Sudeikine had been a founding member of Diaghilev's *Mir Isskustva.*) In February 1921, Diaghilev invited Vera to a dinner at which Stravinsky was to be present, adding: "He is moody today so please be nice to him." And of course she was.

Of this first meeting, in an Italian restaurant in Montmartre, Madame Stravinsky recalls that the composer was "the wittiest, most amusing man I had ever met . . . He was always witty, moreover, but though he could be moody, too, and very caustic, he was never that with me. Most of his tempers were due to impatience with business affairs. Our first '*crac*' occurred in 1926 when I moved to an apartment in the rue Ranelagh. He had asked me to have a priest consecrate the new home, but I didn't, and Stravinsky was angry. I promised to do it the next day, but with him everything had to be immediate." Vera had a pack of cards with her at that first meeting, and she told the composer's future, presumably saying something about the queen of hearts.

Each of Vera Stravinsky's three artistic careers flourished in a different country. She was an actress in Russia (except for a two-month stint in London in 1921 as the Queen in *The Sleeping Beauty*), a costume designer in France, a painter in America. The scene of the middle career was a Parisian atelier which she directed and which employed more than a score of midinettes to make costumes for the Diaghilev ballets and the theater. Her first commission was to design and make the costume for Markova as the Nightingale in the 1925 revival of Stravinsky's ballet. Then she redesigned Marie Laurencin's sketches for *Les Biches*, Diaghilev having found them incomprehensible. Drastic adjustments were also required in Rouault's designs for *Le Fils Prodigue*, a project Diaghilev again entrusted to her. Later she herself designed and supervised the making of some three hundred costumes for a production of *Carmen* in Amsterdam that was conducted by Pierre Monteux.

In January 1925, Stravinsky, on an American concert tour, experienced a public but incomplete meeting with Sudeikine. This occurred at the Metropolitan Opera during a double bill of *The Nightingale* and *Petrushka* for which Sudeikine had designed the sets. Acknowledging the applause at the end of the performance, Stravinsky started on stage, saw Sudeikine approaching from the other side, froze, bowed alone, departed in haste. The *Philadelphia Inquirer* Magazine Section, March 29, 1925, devoted a full page of its Sunday sensation space to the "feud" between Stravinsky and Sudeikine[2] ("Tragedy of the Famous Artist's Lost Wife"), illustrating the story with a cover photograph of Vera.

In February 1925, while Stravinsky was still in America, Vera met with his first wife, at her request and Stravinsky's, in Nice. Three years earlier, in Biarritz, Stravinsky had told his wife about Vera, and described the scene to her in a letter that could compete with the best of Dostoievsky. The two women instantly understood each other, at the luncheon in Nice, and maintained a high mutual respect until the death of Catherine Stravinsky in 1939.

Returning from America on the *S.S. Aquitania,* Stravinsky purchased a Renault, and both he and Vera acquired driver's licenses. Vera eventually sold the Renault to buy a Mathis. The Mathis was sold to buy a Citroën, with which Stravinsky had bad luck. He was given a ticket for parking at the wrong hour in front of Hermès, where he had gone to purchase a cravat, and shortly after that he drove all the way to St. Germain-en-Laye in low gear and burned up the motor. The Citroën was exchanged for a Peugeot *bleu-nuit.*

Vera, arriving in New York on the *S.S. Rex,* January 12, 1940, married Stravinsky on March 9, in New Bedford, Massachusetts. The marriage between this tall, gentle, always calm, soft-voiced, quintessentially feminine woman, and the tiny, bony, always anxious, basso-profundo, quintessentially masculine man was made in Heaven. When the two did not

2. Sudeikine later married the American singer Jean Palmer. He died in 1946 and is buried in Woodstock, New York.

complement each other in their likes and dislikes, it was only because these were the same: their love of birds and flowers, for example, and of animals and paintings. Every day Vera would make a list of errands and business chores to be accomplished, and every day Stravinsky would write at the top of it: "First you have to kiss me." In the spring of 1940, when the Stravinskys moved to Hollywood, Vera opened an art gallery, La Boutique, and resumed the painting that she had not practiced since Yalta. On a visit to Hollywood in 1954, Gasparo del Corso, director of the Galleria Obelisco in Rome, invited her to exhibit there, which she did the following year, her first one-woman show.

Nature—leaves, flowers, seashells, clouds—is the material of Vera Stravinsky's painting. But she prefers nature in a certain mood, rainy rather than sunny. "I like the *mélancolie* in a landscape," she says, "and I like early morning mists, woods and fields blurred by rain, night scenes with mysterious explosions of light." Her first American pictures were inspired by automobile trips through the swamps of Louisiana and the redwood forests of the Northwest. (The Stravinskys traveled extensively by automobile in their early years here.) Oil rigs in the ocean near Ventura, California, were another source of inspiration, "but at night, when they look like Christmas trees." She continued to paint in Europe, too, on each return there in the fifties and sixties, most rewardingly on the Bosphorus, in the great city her boat did not reach in 1919.

Yet her pictures are not really "of" any of these places or "of" any "thing." She does not copy and does not sketch, or even take notes except for verbal reminders of the colors in a composition of Nature. To her, color *is* composition, and her greatest gifts are an infallible color sense and skill in color manipulation. "My imagination is ignited from the outside," she says, "but I paint entirely from the inside, depending on imagination alone. I try to forget the relationship with the object when I begin to paint. Birds, fish, fragments of objects, *natures mortes:* they must retain no more than a *soupçon* of reality in the painting."

Vera Stravinsky's techniques are her own. She has been a gouache painter, first and foremost, partly because she likes the velvety texture, partly because of circumstances. Oil painting was impracticable while she was on concert tours with her husband, since he was seldom long enough in one place for her pictures to dry. (This was before acrylics and modern siccatives.) Needlework was another occupation on these travels, and Madame Stravinsky used her time backstage designing and stitching more than a score of very attractive rugs.

Vera Stravinsky applies paint with any implement, spatula, sponge, palette knife, sable brush, the flat of her hand. She then treats it by any device, rubbing it with paper, scratching it with a table fork, even washing it in her bathtub. In the case of work that displeases her, and her touchstones tell her immediately, this washing is an act of purification, the need to begin with "a clean slate." She will briefly immerse a gouache in the bath, and after the baptismal waters have dried, paint a new surface on the palimpsest of the old.

Vera Stravinsky did not paint after her husband's death. Then one day, after many months, she copied a poem by Kusmin, forming large Russian letters in bright colors and surrounding and intertwining them with flowers, weeds or seaweeds, starfish or stars. It was the most Russian picture she had ever painted, but as a picture of her feelings it was painfully revealing, a vision of Stravinsky's grave in the Russian corner of the cemetery island in the Venetian lagoon. At the same time, it was a good painting, and it broke the barrier. She began to work regularly thereafter, and with new inventiveness, for she has some of her husband's phenomenal powers of self-renewal. More than once, in the dreaded lonely moment of finishing a picture and wanting to show it, she would start toward his room, which she had never entered since his death. Eventually she did go there, and begin to paint there, until now she works exclusively in his room and seems happier in it than anywhere else in the house. Stravinsky, of course, would be—or, as I prefer to think, *is*—happy too. The answer to his "Where is Vera? Is she painting?" is "Yes."

ELEGY AND IAMBUS

April 10, 1972—We drive from Rome, hardly visible beneath election posters ("*Vota Liberale*," "*Vota Communista*") and advertisements for the Banco di Santo Spirito, to the Manzù museum at Campo Fico, where our cicerone is the sculptor's model, Inge. So many of the maestro's figures are of the nude Inge herself, however, that it is impossible, if impolite, to refrain from mentally undressing the original. In fact Manzù's world centers so closely on Inge—straying to any large extent only to *natures mortes*, helmets (he is obsessed with headgear), priests and their raiment—that one looks for her features in all of his women, including the female partners in two tempestuous copulations in bronze. The part of the museum devoted to theatrical designs is more revealing of the artist as a whole. But whereas the sets are generally successful, friezes exploiting pleated drapery in the same way as the sculptures, the costumes are often naïve. And Manzù *is* naïve, in Schiller's sense, a naïve of genius, as at least one of the costumes, that of the Devil in *Histoire du Soldat*, shows: the fallen angel has a tattered black wing and he wears a fig leaf of solid gold.

The gate to the artist's hilltop home still threatens intruders with canine dismemberment, but the hounds are nowhere in evidence (bite each other and die of rabies?), and the barbed wire is less obviously dangerous now than the cactus. The maestro greets us outside, against a landscape as undulant as the flanks and *fesses* he loves to sculpt, for Manzù is an "old man mad about hills."

His studio could serve as a B-52 hangar, yet is not tall enough to shelter a mammoth opus-in-progress that stands just outside the entrance as mysteriously as the Trojan horse. Whatever it is, the scaffolding and canvas covering suggest that the sculptor has struck oil and that he prefers to keep it secret. What the studio does contain are plaster nudes; mitred heads, both in relief and in the round, the latter including two of Papa Giovanni; numerous drawings; three dollhouse-like models of a set for Strauss's *Elektra;* and, oddly, a clump of Winterhalter-period trumpets and hunting horns tied to the wall like dead game, yet not oddly at all, as one looks a second time at the instruments' rounded tubing, flared, infundibular bells, female curves.

The *bozzetto* of I.S.'s tomb is a flat oblong block, actual size, set in a troughlike frame later to be capped with porphyry. Manzù brings out a piece of the milky marble of his choice, but for the lettering asks V. to decide between lapis lazuli and a light green stone. "Blue was our color," she says, but the green is unsuitably veined in any case. Manzù draws the cross, to be encrusted near the foot of the stone, on a square sheet of gold, and draws it at high speed, in contrast to the way he writes, which is like a backward child. In fact he succeeds in writing the difficult word "Stravinsky" at all only thanks to Luisella, his American-speaking secretary (her favorite comment: "He's not kidding") who somehow pulls him through, though for a time the outcome is in doubt. V. wants to be certain he does not make a "w" of the fifth letter, which is the German spelling, and an "i" of the final one, which is the Polish.

He promises that the *pietra* will be in Venice by June for the *sistemazione* and tells V. that he wishes to make a gift of it, and not only of his art but of the materials. Then, as we leave: "I would like to have made something that could last as long as Stravinsky's music, but stone, which won't, is all I have."

April 11—The via Flaminia is decked with advertisements for the forthcoming Florentine exhibition of Henry Moore. The viewer will at least be able to see the Tuscan landscape through the holes.

During the drive to Venice I am obsessed by the thought that I.S. is happy V. is coming, just as he used to be when she returned from a drive in Hollywood. Our arrival is an unbearable, empty homecoming, therefore, made all the more depressing by an unseasonable inundation: half of the Piazza is submerged and the Molo is impassable. Venice is dying on its feet (fins?).

April 13—The Archimandrite—in mufti: black suit, black shirt, gold cross on a gold neck chain—comes to discuss Saturday's Panikheda service. He says that souvenir hunters have stolen three crosses, scrawled with signatures, from the grave, but that the mayor has now had a name plaque cemented to the wall behind it. Apart from Greek, the Archimandrite's only language is the Venetian dialect, and conversation is limited.

April 14—The high waters having receded, we go to the cemetery, where a transformation has taken place. In the midst of death we are in life, the secluded corner being a five-star tourist attraction now, to which arrow-shaped STRAVINSCKY (*sic*) signs direct the traffic. Business at the florist's has doubled, the postcard and curio stall is sold out, and the *ortodosso* wing, I.S.'s part of it anyway, has actually been weeded. Above all, the surly gardeners of last summer have become obliging receptionists, proud, like the gravediggers, who seem to have taken a new lease on death, of the newfound importance of their island.

Passing the tightly packed, pectinate tombs of the poor, my thoughts turn to *ex*carnations, to "A bracelet of bright hair about the bone," to "dogsbody" and "nobodaddy," and to the likelihood of "God" *versus* the likelihood of accidents and chains of events leading over millions of years from amino acid in volcanic lava to Stravinsky; and, more concretely, to the underlying attraction of cemeteries, which may be in the answer they offer to the pretense to equality in the institutions on *this* side: namely that rich and poor, great and humble, are alike, for in San Michele, at least, apart from the price of the name plate and *memento mori*, they *are* alike. Thus "God" is an invention before which, at last rather than at first, we can be equal.

It is Easter Week in the Eastern Church, and many of the graves, including I.S.'s, have lighted candles. Placing her flowers on the still tombless ground, V. says: "I am unable to believe it even now, except that the marker says so" ("Stravinsky, Igor" in black paint on the mayor's plaque). Just then a loudspeaker startles us, "*Attenzione, Attenzione*," as the word sounds in airports and railroad stations. "*Quattro spiriti sono . . .*" But the disembodied voice is interrupted by static—supernal, it may be—until the final words, "*al porto principale*." Workmen are apparently being summoned to receive four newly arrived coffins, unless four escapees have been discovered and the authorities are trying to close all exits including resurrection.

April 15—The Panikheda this morning begins in San Giorgio dei Greci and ends, an hour and a half later, at the graveside. In the church we stand with Nicolas Nabokov before a laurel wreath on a table covered with red cloth (the Red Table of *Les Noces*), this being in the same position in the bema where the bier had been in the Zanipolo a year ago. Small golden balls, like the silver rattles of the censer, are attached to the wreath. (Are they related to the golden balls, clustered like stars in the firmament, on the domes of San Marco and of the Zanipolo?) On either side and beyond the table are tall candelabra and silver lamps on silver chains.

Much of the service, which includes a Mass, takes place behind the iconostasis, some of it visible through the open door, some merely audible. It begins with a procession (*vkhod*) through the iconostasis into the church, the Archimandrite (bareheaded, vestments of brocaded gold) from the center, censing to right and left as he enters, a server, carrying a tall candle, coming from one side, and a deacon, who proceeds to an agalogion to sing the responses, from another. The Archimandrite then turns to the altar and begins a chant, and in an instant that day a year ago is brought back. The music is unornamented, apart from cadential échappées, and at times the deacon, in a hollow voice, joins in, an octave below. At the high point of the service, the Archimandrite lifts the great red book of the Gospel to his forehead for our veneration, then turns to the altar and in a radiant voice sings a verse from St. John. At the end, he dons his black crepelike klobook, another reminder of a year ago, and places a piece of the antidoron in V.'s cupped hands.

On San Michele, the deacon shakes smoke over the grave while the Archimandrite lays the laurel wreath at its head and sings a prayer ("*sophia,*" "*makarios*"). As it was a year ago, the most painful moment is when he invokes the name "Igor."

October 2—Venice. Manzù's stone, expected at Mestre since last week, is still not there, for the reason, we are told, that last-minute authorizations by bureaucrats both Roman and Venetian had been overlooked. V. telephones to the sculptor himself, who assures her that the stone is on its way and will certainly reach Venice "*domani.*" All wrapped up in red tape, no doubt.

Gravitating to familiar places first (looking for a former self and the reasons why the new one is different?), I go to "Mozart's house," next to the Barcarolli bridge, and to the Legatoria Piazzesi to talk to the bookbinder who used to make I.S.'s sketchbooks and who still wears a black smock, as he did then. But I feel lonely afterward, intensely so in the Basilica at sunset, and walking in the white and gold Piazza after dark.

Dinner at Harry's Bar with Nicolas Nabokov (scarlet socks and braces, psychedelic tie). The restaurant is like a subway car at rush hour, and only fragments of Nabokov's talk—about Mediterranean bull culture *versus* Persian lion culture—are audible. Yet he manages to bring I.S. to life by quoting a single one of his expressions: "*On compose la musique avec la gomme.*"

October 5—The stone has finally arrived and, thanks to the mayor's intervention, has already been ferried to the island and entrusted to a *marmorista.*

Bill Congdon comes for lunch, all the way from Subiaco, where he lives in monastic retreat (nearest telephone: ten miles) not only from the U.S.A. and a New England Brahmin background but from the last fifteen centuries as well. Of all those who knew I.S. more than superficially in his later years, and whose lives were profoundly affected by him, Bill is one of the most extraordinary. He remembers I.S.'s every word, gesture, inflection, from their first meeting in an airport canteen in the Azores in March 1955, to their two final meetings, in Assisi, October 21, 1962, the day I.S. learned of Goncharova's death, and, in Rome, November 24, 1963, the day he learned of Aldous's. But it was during the summers in Venice, from 1956, that the camaraderie developed.

Painting is Bill's art, yet he is equally gifted in languages. He speaks the Venetian dialect, having at one time been a gondolier, and is fluent in a half-dozen Mediterranean tongues, as well as in at least one African. His leaves of absence from the cenobitic life in Subiaco are spent in Africa, especially Mali, from which he has just returned.

I do not know whether Bill ever took the Franciscan vow of poverty, but he is a voluntary have not, uncharitable only about the American System. At lunch he complains that "even the grissini wrappers have been desecrated with American-type advertising," a remark that leads to "protest art." This, he argues, "cannot be of any value if the frustration is at the creative level. Besides, the artist's first problem is always the same, to understand his motive. The second is to be patient." I admire this man, though I do not share his intellectual religiosity; for Bill is an "intellectual" despite himself, forever discussing concepts and making distinctions, always acutely self-aware. At one point he remarks that "if the maestro had been younger he would never have accepted me. He was too crisp and precise as a young man for the likes of me. Age expanded him."

When V. and I go to San Michele in the afternoon, Bill returns to Subiaco and the world of the sixth century—

except for his collection of I.S.'s recordings from the world of the twentieth. But he will come every April, as he did last year and this. Nor will I ever forget his words when he first raised his glass at lunch today: "*A noi quattro.*"

The tide is low, exposing scablike remnants of plaster on brick walls that make the city look more emaciated and diseased than ever. Rickety docks, loose moorings, creaky pintles: the whole of Venice seems to rattle, scrape, and grind. The cloacal function of the canals is especially conspicuous, too, the wash in the wake of our boat, and the drains from pipes and spiles suggesting that the city is either flushing itself or foaming at the mouth. The low water level also affects San Michele. Today the Archangel seems to promise not that the graveyard will ever yawn but only that Death Will Out.

"*Vietato Fumare,*" reads a Dante-like sign above the inner entrance. (A question of "no smoke without fire," hence the fear of connection with the eternal flames?) The thin autumn foliage within the walls exposes the grotesquerie of the decor, both iron (a raven, wings spread above a monument as if violently struggling to fly) and marmoreal: wreaths, roses, *putti,* coats-of-arms, busts—of Garibaldian males and weeping-willis (*le villi*) females, the latter with bindweed in their hair. In the lane segregating the ranks of deceased "*Religiosi*" and "*Suore,*" we fall behind a procession: a priest, preceded by a cross-bearer, followed by a coffin cart pushed by four men in black suits and black caps like tam-o'-shanters, moving in step as if performing some macabre pavane.

The names in the *Reparto Greco* read like the cast in *War and Peace:* Wolkoff, Potemkin, Galitzine, Bagration (Princess Catherine, whose tomb is under a fig tree with large, blush-sparing leaves). I.S.'s stone is not yet here, and a litter of kittens is romping on his grave. (Why, in all the length and breadth of the island, at this one place? Because if ever a man possessed what Novalis described as "the awareness of the inter-relations of all things, of conjunctions and coincidences," that man was I.S.)

Suddenly looking up, I discover that *my* grave, Number 38, is occupied! And *newly* occupied at that. I touch the ground, flex my limbs—as Lazarus must have done—say "*Cogito ergo sum*," ask V. to verify me. But neither of us recalls any mention of the event of my death in the recent obits (no epipsychidion in the *Daily American*?). So if I am still *here*, who is *there?* And, in the language of "The Three Bears," what is he or she doing in my grave?

October 6—The stone has finally reached the *Reparto Greco,* though not yet the actual site of the grave. Since its two sections have not been joined, we are unable to form any impression of it, even after workmen unwrap the upper layer from its bed of excelsior, and then stand by, brown paper hats in hand, awaiting tokens of the widow's appreciation.

The cemetery's administration building, where I go to pick a bone with the Direzione about who has usurped my grave, is a lugubrious room piled with ledgers, each with a year stamped on its spine. A sallow bookkeeper, Signora Mondovecchi, coldly listens to my case, grimly removes "1971" from the shelf, opens it to a map showing coffins stacked like bottles in wine cellars. Pointing to an area marked "*Spazi Perpetuità*," she explains that in practice "perpetual" means only ninety-nine years, to which I reply that this will not be long enough in I.S.'s case, whatever may become of Venice. *His* name has been entered in red ink, V.'s, next to his, in black. But in the place where *I* had expected to be stretched out, the mortal remains of Princess Aspasia of Greece now languish, her name freshly blotted on the page. A greatly flustered Mondovecchi assures me that the Principessa is to be transplanted to her native country, "as soon as money has been raised to pay her debts in Venice." (A case of squatters' rights, then?) But another thought seizes La Mondovecchi: What if this money is not found, if a moratorium is denied, and if the exhumation does not take place? Then the sale to me will have been lost. Whereupon La Mondovecchi, and she is very "old world" indeed, urges me to put a deposit on the plot adjacent to the Principessa, for the reason that *her* companion and closest friend, the morganatic Queen of Greece, is rumored to be "*molto malata*."

As La Mondovecchi turns to shut the Domesday Book, I inquire about the mosaic-encrusted mausoleum facing I.S.'s grave on the other side of the path and covering a hundred times the territory, a sarcophagus of such dimensions, in fact, that one pictures its cadavers not resupine but striding about. In La Mondovecchi's ultimate roll call this House of the Dead is registered under the name Messimis, which, I suppose, out loud, to be that of a Greek shipbuilder. But La Mondovecchi corrects me. "No, Signor. Maestro Messimis is a very important music critic."

June 10, 1973—Venice. The city has escaped death by drowning for yet another winter only to succumb to an invasion by the Japanese—aerial units alone, thus far, to judge by the 727-size contingents in the Piazza, and unarmed except with cameras, maps, yen. "The Americans of the seventies," the Italians call them, except that the Japanese reportedly clean their own rooms and make their own beds.

At San Michele we are obliged to wait for the departure of a *convoi funèbre*, led by a gilded water hearse with gold-winged orb. The Orthodox section is a blaze of poppies found nowhere else on the island, which raises the thought that they might be an ancient mark of heresy. I.S.'s stone is unexpectedly small—too nearly the size of his own body—and so narrow that the letters of his name look crowded on their single line. In the brief time we are here, flowers are brought by several visitors, one of them an ex-ballet dancer, I suspect, to judge by her legs and her interest in the Diaghilev monument. We search among the newer graves for Ezra Pound's but find only those of one "Oreste Licudis" and one "Pericle Triantifillis," the company of whose *names,* at any rate, the late poet would have appreciated.

Back in Venice I go to the Scuola de San Rocco, my first visit there without I.S., to hear a Ravel concert. This reminds me of I.S.'s comment on the Trio when we last heard it together: "*C'est comme une très longue conversation dans un boudoir.*"

June 11—To Torcello, via the rio della Pietà, a sewageway of empty bottles and assorted offal—the lees of the last minstrel, as it were. But in the lagoon several boys are diving from a barge that has been girded against the bruises of stone corners and canal traffic with rubber tires. At Torcello weeds writhe behind our boat—"like souls in torment," V. says, no doubt thinking of the island where "all flesh is grass." The beautiful floor of Santa Maria Assunta, in Torcello, is now covered with pews, and the beautiful walls are marred with dial-a-lecture telephones.

June 12—San Giorgio dei Greci is heavy with incense this morning, and the images of Simeon Stylites flanking the center portal of the altar are obscured in smoke. The Panikheda seems to differ from last year's in that the genuflections are fewer and the tempi of the chanting faster. The larger share of the latter is done by a boy in jeans and striped shirt—who loses his place, however, whereupon the

Archimandrite sings the page number to him, disguised in melismas. We are able to follow most of the service, from the first "*thanatos*" to the final "*makarios*," and can join in the repeated Kyries

and Alleluias

V. stands before a fresh laurel wreath, and at the end of the service the Archimandrite places a crust of consecrated bread in her hands. The name "Igor" occurs six times in his prayers.

Afterward, on the way to the island, the Archimandrite chats with us about the fame that has come to him from I.S.'s funeral. (He cannot pronounce the Italian *ci, che,* or even *gio,* saying *unditsi* for *undici, vetsio* for *vecchio,* and greeting a workman on the dock with "*Buon zorno.*")

The crown of laurel is on the stone when we arrive, and lighted candles have been planted in the ground at its head. Once again the grave is like a bier.

THE NEW MUSIC—
Sound and Sense

"Instead of spreading art among the public," Debussy wrote, "I would suggest founding a Society for Musical Esotericism." To a large part of the public today, the New Music is evidence that this is precisely what happened. Which is the reason that a reliable new book for general readers, in so far as the problem is concerned with books, is almost more valuable, and certainly rarer, than a reliable new specialist book for specialist readers. Mrs. Peyser's *The New Music*[1] is in the first category. In the second it may conveniently be compared with the recent *Perspectives on Stravinsky and Schoenberg*,[2] for these antipodeans also occupy about two-thirds of Mrs. Peyser's pages.

The second category is naturally marked by a more thorough sifting of musical fact than the first, for which reason different, but not double, standards should be applied, the differences corresponding to the needs of the reader. The principal question for the reviewer, therefore, is: to what degree does simplification misrepresent? In Mrs. Peyser's case, the answer is that while much which she describes is far more complex than her account of it, nothing of great importance is either "wrong" or misleading. Nor is this a

1. *The New Music: The Sense Behind the Sound*, by Joan Peyser (Introduction by Jacques Barzun), Delacorte Press, New York, 1971.

2. Edited by Benjamin Boretz and Edmund T. Cone, Princeton University Press, Princeton, 1968.

backhanded accolade. If possible books of the sort are scarce, as I have already said, good ones are practically nonexistent.

The survey is rapid, hence selective rather than compendious. Moreover, it is conducted in terms of movements and schools as personified in only three composers, for Mrs. Peyser's "new music" is classified under the influence, in the broadest sense, of Schoenberg, Stravinsky, and Varèse. By and large, the advantages of her method outweigh the disadvantages. The representative composer can be cast in a role, his story dramatized, the life related to the work, and, above all, that general reader kept in mind. The disadvantages are that the emphasis on the founding fathers tends to slight the share of the favorite sons, Alban Berg, for one, getting short shrift; and that "the new music," like the old, will survive not because it exemplifies an aesthetic, ideology, or tradition, but because of its musical qualities. Thus Stravinsky's Octet, exhibit A in Mrs. Peyser's discussion of neoclassicism, endures without regard for the label.

Edgard Varèse is Mrs. Peyser's covering figure not only for experimental music but for most music outside of and since the two S.'s. His is the widest of the three roles, and not all of the material relegated to the part of the book devoted to him fits very snugly into the suitcase. Some readers might have expected Ives to have been Mrs. Peyser's choice of protagonist here, which is not to say that the two are comparable, even as prophets. But Varèse has had the greater impact abroad. And as a pioneer of electronic music he brings the chronicle down to the present, for, unlike Ives, the Old Lion of Sullivan Street did break his silence toward the end, roaring not only effectively but also electronically.

If my personal associations with the three composers and my involvement with their music disqualify me as a juror, let me say—speaking from my prejudices—that Mrs. Peyser seems to be admirably balanced. Nor does she ever force the reader's choice. Moreover, she has an astute eye for quotation, judiciously interspersing the composers' own words to support and pace her narrative. But she may well find herself quoted for at least one remark, the suggestion that Stravinsky dedicated *The Firebird* to a son of Rimsky-Korsakov "as though to compensate the family for what he borrowed from the father."

A few errors have crept in. It should not be said that "no musical idea [in *Erwartung*] is ever repeated"; add: "in exactly the same way." Or, that "Webern and Ravel did not establish schools of musical thought, for to do that required the unbridled narcissism of Schoenberg or Stravinsky." (And a lot more than that!) Also, one argument seems to me fallacious. Mrs. Peyser believes that the source of the "anxiety" with which Schoenberg identified in the song *Vorgefühl* was the "threat" of Stravinsky; and she says that the text for a chorus composed a decade and a half later "must surely have been motivated by Stravinsky's rise in prestige and his own decline." I doubt it, in both instances. The "loneliness" in the song was that of the composer's own artistic isolation, and as for the "rise" and "decline," Schoenberg was never that much aware of Stravinsky.

Mrs. Peyser makes a great deal of Schoenberg's mathematical superstition, as well as of the effect on his music of the tragedy of his first marriage: his wife eloped with the painter Richard Gerstl, who then committed suicide. "The Gerstl affair . . . precipitated Schoenberg's move into the atonal world," Mrs. Peyser says. Yes, possibly. But how? Wasn't his musical logic taking him there already? And, conversely, in the special, involuted case of Schoenberg, mightn't such a trauma have thrown him back into the *tonal* world? Incidentally, an example of the same sort, but the other way around, the work affecting the life, was the dissolution of

Bertrand Russell's first marriage as a result of the "antinomy paradox" which he discovered after completing the *Principles of Mathematics* and could not resolve.

It remains to be said that the neophyte who turns from the book to the musical life around him will be disappointed. So little of this music is played. In New York, revivals of Cilèa and Zandonai appear to be more in demand than of Schoenberg, while the instamatic "opera" by the latest playboy of the multimedia is more likely to be staged than Berg's *Lulu*—timely as that would be, what with all the recent speculation on the Duke of Clarence as Jack the Ripper. The neglect of Mahler now having been overreversed, it is high time for real live performances of Schoenberg's *Jacob's Ladder*, Stravinsky's *Abraham and Isaac*, Varèse's *Amériques*.

A BELL FOR ADORNO

Turn Adorno's[1] deterministic theory of music history the other way around and *start* with the present pandemonium of "new resources," "new media," "unlimited possibilities." Then along comes "historically necessary" Schoenberg, who reduces the field to twelve pitches, to forms closed at the ends, to the "media" of human voices and string, wood, brass, keyboard, percussion instruments. Schoenberg system-

1. *Philosophy of Modern Music*, by Theodor W. Adorno, The New Seabury Press, New York, 1973.

atizes the dozen notes in a somewhat rigid way at first (from Opus 50 up to Opus 23), but later "progresses" in the direction of a more pliant music (Opus 22 up to Opus 1). The torch passes next to a composer who carries Schoenberg's ideas "to their logical conclusions" and who exploits, at the same time, a still more restricted palette of pitches and sonorities. Then the next, no less ruthlessly "logical," composer in line discovers, in the greatest of all evolutionary leaps forward, that powerful form-building identities can be established by "structuring" the pitches "hierarchically." And *his* successor, pursuing what deterministic philosophers are by this time referring to as "irreducible principles," institutes even more stringent economies and composes the most affecting music of all. Finally a supreme musician appears, reduces the resources still further, and composes whole operas using only a handful of harmonic combinations. This ultimate innovator, economist of means, radical, is W. A. Mozart.

Adorno's musical historicism, as expostulated in this classic of ideologically "committed" criticism, is, as I have said, aimed in a different direction. And as a direction finder for young European musicians immediately after World War II, it amounted to a creed, incredible as that seems now. For this first English translation comes twenty-five years too late to exert any active influence. Not that Adorno's interpretation has been proved or disproved. It simply has been passed by, relegated to academe when the music finally escaped the custody of theoretical critiques and entered the live performing repertory—a more useful place for it, one might think, and not merely, as Adorno would say, to determine its "pragmatic value as emotion."

Yet in spite of many near-fatal handicaps, the book survives. For one thing, small but redeeming chinks of "regressive humanism" show through the heavy armor of Adorno's

Marxism. And for another, a mind of exceptional subtlety is in hiding somewhere in this loftily wrongheaded philosophy. "The basis of the isolation of radical modern music is not its asocial but precisely its social substance. It expresses its concern through pure quality . . ." This is paradoxical, but the trick of hitching Schoenberg's super-elitism to a reductive progressivism entails, at the very least, a great deal of paradox. And it is obscure, for "substance" and "quality" refer as far back as Anselm's distinction. But it is well said, all the same, and it speaks for anyone who tries to apply artistic standards to his work and who for that reason is anomic in a social system that Adorno terms "the context of deception."

Thus Adorno earns at least a temporary claim on our attention to his other views. The most valuable of these, almost worth the many pains of reading the book, are his comments on our "capitalist music industry," with its "fetishization of cultural commodities" and its endorsement of advertising as the metaphysics of the age. Regrettably—for the subject suits Adorno's philosophy and erudition better than his actual one—this is only incidental. Yet partly for these incidentals, partly out of interest in Adorno himself, one persists in the excruciating effort to read him even after losing confidence in his main arguments.

The obstacles are formidable. Even the simplest meanings are difficult to dislodge. The reader not only fails to catch the drift of the commonplace idea struggling to surface in the following, but he risks lockjaw:

> When the immediate self-certainty of unquestioningly accepted materials and forms has vanished from the foundations of art, then at least one region of obscurity will have healed over, will have relieved that boundless suffering whereby the substance of intellectual conception is brought to consciousness.

Elsewhere, when Adorno tilts at

> . . . falsifying ameliorations which prevent the consequence of unpragmatic concepts inherent in the object

or claims—circularly, it seems to me—that

> The absolute liberation of the particular from the universal renders it universal through the polemic and principal relationship of the universal to the particular

he loses me entirely. One does not like to say so, for the existence of a book of this kind is commercially precarious, in danger of remaining a closed book literally, as it nearly is at times in content. Yet a more convoluted, abstruse, and floridly unintelligible style is scarcely conceivable. It can have been designed for one purpose only, that of maintaining the highest standards of obfuscation throughout.

Nor is "style" the only fortification in Adorno's defense system. He is, in addition, a master of arcane terminology, of the half-truth, the false parallel, the hysteron proteron, the nonsentence—though whether this last is his dodge or his translators' I cannot say:

> And it is not only that the perceptive faculty has been so dulled by the omnipresent hit tune that the concentration necessary for responsible listening has become permeated by traces of recollection of this musical rubbish, and thereby impossible.

It does not matter, furthermore, that I am quoting out of contexts. On the contrary, many of these sententious muddles are still more obscure *in* them, connected by pronouns referring to complex concepts set forth in five or six clauses and strung together in paragraphs several pages long. The next edition should introduce a typographical aid, such as printing the punctuation in red, or would that constitute a "falsifying amelioration"? At present the only help with the indigestible lumps between is a supply of amphetamines and a strong conviction that Adorno's philosophy is worth pursuing.

Often the terminology is so remote that the ostensible topic disappears from sight, leaving the less than doggedly attentive reader uncertain which is the metaphorical and which the real. A reference to a "solipsistic piece for large orchestra," for instance, or to "the reduction of music to the absolute monad" might lead one to suppose that the discussion was connected with Leibniz. And *what* terminology! It can only represent a resolute effort to be uncommunicative, drawing, with singular inappropriateness, on botany (a "revolutionary idea" is said to have hidden under a "cotyledon"), and a sociological jargon whose keywords are used in an idiosyncratic way that Adorno is too self-involved to define, and on a psychiatric lingo that, whatever its pertinence, is bizarre in itself ("hebephrenia"). As a further unhelpful ingredient, Hegelian phenomenology is so much a part of Adorno that one reads from him into Hegel and out again, hardly aware of a difference. At one point Adorno warns us to "come to terms with Hegel's statement, 'Consequently, we do not require to bring standards with us, nor to apply our fancies and thoughts in the inquiry; and just by our leaving these aside we are enabled to treat and discuss the subject as it actually is in itself and for itself, as it is in its complete reality.' "

But how on earth is anyone to "come to terms" with *that?* As for those specious parallels, Adorno says that

> This "second nature" [of the tonal system] owes the dignity of its closed and exclusive system to mercantile society, whose own dynamics stress totality and demand that the elements of tonality correspond to these dynamics on the most basic functional level.

Most basic is probably more basic than just plain basic, but apart from that, *how* do the "elements of tonality" actually "correspond"? Another "parallel," that the "liberation of modern painting from objectivity was to art the break that atonality was to music," is more obviously meaningless, unless Adorno had discovered correlatives that he was keeping to himself. It is clear that he believed in them, I should add, just as he believed in a philosophical "reality" underlying mere musical "appearances." How otherwise explain the preposterous notion that Schoenberg "construct[s] modes of expression and various forms of the row according to these modes"? And that "Wagner . . . knew how to manipulate the impulses of the psyche by finding for them the most penetrating correlates"?

Finally, when it comes to facts, Adorno is so extremely accident-prone[1] that broadly representative examples are difficult to choose. Perhaps the most common type is the result of exaggeration. He says that "the various dimensions of Western tonal music, melody, harmony, counterpoint, form and instrumentation"—not rhythm?—"have for the most part developed historically apart from one another . . ." But what he means is that the growth and exploration of each of these "dimensions" was intensified at different times, any and all "developments" necessarily being interactive. And though he defines Florentine Ars Nova as "the combining of voices without concern for harmony," he means simply that harmonic innovation was not the main impetus of the movement. Another, no less common, type of error results from disregarding dates. A passage in *Petrushka* "would be difficult to imagine without Schoenberg's *Orchestra Pieces*," he says, yet somehow this difficulty must be overcome, *Petrushka* having been performed first. Perhaps it is asking too much of a

1. Not Adorno, however, but his translators confound Schoenberg's *Kol Nidre* and Suite for String Orchestra, on page 120.

thinker burdened with cosmic historical processes to trouble himself with details of this kind. And it may be that a philosopher of history is entitled to proleptic license, as a poet is to the poetic kind. But in the statement "radical music was forced into complete isolation during the final stages of industrialism," it would be interesting to know, as one looks out the window at the smokestacks, approximately how long ago those final stages took place.

Stravinsky, as Schoenberg's Manichaean opposite, the archetype of "historical innervation" as Schoenberg is of "historical progressivism," is scarcely recognizable. But Adorno writes about Stravinsky with a belying emotion that redirects the psychoanalytical thrusts to a target nearer home. This is not to deny that Stravinsky may have suffered from "the lack of a libidinal possession of the objective world"—although the diagnosis strikes one as more appropriate for a type of *Playboy* reader. Or that—again I am no judge—"*Histoire du Soldat,* Stravinsky's pivotal work" (but surely no more so than a dozen others) "ruthlessly weaves psychotic attitudes and behavior into musical configurations," its "depersonalization" acting as a "defensive reaction against the omnipotence of narcissism." What I *do* know is that when Adorno steps from behind this Freudian folklore to examine the music, he succeeds only in betraying how foreign it is to him. The *Histoire,* he says, "places immoderate demands upon the trombone, percussion, and contrabass." Yet these demands have delighted every good player of those instruments since the piece was composed.

Adorno garbles even the well-known account of the conception of the *Sacre:* it occurred during the composition of *The Firebird,* not *Petrushka;* nor is this a trivial mistake for it shows that he has not perceived the strong ties between the earlier and the later works. Much is explained when he acknowledges a personal objection to "emphatic and overly precise rhythm"—except in what way a rhythm, in itself, *can* be "overly" precise. But the full extent of Adorno's confusion is best revealed in a remark about Stravinsky's "attempt" in the *Sacre* "to evoke the spiritual landscape of Strauss's *Elektra*." One wonders whether an attempt has ever failed with such spectacularly flying colors.

"It would be meaningless to reproach the artist for not doing what his principle does not indicate," Adorno counsels, doing just that. Not understanding Stravinsky's principles, which are neither more nor less than Stravinsky's music, he turns to those old stand-bys, "parody" and "music about music." These are of limited relevance, in any case, but *a priori*, without consideration of transcendent and self-sufficient individual qualities, are by no means illegitimate categories, no matter what the ruling of "historical force." Besides which, the view down the wrong end of the telescope is too small, negative criticism on such a scale too large.

Webern and Berg, *sub specie* Schoenberg, offer more rewarding material. Berg is described, not far from the mark, as only "coincidentally a twelve-tone composer" whose "every effort in the composition is aimed at rendering the technique unnoticeable." But then, Schoenberg himself, whose "great moments . . . have been attained despite the . . . technique as well as by means of it . . ." composes twelve-tone music "as if there were no such thing as the twelve-tone technique." Only Webern, with his "fetishism of the row . . . realizes twelve-tone technique and no longer composes"—or, less paradoxically, "Webern's rows are structured as if they were already a composition." This, for the time when Adorno wrote, is perspicacious and shows him to have been among the first to recognize the rift that, in part, determined the course of post-World War II music. Moreover, he seems almost to be on the verge of elucidating the vital distinction: "The mysteries of the row . . . limit themselves to the mathematical relations of the material and are not borne out in the musical form itself."

Adorno's ambivalence with regard to Schoenberg's "twelve-tone music" is the result of a conflict between music and ideology—for which reason, perhaps, the difficulties in extricating the true from the partly true are even greater than usual. "The twelve-tone technique [is] retrogressive in itself, and infinitely static by virtue of its total independence of any historical forces." Static, in a sense, it may be, but for a different reason: the question cannot be understood outside of music. After all, the twelve-tone technique came into being for musical reasons, one of which is that "chromatic tonality" had been "modulated to death." It should be said, however, that Adorno's denial of "historical process" is at variance with Schoenberg himself, who expressed the belief that the twelve-tone technique would "assure the supremacy of German music for another hundred years"—a remark that unfortunately echoes the longevity claim of an all-too-recent German government which was to have lasted "a thousand years."

But Adorno's criticism of the technique—which at one point he describes as a "number game" that "borders on astrology" and "approaches superstition"—is ideological and logical rather than musical. When he observes that "in the totality of variation there is no longer anything which undergoes change," a logical argument is being substituted for a musical one; musical experience refutes the assertion. The same may be said of the statement that "twelve-tone music maintains in all its moments the same distance from the central point," though this contradicts an earlier, hardly less dubious postulate to the effect that "in Schoenberg's twelve-tone themes," because of the diminishing possibility with each successive pitch for each remaining one the ear not only anticipates the last pitch but "participates spontaneously in its perfection." This in turn is contradicted by another pronouncement, equally false, that "the twelve-tone system . . . unaware of forceful harmonic necessity . . . relegates harmonies . . . as well as the succession of sounds, to coincidence." Which is incompatible with "every single tone is transparently determined by the construction of the whole," a claim that is difficult to reconcile with "the correctness of twelve-tone music cannot be directly 'heard'—this is the simplest name for that moment of meaninglessness in it. Only the force of the system rules . . ." In sum, "the unperfected aspect of Schoenberg's work with the twelve-tone technique is harmony." And so on, false corollary following false corollary until the reader collapses from a true corollary thrombosis.

Adorno's analysis of *Erwartung* and *Die glückliche Hand,* Schoenberg's pre-twelve-tone masterpieces, depends to a lesser extent on music than on "psycho-social content." But the perplexities continue to outnumber the clues. Thus a chapter on *Erwartung* and the "Dialectics of Loneliness" never tells the reader *why* "lonely discourse reveals more about social tendencies than does communicative discourse." Adorno believes that *Die glückliche Hand* is "perhaps [Schoenberg's] most significant work." But in this case he should have said something less vague about its music than that "the construction is based on the stratified structure of harmonic sound levels." In fact, his most explicit musical comment is on the negative side: discussing "the lost wealth of the differentiation in tonality" he remarks that "dissonances which arose as the expression of tension . . . [are] no longer the media of subjective expression."

Die glückliche Hand was formerly thought to be concerned with the vicissitudes of the artist's ego (Schoenberg's in masquerade), the artist who, denied his "place," then makes a virtue of despising it. But in Adorno's view the true dilemma of Schoenberg's protagonist is that of a man "alienated from the actual process of production in society" and unable "to recognize any relationship between labor and economic system." In the course of an elephantine exegesis, Adorno defines "the chaotic" as "allowing the obscure to remain obscured." Which may explain why he explains the obvious. Thus he describes a simple remark, "That can be done more simply," as a "symbolic criticism of the superfluous." But surely it is a superfluous criticism of the symbolic! *Die glückliche Hand* needs this sort of "hermeneutics" much less, in any case, than it needs a good performance.

"Historical force prohibits an aesthetic compromise," Adorno concludes. But what *is* this historical force in music? Is it analogous to evolution? Yes, according to the Lamarckian hypothesis to which Adorno still subscribes. But in any larger sense, no. For evolution is not uncompromising. It moves by hybridization, mutation, coadunation, the ever-changing means that can even change "historically inevitable" ends. It is impossible to trace a sequence of evolutionary ascent or descent from Bach to Bach's sons, let alone an unbroken trajectory over several centuries. Music history not only backtracks and switches directions but in the persons of its greatest composers is remarkable chiefly for its *un*predictability. And, in sum, causality and antecedents account for everything except the differences that matter most.

Is "historical force" a form of functionalism, then? For Adorno proscribes "the medium of tonality not simply because these sounds are antiquated and untimely . . . but because they are false. They no longer fulfill their function." This function is never explained, however, and the assertion involves him in an inconsistency concerning Schoenberg's "conciliatory"—*i.e.*, tonal—"music." The Schoenberg brand recognizes "the right to music which, in spite of everything, is still valid even in a false society." This, politely speaking, is overingenious. Plainly speaking, it is double-talk.

Whatever Adorno means by his unidirectional, incontrovertible abstraction, the narrowness of the terms of his argument dates the book. Social anthropology has no place in it. And neither have "cultural traditions," though they offer the only criteria that Stravinsky, a cultural transplant, and Schoenberg, who never left Vienna even in Los Angeles, would recognize. It is a measure of the twenty-five years since Adorno published that the approach to a philosophy of music today would be primarily anthropological (Lévi-Strauss). And that this new philosophy, after dealing briefly with composers as an endangered species—and endorsing Gresham's Law about the worse driving out the better—would go on to consider everything Adorno regarded as inconsiderable, including the music of Oriental, African, and other "exotic" cultures, Western preclassical music, the music of the byways and of the wayward. The new philosophy, in short, would respect the rights of minorities, including the "primitive peoples" whom Adorno dismisses, but in whom the *impulse* to musical expression is the same as it is in Beethoven.

Finally, if music had a *telos*, an end to which its history has always pointed, that pointed-to end would mean the end in the sense of "the rest is silence"—at least in Adorno's dialectics, which amount to a *reductio ad nihilo*, for if art is a "catalyst for social change" the perfected society has no need of the commodity. Meanwhile, his progressivism is extremely depressing. What it narrows down to is "expanding means." Not art, but putative materials of art. "Traditional music had to content itself with a highly limited number of tonal combinations . . ." Well, poor Mozart, lucky Stockhausen.

SUMMER MUSIC

Table d'hôte hinterland America must have its attractions. With that shaky hypothesis in mind, I sortied three times last month to the outdoor music festivals, and was three times turned back, ignominiously scratching mosquito bites. Not that I was an especially favored target: the applause at oddly inconclusive moments during a violin concerto proved to be insect slapping, and the soloist, deliberately attacked while his hands were committed to a cadenza, had by the end of the performance grown a bump on his forehead that would have excited even the most blasé phrenologist. I returned to New York from dragonflies (Santa Fe) and fireflies (Saratoga) to just plain flies, for the city is no less pestilential. And came back to an indoor festival on the turntable, subject to black-outs and candlepower, and to the choice of suitable summer-wear music.

This, experiment revealed, was produced routinely in the Renaissance, for its music comes only in small sizes, is very quiet—wholly inaudible by Mick Jagger's standards—and generates no body heat, its passions being of a higher order. It was recognized in its time as the best of palliatives for the torpors of the season, some of it having been summer music then, as well. The composer Vincenzo Galileo, less noted for his music than for his astronomer son, refers to summer-night madrigal singing at the Zeferini Gardens in Siena. Mosquitoes very likely abounded at that time also (the "squashing" of one of them is evoked in a celebrated madrigal) but presumably not on anything like the scale of their current population explosion.

It is difficult even to keep abreast of the spate of Renaissance recordings, let alone to choose representative ones, and the task occupied the whole of my itchy convalescence. But our live repertory has been standardized to the extent that this music is accessible only through records. Concert performances of it are so rare and single impressions so fleeting that a lifetime of attending them would provide only the sketchiest notion of the riches of the era. But "concert" is an anachronism. Most of the music was composed for the court and hence was comparatively intimate; or for the church, where it was incidental. Rebecs and regals, sackbuts and krummhorns are rare, too—not altogether unfortunately, perhaps—while performing editions of the music or even reliable transcriptions are virtually nonexistent.

The period of the records I have chosen is bounded at one end by the late *quattrocento* and at the other by the early Monteverdi, *ca.* 1600. But this covers, or opens up, an unmanageably long span. Which is precisely the fault of the majority of the records: they skim over decades and even centuries without allowing for differentiations of time, cultures, schools. Too many of them, moreover, are anthologies. What is needed are fuller views of particular styles and of individual composers.

Relatively good marks should be awarded to Arion's *Spanish Vocal Music of Charles V's Era.* The original French title of the same record, *Chants à la Cour de Charles Quint,* is not only different but misleading, the music being only supposititiously associated with that monarch. In fact about half of it, including two delectable *villancicos* possibly heard by luckless Columbus's King Ferdinand, dates from the previous century, while other pieces were composed for John III of Portugal and for Charles's son and successor. In Spain, however, and in this genre of popular song, the hundred-year period does not encompass the drastic stylistic changes encountered in Italy. Stylistic consistency of a sort is also imposed by the restriction to a single singer—a dubious blessing usually, the one style of the performer homogenizing the several styles of the music; concerning this, however, I am in this instance too ill informed to be able to assess the validity of the criticism. The most attractive piece in the collection is *Duelete de Mi, Señora,* but half a dozen others are hardly less enjoyable. I should add that the accompaniments by vihuelas (guitars), zinks (an early species of cornet), and flutes that sound like a carrousel, are genuinely, and therefore satisfyingly, out of tune.

The purely instrumental music of the time is infinitely more limited than the vocal. CBS's *Musique pour les Instruments Anciens* is bearable for most of side one only because of extreme changes of timbres—bombardons, bells, bagpipes, serpents—from one piece to the next. The music itself never attains a degree of interest to compete with the "juvenile" passages in Haydn's *Toy* Symphony, which the "instrumentation" of one of the pieces brings to mind. But the remainder of the record, a contemporary version of *Aucassin et Nicolette,* is *un*bearable. The composer, born in 1933, has updated various kinds of war found in the popular fable of the *moyen âge*—war between the generations, the races, the classes—which is precisely what most people bought the record to escape. But to revive these half-extinct instruments only to submit them to electronic distortion, and to require them to play clichés of contemporary music, is pointless. They forfeit their character and no longer sound like their former *jolie laide* selves.

One side of Argo's *A Florentine Festival* contains twenty pieces by twenty composers (unless the medley of sixteen by Anon. includes more than one by the same person). The other side begins with a fanfare by Monteverdi, but for good measure only, since it is not by any definition Florentine. This is followed by two of six *intermezzi* performed in 1589 at the nuptials of Ferdinand de' Medici. The composer of one of them, Luca Marenzio, is associated in musical style with three or four Italian cities, but notably *not* with Florence. (Ferdinand apparently knew Marenzio in Rome—the composer had a *pied-à-terre* in the Vatican, no less—and had enlisted him in his entourage for the occasion.) But whether Florentine or not, the alternation of instrumental and vocal pieces is tedious. Furthermore, the shallowness of the instrumental sound invites comparison with the earliest experiments of Edison, while the individual parts in the vocal groups are so indistinct that one pictures the singers huddled around an early funnel-shaped recording apparatus. As for the quality of the singing, the solos are acceptable but the ensembles range from bad to abysmal. Though one does not expect music such as the trio, *Tri Ciechi Siamo* ("three blind men"), to be sung like a lyric from *Finian's Rainbow,* this performance sounds as if it had been recorded by a coven with the microphone in the pot.

Yet the album contains an unblemished performance of a small masterpiece, scarcely two minutes long but worth the price of the whole. It is a song in four brief stanzas, which say, in effect: "I am a bird without flight, at the mercy of the stars . . . buffeted by the gods and by fortune . . . Careless am I of my destiny, since heaven alone rules that of each one of us." The verse is *ottava rima* (Ab, Ab, Ab, Cc), as in Byron's *Don Juan,* and the verse and musical form are interdependent, the musical lines A and b exactly corresponding to the verbal ones. But despite the strictness of the scheme, the composer, Bartolommeo Tromboncino, found room in it for ingenuities of art. In the line "*Ve sforzano de stelle aduna, aduna,*" for example, the syllables of the repeated "*aduna*" fall on different beats of the music from those of the first one, with the effect of a triple meter concealed within a quadruple (although today most of us hear these accentuations merely as syncopations). Tromboncino was justly noted for his fastidiousness in choosing and setting verse. One of his poets was Michelangelo, whom he must have known: a certain madrigal text by the great artist could have been obtained only directly from him, for it was not published until after his death.

Like Gesualdo at the end of the *cinquecento*, Tromboncino, at the beginning of it, murdered his wife-*cum*-lover. Also like this colleague in homicide and art, Tromboncino's music is introverted and tormented. An itinerant musician, as were most composers of the time, he was employed by the Medici, the Gonzagas, the Estes—Isabella herself—and he wrote music for the wedding of Lucrezia Borgia. His patron in Venice, for at least one documented event, was the doge. Tromboncino's fame in that city outlived him, moreover, for Aretino invoked him in a popular comedy. This song of the grounded bird could have been performed by Giorgione's musician, even perhaps by the painter himself, whom Vasari describes as a skilled lutanist and singer, except that we have no frame of dates for Tromboncino, only "*floruit.*"

To return to the recordings, the most completely successful is Vanguard's *Music from the Court of Mantua: Giaches de Wert.* Its shortcomings are inconsequential. The inclusion of a sacred piece (*i.e.*, unconnected with the court) is a miscalculation, for it slows the pace. One madrigal, *Vaghi boschetti,* from *Gerusalemme liberata,* is seriously out of tune, and the bass voice is too prominent in several others, impairing balances. The treble viol, on the other hand, is too faint and could have benefited from amplification. Ornaments are added at some of the cadences, more elaborately in the *Fantasia à Quattro* for viols than in the vocal pieces, but so tastefully that one regrets the performances are not more "encumbered" with them.

Wert is a great composer, of a stature demanding not only

a full record but a "complete works," in many albums. Though born in one of the Low Countries, his style seems indigenously northern Italian, especially Mantovan. As in the cases of Tromboncino and Marenzio, he was a peripatetic whose art developed with a consistency of style reflecting nothing of his travels. He composed *canzonettas* in Greek and Spanish, as well as in French and Italian, and good examples of all four are included in the record.

The inexperienced listener would be well advised to single out two masterpieces and to play them over and over. These are the five-voice madrigals *Datemi pace* and *Ecco ch'un altra volta* (a text also set by Marenzio); in this performance of *Ecco* only the fourth voice is sung, the upper voices and the bass being sounded by viols. These are late pieces, and though Wert was "in his stride" from the first, his final books of madrigals transcend not only his own earlier music but the finest compositions of some of his most illustrious contemporaries. The suspensions at the end of part two of *Datemi pace* scoop Gesualdo, as the chromatic cry, "*le lagrime mie,*" in *Ecco ch'un altra volta* does Monteverdi.

On a night of heat lightning outside and hot flashes in, when a lid of foul air is clamped over the city's noise-besotted streets, one of these songs by Wert, or that heart-aching lament by the "Little Trombone" is guaranteed to bring relief. The forms are minuscule, but not the emotion. It retains a freshness across four and a half centuries that some more recent and more "searing" musical passions have lost.

ON PERFORMING THE BACH CANTATAS

Those who love the music of Bach, and therefore hunger for more of it, must welcome the recent Telefunken recordings *Johann Sebastian Bach: Das Kantaten Werk* (Vol. I, Cantatas 1–4; Vol. II, Cantatas 5–8; Vol. III, Cantatas 9–11). For if one were to divide the world of Bach—with a papal gesture but trying otherwise not to pontificate—the cantatas will comprise the lesser-known half. (Among the many purely practical reasons for this, one is that the instrumental parts for several of these masterpieces do not exist even now, and anyone intending to perform them is obliged to extract the music from the century-old "complete works"; but of this aspect of Bach, more later.) Nor is this division merely quantitative. Although we tend to think of Bach as a great musical computer, in his case quantity does not imply any diminution of quality. Not all of the music is on the same level, of course, yet none of it is mediocre or unrelievedly dull: the dullness is that of the performances to which the music is usually subjected.

But here, at last, is a beginning, and I, for one, am so grateful to have this incomparable music in clear and intelligent performances, whatever else, that I am reluctant to criticize them. Congratulations all around, and a distribution of baccalaureates to the musicians, the engineers, and to Telefunken itself. The "complete Bach cantatas" is one of the most valuable recording projects ever undertaken.

For all the claims to musicological authenticity, however, the results are better described as musicological timidity. The performances are surprisingly straight and "as-written." Not that the stylistic adjustments are inconsiderable; but they are confined to a secondary category. To count the blessings first, metrical accents are correctly emphasized (overemphasized in the aria *Durch's Feuer wird* in Cantata No. 2), and this is rare. Then, too, the double-dotting properly lengthens the silences after the dotted notes, rather than the notes themselves. And, *mirabile dictu*, Nikolaus Harnoncourt, the conductor, understands the staccato style so well that listeners bred on Philadelphia Orchestra sostenuto risk apoplexy if they begin with his performance of the *Sinfonia* from *Christ lag in Todesbanden.*

The principal authority against "as-written" performance is Bach's contemporary, J. J. Quantz. Yet few statements in music history have engendered more debate than Quantz's observation that notes of equal value are more pleasing when played unequally. The difference between notation and performance in Bach may be compared, however loosely and inexactly, to the difference between notation and performance in jazz, except that Bach's performance style has been lost and must be reconstructed and relearned. But other contemporary music besides jazz relies on living traditions of performance, and few composers today believe that all performance characteristics *can* be notated. The written note-values in the fast movements of Stravinsky's Octet, for example, are in practice approximately halved.

These recorded performances do not experiment with rhythmic alteration in Quantz's sense. The soprano's second phrase in Versus VI of *Christ lag,* for example, begins with an eighth-note upbeat. It is immediately evident to the ear that the note should synchronize with the skipping rhythm of the accompaniment (and the basic rhythm of the whole piece), not stand out against it, and that the upbeat must therefore be sung more like the third of a triplet than like an eighth. The same obviously applies to all of the written eighths in the movement: although grouped as twos they should sound like triplets, or, rather, *more* like triplets—actually a "long" note followed by a "short"—since we are not dealing with exactly notated values. In other contexts and with different emphases the pattern might be reversed, a "short" note followed by a "long"—a principle felt more quickly by amateurs, incidentally, than by musicians trained in strict obedience to notation.

Needless to say, other elements than rhythm are involved in an "authentic" Bach performance. Thus the changes of harmony in the *secco*-recitatives are indicated by figurations in the bass part, which is the only written-out part, the upper ones being entrusted to keyboard (organ) improvisation. In these recordings, however, the upper parts are realized with something less than the barest minimum of embellishment. In two cases, moreover, changes in figuration have been ignored, probably because the bass notes are not sustained—which is stylistically correct, of course, but not when the harmony shifts. Bach may have been a WASP–or, more correctly, a WSP—but his music is more flamboyant than this. Like the other arts of the Baroque, the music of the period is highly ornate and even euphuistic. Herr Harnoncourt, however, is sobriety personified. His ornamentation is limited largely to cadential trills, and not always there; nor does he ever employ *messa da voce,* the "natural" crescendo and decrescendo on long notes.

Harnoncourt's own performance notes amount to little more than a defense of old instruments. But this is unnecessary, for with a single exception the listener would probably prefer the softer, more varied sonorities of Harnoncourt's museum instruments to the "equivalent" modern ones; the trumpet in

Cantata No. 5, for instance, though apparently unable to trill, is rounder, less penetrating in tone, and, to our ears, sounds more like a member of the horn family. The exception is the organ, but it is exposed only in the recitatives. It reminds one of the calliope in Popeye cartoons, and the boy soprano's recitatives are unendearingly reminiscent of duets between Popeye and Olive Oyl. But the characteristics of an instrument's articulation, phrasing, and range are no less important than its sonority. Range especially: the upper tessitura of the viola da gamba is awkward for the modern cello. Once again, the superiority of the original instruments is a *prima facie* truth that the amateur grasps more readily than the professional.

The beginning of Cantata No. 8 (last side of Vol. II) provides an ideal introduction to Bach's orchestra; except that "Bach's orchestra" implies a fixed ensemble, whereas, even when comprised of the same timbres, it is never the same from cantata to cantata, partly because of the variety and rotation of the solo instruments. Not only is "Bach's orchestra" a far less standardized instrumental body than the orchestra of Beethoven and Brahms, but so far as instrumental color is concerned the listener can pile these discs like a platter of pancakes and play them from beginning to end without ennui. And if the opening of No. 8 is particularly delectable, so, I might add, is the succeeding oboe d'amore aria, with pizzicato bass, and the next piece, and in fact the whole cantata.

Herr Harnoncourt might have said more by way of preparation for the sound of the male treble, since the shallow, fragile, and sexless tone of the boys' voices could very well disturb the listener accustomed to bosomy opera sopranos. As in the case of the instruments, more than tone quality is involved, yet a taste for the purity and lightness of the vibratoless soprano and alto will grow together with an appreciation of the style and idiom. Like the boy actor in Shakespeare and Kabuki, the ten-year-old boy soprano cannot "load" a word (such as the *sterben* in the recitative in Cantata No. 8) with the "tragic sentiment" that a woman of mature years can hardly help but inject.

The duet, *Wenn Sorgen*, in Cantata No. 3, as attractive a piece as any in the three albums, provides an ideal introduction to the sound of these prepubertal male trebles. The intonation is exceptionally good, for one thing, with only some intermittent, not overly painful, flatting in the soprano. For another, the voices contrast rather than blend, which helps to delineate the counterpoint and the melodic design. Still another instance of the advantages of a light, "cherubic" boy soprano is displayed in the aria *Jesu, deine gnaden Blicke*, from Cantata No. 11. Here the instrumental obbligato is a trio for flute, oboe, and a "bass" line of violins and violas in unison. Whereas a woman's voice might well have relegated the wind parts to accompaniments, the boy's voice equals the instruments in volume and matches them in quality, like a third woodwind.

The most important element of performance is none of these—not color, not volume, nor even any point of style—but tempo. Herr Harnoncourt's tempi are just and convincing. He is brisk but never to a fault, though if the tendency *were* a fault it would be a lesser one in my book than dragging. Tempi in the cantatas are determined by phrase lengths, by the mechanics of instruments—the action of the pedals on Bach's organ, for one—by musical instinct, and by uncommon sense, assuming that the last two at least resemble the same faculties in musicians two centuries ago. With these recordings the listener is never anxious lest the singer run out of breath, or seem to be nearing the end of his vocal rope, or cords.

The next most important aspect of performance is that of

balance, and this, too, is consistently good, instrumental and vocal together and each within itself. The chorus and solo voices are on the same level as the instruments, separated but not stratified, and no part is ever lost. Our baroque specialists affect an indifference to this, but the contemporary listener wants to hear everything, and to hear it in balanced relationships.

To begin on Side One, and, in a sitting or two, to play through the eleven cantatas in order, would be a mistake. The very first cantata, for one objection, is by no means the treasure of the lot. But then, the wisdom of releasing the cantatas in the order of the "complete edition" is questionable. Not that I would advocate the alternative of a chronological grouping, or attempt at one, for that would have resulted in an almost indigestible feast at the very beginning, the Italian-style Mühlhausen cantatas, *Gottes Zeit* and *Aus der Tiefe* among them, comprising many of the very greatest. Another possible ordering would have been to follow the cycles of the Lutheran Church Year, although only about three-fifths of the five that Bach composed have survived. Thus, in the second year, Cantata No. 7, *Christ unser Herr*, follows Cantata No. 2, *Ach Gott*, both from June 1724, while Cantata No. 1, *Wie schön leuchtet der Morgenstern*, concludes the cycle in April 1725. Nor does it matter that the Lutheran calendar is less than universally observed; but so far as the sacred use of the cantatas is concerned, many people will agree with Schweitzer that "any room in which they are performed is turned into a church." I should add that the literature on the subject is extensive, and that Terry's *Bach's Cantata Texts* (Holland Press, 1964) can be recommended to anyone wishing to pursue it.

The printed matter accompanying the recordings includes miniature scores from the "complete edition," reproductions of the original manuscripts, photographs of the instruments. (Examples of the instruments themselves are superbly displayed in the Mertens Collection in New York's Metropolitan Museum of Art.) The texts are also included, along with English and French translations, and notes by the Bach scholar Alfred Dürr (same trilingual arrangement). Professor Dürr is always enlightening on the libretti but confusing at times on the music.

Much of the musical substance of the cantatas can be understood as symbolic, the symbols themselves being based on conventions inherited from, and, in turn, developed by, Bach. The word "*Freudenhimmel,*" for example, is set to a laughing figuration, "*Glocken*" to repeated flute notes, "*Wasser*" to wavelike arpeggiated accompaniments, "*Pein,*" "*Schmerz,*" and "*Tränen*"— which sounds like Churchill in German—to dissonances. Yet one cannot agree with Professor Dürr that "an oboe d'amore depicts the frightened agitation of Man in view of death." In the first place that agitation is hardly "depictable" by an oboe d'amore, which is not to deny that the *music* which the instrument plays may have stood for something of the kind. One's awareness of these conventions is not irrelevant, any more than is one's awareness of the iconographic interpretation of a *quattrocento* painting, and certainly the listener's stylistic understanding of the cantatas is increased by his knowledge of them. But the purely musical values are unaffected by such questions, nor do they preclude our musical delight.

ONE MAN'S MOZART

Much is to be said both for and against establishing one's image of the Mozart piano concertos through the perspective of a single interpreter. Yet after comparing many performances of each concerto, I am decidedly in favor of at least this one-man view of them: the twelve-record album by Géza Anda and the Salzburger Camerata Academica (Deutsche Grammophon 2720 030). Whereas a variety of performing styles tends to focus on the differences between players, the one-man, one-style reading helps the listener to concentrate on the individual qualities of the concertos themselves. In the long run, and this is a marathon, the shortcomings of the lone-star presentation may turn into virtues, as they do in Herr Anda's case, a happy outcome that requires forbearance on the part of the listener, and the withholding of judgment.

Hearing Herr Anda in only a few of the concertos, one is troubled with the impression that he too conscientiously avoids rubato, does not "moon" enough over the slow movements, fails to communicate the music's ardor; and that, in short, the profile he has adopted may be too low. On limited acquaintance, moreover, his conceptions seem somewhat straight, his executions a bit hurried. And, still on minimum exposure, one regrets that Herr Anda chose to conduct as well as to play. With a collaborator on the podium, the ragged attacks of the strings (in the Andantino of K.271, for instance) could have been avoided, and a separate conductor might have given more shape and meaning to the orchestral parts. The woodwinds following the second movement cadenza of K.453, for example, should register some effect from its development, but here the players sound as if they were sight-reading.

Yet the unity of view resulting from a pianist-conductor is more valuable than the greater meticulousness that the separate conductor might provide. Brilliant as are the orchestra parts, the piano is the core of the music, and, with the help of a good concertmaster, even the most indifferent conductor among pianists can achieve a cohesive performance around that core. But then, of the versions I listened to that used this division of labor, none was very impressive even in the matter of precision. Thus the orchestral accompaniments in the Rubinstein recordings generally trail the pianist and often lose the tempo in the tutti. (Anda himself does not consistently sustain the tempo of his own orchestral introductions, and in K.503 contradicts it jarringly.)

Ensemble, however, is not the most important consideration. Comparing Anda's performance of K.459 with a widely touted newer release of the Concerto played by Brendel with an orchestra led by Marriner (Philips 6500 283), the latter seems overconducted. The mildly tristful Allegretto becomes positively mournful in consequence, owing to the tempo and to the heavy accentuation of the on-the-beat appoggiaturas in the woodwinds, while the sixteenth notes in the strings, last movement, mumbled through in the Anda, are so cleanly articulated here that they call attention to themselves. Finally, in spite of the objective ear of the separate conductor, the piano, before the return of the ghostly first theme, is obscured by the strings and horns (*cf.* measures 358–59). Brendel, incidentally, blurs the arpeggios with too much pedal at measures 215–16 but, as always, phrases intelligently.

Technically the Anda recording is fine but not flawless, the piano sometimes being overmiked. The same can be said of the musical supervision (one of whose flaws is that just before the D-minor episode in the slow movement of K.453, the second bassoon, and hence the bass line, was not recorded at all). A very handsome booklet accompanies the album, but the reader would be well advised to disregard its value judgments. (Mine, too, for that matter: make your own!) These have been determined not by any comprehensive criteria but by what might or might not be evidence of Mozart's own preferences as suggested by his performances of particular concertos. The booklet proclaims that "K.456 begins the series of eight master concertos," thereby excluding K.453, in my opinion the prize of them all. But beginning with No. 9 *all* are master concertos, and their mastery is absolute and incomparable. The booklet simply subscribes to the price-list fallacy: the higher the Köchel number, the higher the quality of the work.

I must take issue with two further tenets. First, "It is a remarkable fact that . . . Mozart did not give up the continuo function of the solo instrument, as is shown by the bass line which runs uninterruptedly throughout the tutti sections . . ." But so do the solo violin and viola parts run throughout the tutti sections of the *Sinfonie concertante;* which is not to doubt the continuo function even in the last piano concertos, but only to say that this argument does not prove it. Second, the booklet stresses the symphonic characteristics of the concertos to the neglect of the operatic, and, as it happens, the latter are dominant in the three I would choose as the greatest, two of them already mentioned: K.271, in E flat, whose slow movement is a dramatic recitative, and K.453, in G, whose first movement includes a passage that might have come from *Don Giovanni,* and whose entire last one pre-echoes *The Magic Flute.* My third choice, K.467, the "*Elvira Madigan,*" has an opera aria for a middle movement.

The piano concerto is the apotheosis of the forms of

Mozart's instrumental music. It not only adds a rich new dimension to the serenade, the symphony, the string quintet and quartet, but also subtracts a cumbersome and antiquated formal one, the double-repeat minuet-with-trio. The piano is Mozart's instrument, but the concertos draw a new poetry from it not found either in the solo piano music or in that of the piano with chamber ensembles. One of the reasons is in the opportunities offered by the orchestral frame. The new effect of slow, isolated notes describing wide intervals in the middle movement of K.488, for example, is made possible only because of the structure given by a sustaining orchestra. Then, too, Mozart's merely five-octave and probably out-of-tune piano was a match, and as a chromatic instrument more than a match, for Mozart's orchestra.

Without changing the essential fast-slow-fast format of the concerto, Mozart creates new forms. And, like the little child, it is the piano that leads him—into "free" fantasy cadenzas; into new combinations of sonority; into exploratory chromatic music (for sheer contrast with the orchestra, it seems, as in the finale of K.453). The instrument is the entelechy of discovery, then, and Mozart follows it wherever his fingers and fancy take him. Thus the melody beginning at measure 163 in the last movement of the C-Major Concerto, K.503, is never repeated (and is therefore something of a waste), but the flexibility of the form easily accommodates the divine digression. This power of the Mozart concertos, moreover, is one that no other composer ever succeeded in recovering, for like all great art, and despite the "derivations and influences" industry, the Mozart concertos are their own beginning and end.

Each concerto in the succession of masterpieces from No. 9 through No. 27 differs strikingly from the others. (I do not count the one for three pianos, which is an arrangement.) Each is an individual, with a unique personality and mood. Without attempting to compare them, therefore, but in justification of my choice of the three that seem to me to shine in even this glittering company, I shall simply mention what in effect are some of the idiosyncracies of my own taste. According to my lights, the second movement of No. 15, in B flat, for example, fails to develop, while the slow section in the last movement of No. 22, in E flat, is mere filler: not only has the vital nerve that runs through the first two movements stopped running here, but the composer is strangely unable to extricate himself from the key. As for the popular concertos, the D-Minor, the A-Major (K.488), and the *Coronation*, they are hardly in the same league. Yet these may well be the ones that Brahms had in mind when he remarked, endearingly: "The fact that people do not understand and respect the very best things, such as Mozart's concertos, is what permits men like us to become famous."

The history of the concertos is a miraculous one: Mozart composed no fewer than twelve of them in two years (1784–86), and two in a single week. Yet the most astonishing event of all is the birth of No. 9, that offspring of a mere twenty-year-old. Mlle Jeunehomme, the pianist who evidently inspired it, is almost as mysterious a quantity in Mozart's biography as the Dark Lady is in Shakespeare's. (How can the ambiguity of gender in her name have failed to spawn theses developing closer analogies?) One is curious to know more about Mozart's relationship with her. Certainly he experienced an emotional upheaval in that month of January 1777, when he wrote the Concerto, for he never equaled it, the slow movement anyway, in all of his music—though it must also be said that he never returned to the same path. But the Concerto is very good as a whole. Of the many excellences that should be remarked in the first movement, let me mention Mozart's discovery of the possibilities of the cadenza as a vehicle for *musical*, and especially harmonic, invention, as well as for virtuoso display. I should add that his cadenzas are feats of invention and of suspense that should long ago have discouraged the poor stylistic parodies, the tedious technical exercises, and the anachronistic wanderings that are too often substituted for them. The third movement is good, too, even though the middle section never really gets off the ground. But this generally fast movement is unfairly annihilated by the preceding slow one, whose profundity, in spite of its early date, Mozart never surpassed. Which ought to demolish standard arguments of chronology and development in connection with genius.

All of the mystery of art is in this second movement, and fortunately nothing that can be said about it will solve the mystery or explain why the music is so haunting. Technical comment —on the canon between the violins and the piano, for instance, and on the interweaving of piano and orchestra–is unhelpful. All is convention and all totally unconventional, the figurations, rhythms, melodies sounding like thousands of others and no other. The movement seems to leave even Beethoven nowhere to go, yet does not evoke him, being simply another perfect mansion in the kingdom of Mozart.

If Mozart's prodigality astounds the contemporary imagination, what can that beleaguered faculty make of his almost continuous euphoria, for the joy of this music, to an age "spacing itself out" with the many forms of anti-art and with philosophies of despair, is scarcely comprehensible. Here are twenty-four record sides containing not a single dark moment, the composer's object being simply to give pleasure, whatever the bonuses in sublimity accruing in the process.

No one has ever spoken more wisely on art and aesthetics than Mozart in the letter to his father dated December 28, 1782. It should long ago have stopped criticism, and not only of music: "The concertos are . . . agreeable to the ears . . . here and there are things which only connoisseurs can appreciate, but *I have seen to it that those less knowledgeable must also be pleased without knowing why . . .*"

THE TRUE VOICE OF FEELING

Schubert: The Final Years by John Reed (Faber, London, 1972) is that *rara avis,* a successful fusion of biography and musical analysis. A book with a seemingly limited thesis–that "The Great" C-Major Symphony was composed in 1825 rather than in the year of Schubert's death, 1828—it nevertheless illuminates the whole of the man and his music. Mr. Reed contends that this error in chronology must be recognized in order to understand the development of the composer's last years. The argument, based largely on reappraisal of well-known evidence, is not new, but it has never been more convincingly presented. Mr. Reed does not offer microscopic examinations of the internal musical clues, a difficult assignment in Schubert's case, the boundaries—early, middle, and late—as established by musicologists having so frequently been disregarded by the composer. Instead, Mr. Reed points out what should have been obvious, namely that the exuberant dance symphony is unlikely to have been written soon after the *Winterreise*, that profoundly bad trip for Schubert himself, however enjoyable for posterity. But Schubert defies all preconceived notions as to the logic of an artist's evolution.

Great composers are not necessarily consistent, but Schubert's unevenness—between one piece and another, one movement and another, and within movements—is altogether exceptional. He sometimes seems to have divided himself between Mount Olympus and the beer hall, wasting a regrettable amount of creative energy en route in attempts to gain both a church market and recognition in the theater. Those large gray volumes of the collected edition, nineteen of them, contain fewer *moments musicaux* than *mauvais quarts d'heure*. The explanation for this varying quality may lie in the phenomenal productivity of a pitifully short life. The first and final compositions, after all, are scarcely more than a decade apart. Another important factor—not to mention the most terrible of all, degenerative and fatal diseases—was in the nature and circumstances of many of his commissions. The music that he wrote to other people's specifications is greatly inferior, on the whole, to that which he wrote for himself, in its sense of directness and intimacy of feeling, and of thought and feeling being one. When composing for himself, Schubert sometimes seems to express the attitude, "Who else could care?" He was unable to dissimulate, in any case, as his last opus, *Der Hirt auf den Felsen,* proves. Composed as a display piece for a singer, it includes yodeling for the voice and a clarinet in duet, and concludes with a bumptious polka. This ear of corn, moreover, dates from soon after the masterful Sonata in B Flat!

Forced to choose, in the face of Schubert's awesome abundance, I recommend this B-Flat Sonata as one of the works that most closely fit the description of my title, along with the Impromptus and the finale of the Octet. Each of these examples is radically different, yet each is one of the composer's pinnacles. This choice is to some extent dictated by Mr. Reed's omissions, for he tends to support the current opinion that the middle-period sonatas have been slighted in favor of the later ones, to which, correspondingly, he devotes little attention. The amazing Octet movement does not fall strictly within his province of the later years, but his failure to single it out may be blamed on the deadly minuet that precedes it and that leaves listeners unprepared for its deep experience.

Like this writer, Mr. Reed reserves his highest marks for the Impromptus. But he neglects to stress the difference in quality between the first three in the second group (Nos. 5–7) and the others (Nos. 1–4 and 8); these three are on a considerably lower plane despite the popular, country-Western middle section—Austrian country—in No. 5. To Mr. Reed's observation that the Impromptus are quintessential Schubert, I would add that they are also essential Schumann, Chopin, and Brahms, those heirs of Schubert's most fruitful legacies. (No. 2 is often likened to the Chopin of the Etudes, and resemblances exist, in form, line, rhythm, figuration; but the same similarities are found in Nos. 3 and 4, while the Trio of No. 4 reminds one of the great Polish composer on a good day.) Schubert took his world with him, however, and was in no sense a "composer of the future"—fortunately, perhaps, in view of some of those who have been and who are still waiting for "their time." Innovation and experiment are secondary in his music, despite his use of remote keys and his "daring" modulations, less daring, it may be, in his own era when they were in fashion.

Affinities apart, the Impromptus are unsurpassed, even by Schubert himself. The rambling, sprawling repetitiveness and sentimentality to which he is prone are nowhere in evidence. Technically among the most polished music he ever wrote, these little pieces are perfectly proportioned. The modulations could not be smoother, and the composer does not overindulge his taste for enharmonic pivoting, a facile device at times and one that mars a passage in the Andante of the great B-Flat Piano Trio. The impromptu is his perfect instrumental form, in short, and it is debatable whether any of his sonatas succeed as do these smaller pieces. They reveal, moreover, an aspect of Schubert's personality heretofore only incompletely realized. It is the high spirits that overflow in them instead of, as so often, the recapitulations, for Schubert's "divine lengths" can be as tedious as theological tracts. The Impromptus, Nos. 1–4 and 8 at least, are felicities unspoiled even by those of us who prefer not to listen to them but to pound them out for ourselves, unmindful of the advice of the publisher who returned them to Schubert with the comment that they are "too difficult for trifles."

Going from these "trifles" to the posthumous B-Flat Sonata —which I would preserve of all Schubert, as Mr. Reed would the Adagio from the C-Major Quintet—the listener is disturbed by the overample dimensions of the first movement. It could hardly be otherwise, perhaps, given the expansiveness of the first theme, yet one wishes that the end of the exposition had been tightened, and that the music following the statement of the theme in C-sharp minor had a clearer sense of direction. The episode in D minor, on the other hand, with accompaniment of repeated eighth notes, is both the true stuff of sonata development and one of the beauties of piano literature. The bass trill introduced at the end of the original statement of the theme—at which point a lesser composer might have abandoned it as a mere embellishment—has been held in abeyance for this episode, where it is exploited to wholly unforeseen effect, resolved, at one point, in an unexpected upward change of direction that is an inspired touch.

The second movement cannot be faulted for any miscalculation, certainly not for the surprising, Debussyan harmonies toward the end; these, on the contrary, are a stunning example of Schubert composing for himself alone. The movement is one of his numerous *Schwanengesänge*, I might add, and like the road from the *Winterreise*, to name another one, leads, so one feels, directly to the grave. But while the Sonata as a whole is valediction on a grand scale, this second movement seems even to specify the hour. Like the poet to whom I owe my title, Schubert must have longed to "cease upon the midnight."

The exquisite flicker-of-hope Scherzo contains a marvelous jointure in the return, before the Trio, to the first theme; almost instantaneous, it is as difficult to perceive as a sleight of hand. Nor is the Finale the letdown that finales sometimes are in Schubert. (The legato second section, incidentally, reminds one of Chopin, as much as anything in the Impromptus.) But the movement is often botched in performance. For one thing, the sustained G with which it begins, which recurs, and which, at the end, is progressively and poignantly lowered in pitch, seldom receives its full time-value. Many pianists, too, Rubinstein among them, have not yet learned that, in Schubert's notation, dotted eighths and sixteenths *against* triplets must be played *as* triplets. Having said this, I should add that with the exception of a Beethoven-like and thumpingly articulated reading of the development section of the first movement (it should be veiled), Rubinstein's performance of the Sonata (RCA) has much to commend it.

As for the finale of the Octet, the slow introduction is Schubert at his most mysterious, an apocalyptic mood found in no other work. The eerie beauty of the music is intensified on its return in a different guise shortly before the end, where it interrupts a strangely deceptive—apparently jovial but actually sinister—Allegro. The finale of this too-little-known opus is one of Schubert's most astonishing creations, and one hopes that its audience will be enlarged.

No critic reminds us sufficiently often that Schubert's art is that of a youth. None of the composer's friends appears to have considered him prematurely aged, at any rate, and it is only after the Vienna Music Society's failure to perform the C-Major Symphony ("The Great"), and after his labors on the *Winterreise*, that he was observed to be suffering from unusual depression. But who can explain the miracle of Schubert, of the richest heritage of music the earth has ever received in return for so brief a visit?

GENIUS INTO GENTLEMAN

Not many people are likely to sing "Hark, the Herald Angels" to greet three new books by and about its composer. Which is regrettable, though in most cases probably not literally. Mendelssohn has been underrated, even patronized, owing to his neoclassicism, the classicist in the romantic being stronger in him than in any of his contemporaries. But precisely that reason allows, if it does not account, for the continuing elegance and freshness of the new spirit that, still in Beethoven's lifetime, burst into the world full grown in the Overture to *A Midsummer Night's Dream.*

The body of Mendelssohn's best music is small, though larger than most of us are aware. Before all else, therefore, the biographer, by his advocacy of neglected works, should address his efforts to enlarging the standard Mendelssohn repertory. To some extent, both Herbert Kupferberg, in *The Mendelssohns* (Scribner's) and George Marek, in *Gentle Genius, the Story of Felix Mendelssohn* (Funk and Wagnalls), do this. But neither brings the reader in for a close look at the music (no example of which is quoted in music type), both authors jumping instead to value judgments, concerning which they are in broad agreement, though it must be admitted that the room for disagreement is narrow. Nor do the new books attempt to tell the reader what is quintessentially Mendelssohnian about a modulation or a melodic turn, or idiosyncratically Mendelssohnian about a marvel of instrumentation such as the obbligato for two flutes in the Andante of the *Italian* Symphony, which could have been written by no one else.

First, the book *by* Mendelssohn. It is his translation into German verse of Terence's *Andria* (Officina Bodoni, Verona), published together with the Italian version by Machiavelli and the 1598 English version by Richard Bernard. Mendelssohn was sixteen at the time, yet his versification is no schoolboy exercise but a work of uncommon literary skill. In the chronology of his music it follows the string Octet, a masterpiece surpassing anything by Mozart or even Schubert at that age, not in technique—they all had that—but in the full realization of the musical personality; for sheer precocity, in the same sense, perhaps only Bizet, in his Symphony in C, written at eighteen, is in the same class, except that precocity by itself is a meaningless measure and does not describe the phenomenon of Mendelssohn.

Grateful as we are for the new biographies, a book of a different kind would have been even more welcome. Mendelssohn is one of the two or three most engaging letter writers among the great composers, and a larger selection of his correspondence than is now available in English has long been overdue. As his letters attest, he is a decidedly attractive character. Nor is it a disparagement of the new books to say that he is a wittier and more engrossingly observant writer than anyone who has written about him. His reply, at the age of fourteen, to a composer who had submitted a symphony for his criticism is a model of tact and well-expressed advice, while his letters on the state of music are that rare commodity, readable music history. Thus he reports from

Paris of an opera by Auber that it includes "perhaps three pieces in which the piccolo does not play the principal part. This little instrument serves to illustrate the fury of the brother, the pain of the lover, the joy of the peasant girl." Some of the contents of the letters, moreover, are thoroughly up-to-date, as in the case of this communiqué from Rome, which might have been dispatched yesterday: "Really horrible people sit around in the Café Greco."

But Mendelssohn is undetachable from his ingrown family, and his letters should be supplemented by those of his sisters, which, though of interest in themselves, are much more so in relation to the composer. (S. Hensel's *Die Familie Mendelssohn,* 1882, is one such compilation, which, incidentally, includes a memorable description of Ingres at the Villa Medici.) The Mendelssohn Archive in Berlin contains still unreleased material, the composer's heirs having destroyed much but withheld more. No love letter was ever published, and discreet and reticent though Mendelssohn was, it is hard to believe that he did not write any. More important would be the discovery of letters revealing the degree of self-awareness of his inner mind in his later years. But in any case, a complete "Mendelssohn Letters" in English is greatly to be desired.

Robert Schumann may have been the first to detect the pronounced melancholy in Mendelssohn, then in his twenty-seventh year. The condition is attributable to a number of factors, metabolic as well as psychological. But the clue to the principal one is surely in Mendelssohn's apprehensions, confided to Schumann, about "the sad thought of creativity drying up," together with the realization that he could neither surpass the works of his early years nor continue on the same path. For the phenomenon of Mendelssohn is that at the time of life when the other great composers were barely entering adolescence, he had reached full musical maturity, the fullest, at least, that he was ever to attain. He was in possession of these powers for only a few years, however, after which, failing to broaden or increase, they began to wane. After that he was able to regain the heights of his earlier music only sporadically, as in the Violin Concerto (a comparatively late work, but Mendelssohn died at thirty-eight!), in the not-all-that-serious *Variations Sérieuses,* and in the incidental music to *A Midsummer Night's Dream.* The Intermezzo, perhaps the most perfect of the *Dream* excerpts, was written seventeen years after the Overture, yet the passage of so much time is not reflected by any change of musical language, and it would be difficult to establish chronological order between the two compositions. In short, Mendelssohn did not grow beyond his miraculous youth.

After his visit, aged twelve, to Goethe, it is as if the *Wunderkind* had come away with a Faustian pact of his own; and as if the great magus, having foreseen the works of genius Mendelssohn would soon compose, had cast a Mephistophelean spell on him, to imprison him in his brilliant youth. (Mendelssohn's maturity was by no means confined to music, as I have already said, and as is demonstrated by this remark apropos the poet's attraction to the pianist Maria Szymanowska: "They confuse her unpretty playing with her pretty face.") But for whatever reasons, the stasis in Mendelssohn's creative powers was accompanied by a strange physical deterioration. A doctor who saw him in his thirty-fourth year said that he was prematurely aged, and that his handwriting did not change from his youth until his death, which, whether Faustian or Mephistophelean, sounds like a variant of the story of Dorian Gray.

Whatever the reasons, loss of nerve, critical self-consciousness—Schumann remarked that Mendelssohn was continually amending and rewriting, and that self-criticism was one of his most striking characteristics—some stagnation is evident in the later music, a great deal of it, to my mind, in the larger works, including *Elijah.* No less deplorable, composing gives ground to conducting, which indicates, since he was in no need of a career of that type, that the urge to give birth to music of his own was no longer irrepressible. Furthermore, his greatest achievements as a conductor were in discovering and restoring music of the past, Bach and Handel above all. Not that he was ineffective as a champion of the new, yet he seems to have felt increasingly distant from the romanticism not only of Berlioz, Liszt, and Wagner, but also of Chopin and Schumann.

Mendelssohn's letters describing his work as a conductor, and the qualities of orchestras and musicians, form a representative picture of the conditions of musical performance not only in his time but also in ours; the letter to Ferdinand Hiller, March 14, 1833, is a remarkable document as to how little they seem to have changed. Mr. Marek argues that Mendelssohn's celebrated revival of the *Saint Matthew Passion* could not have been "exaggeratedly romantic"—but was *any* Mendelssohn performance *exaggeratedly* romantic? —"insofar as one is able to judge from Mendelssohn's tempo and dynamic marks in his score." But how far is that, and what *are* those marks? I regret that the point is not elaborated, for Mendelssohn's verbal tempo markings are inconsistent in relation to his metronomic ones. No doubt his tempi were on the lively side, but surely never as fast as Kalichstein plays the fast movements of the G-Minor Piano Concerto (RCA), or as the Claremont Quartet plays some of Opus 11 (DGG). Both of these works, incidentally, contain important examples of Mendelssohn's neoclassicism, the recitative at the beginning of the Presto in the Quartet obviously having been inspired by late Beethoven, while the second theme of the Piano Concerto, especially the episode beginning in D-flat major, might have come from a concerto by Mozart. Wagner thought Mendelssohn's tempo in the Menuet of Beethoven's Eighth much too fast, and it is the Wagnerian tradition that has prevailed—to the extent that Szell takes the Menuet in Mendelssohn's *Italian* at Wagner's, in this case impossibly slow, Beethoven tempo.

Mendelssohn's death has been attributed mainly to depression following the deaths of his father and his sister Fanny. But the composer's self-critical intelligence would have penetrated every natural defense and must also have played a part. Father and son, brother and sister were interdependent to a neurotic degree, even as adults, Felix being far closer to Fanny than to his wife, a situation he well understood, keeping the two women apart for almost a year after his marriage. (At one time, incidentally, Fanny composed music virtually indistinguishable from her brother's.) His wife bore him five children, but her diary of the honeymoon could leave a slow reader's fingers frostbitten. She may well have had a "romantic temperament," however, that Mendelssohn failed to awaken: she admired Chopin to the point of asking him, through her husband, to write a few measures expressly for her.

Some of the gentleness of Mr. Marek's title was the result of repression so strong that it seems to have resulted in fainting spells: Mendelssohn appears to have kept his deepest feelings to himself. (Even his death was "interior," from a ruptured brain artery.) But my title distorts Mr. Marek's in order to point up an outward aspect of the composer's gentility. As the one aristocrat, socially speaking (though not only), among the great composers of his time, the musician uniquely wealthy and educated, he felt at home among English gentlemen. Partly for the same reasons and partly because of his own reserved temperament he was also the only great composer of his time to have had a vital role in English musical life. It is useless to speculate about his musical destiny if, like his fellow townsman Brahms, he had gone to Vienna—still a composer's city, for all of its exasperations—instead of to London. Mr. Marek says that "To Felix, Jew or Gentile made no difference." But I think it did, even if the written evidence yields nothing to support me. Perhaps it even had something to do with his preference for London over Vienna.

As for performances of the music, Bernstein's reading of the *Scottish* Symphony (CBS) would be difficult to better. The strings do not articulate clearly in the first movement, playing ah-ah-ah instead of, as the winds play the same figure, ta-ta-ta; but the tempi are good and the climaxes are not marred by indulgences of the sort that were at one time the bane of his conducting. (Like his first-namesake in *Of Mice and Men,* Bernstein sometimes kills what he most loves by hugging it to death.) And the Bernstein-Stern performance of the Violin Concerto recorded on Mount Scopus, though probably a hundred degrees or so warmer than Mendelssohn ever imagined it being played, is an exciting recording nevertheless.

BELLINI'S BOADICEA AND THE BOYS FROM NEWARK

Norma has the reputation, unfortunate and unjustified, of being little more than a singers' vehicle, the frame for a vocal concert. It is, on the contrary, a concentrated and sustained music drama, and one relatively free of musical diversion for its own sake, its famous display pieces being active links in the dramatic unity. A still more striking paradox is that this inherently theatrical work has become the most static of spectacles on the stage, a state of affairs that we are asked to accept and excuse as a "convention."

The title role is awesomely demanding, both to sing and to portray, for which reason we now consider ourselves fortunate with any performance that is reasonably well sung, seldom taking the histrionic aspect into serious account. The histrionic half of Montserrat Caballé's Norma, currently at the Metropolitan, is limited to a few poses. Some of these have force, and as the High Priestess of the Druids, Madame Caballé is an imperious presence. But she must also play a mother and a jilted woman, and here her acting is inept. Surely, however, it is the responsibility of the *régisseur* to correct her, when, dagger clutched in fist, she simply aims the weapon in the general direction of her former lover and holds it there, as if expecting him to impale himself, the Roman literally falling on the sword. And in her other dagger scene, when the threatened parties are her own children, could she not have been taught how to convey at least some ambiguity of intent? What Madame Caballé does convey is that she has never even entertained the thought of becoming another Medea. Ironically, her most vehement and convincing gesture, in the performance that I saw (February 12), was a sweep of the peignoir that raised a dust storm from the Metropolitan stage (and titters from the hall) more appropriate to *Aida*.

The Metropolitan's visual conception of the opera is occasionally at odds with the score. Not that the music sets the scene, except internally: Bellini's landscape is the melancholy of the soul. But whereas the opera depends more profoundly on its intimate scenes than on its Druid rituals, this production emphasizes the monumental virtually to the exclusion of the personal. The stage picture at the beginning should represent a "Forest of the Druids," in which the most conspicuous tree is the "Sacred Oak of Irminsul." But the Metropolitan limits the view to menhirs, and on the scale not merely of Stonehenge but of the Palisades seen from below. Furthermore, and most inappropriately of all, the Druid warriors enter carrying spears, despite Norma's admonition that Druid *axes* "are not yet strong enough for an uprising" against Roman *spears*.

Instead of leaves, limbs, and woody trunks, a bundle of wire hangs above the stage, symbolic, it may be, of the Druids' mistletoe but suggesting a "sculpture" of the sort for which, not long ago, a certain much-maligned New York museum would eagerly have exchanged a Titian. Yet a "real" forest would have offered two important advantages. First, the sacrificial altar stone would have been the cynosure that Bellini and his librettist must have intended. Second, a patch of sylvan surroundings would have helped to foster a measure of credibility for the concealment of the "virgin" Priestess's motherhood; this, incidentally, is the main flaw in an otherwise near-perfect libretto, for even in the depths of the forest how could a High Priestess keep her vestal attendants from revealing the existence of her two strapping sons? The public reason for Norma's self-immolation, after all, is the betrayal of her vows of chastity.

The musical performance at the Metropolitan was in some ways superior to that of the new recording (RCA LSC-6202) by the same conductor and female principals. Caballé is intermittently and more frequently flat in the record album than she was in the theater. Nor does the recorded singing fulfill Bellini's impassioned demands—"*Con voce cupa e terribile,*" "*abandonandosi*"—which *were* met, however, and more than once, in the staged performance. But the most obtrusive musical fault at the Metropolitan was the torturous fraction of a beat by which the chorus anticipated the orchestra. This is not an unusual occurrence and not one to be blamed on the conductor, Carlo Felice Cillario, who managed to keep the singers and orchestra more or less together in the recording. The culprit is that unnecessary intermediary the prompter, who is easy to see but often disastrous to follow. Aspiring maestri, incidentally, would do well to study one of Cillario's techniques, a slow, two-handed, parabola-like dive in which he both guides and follows Madame Caballé through one of her most effective vocal stunts, a downward portamento that goes up the listener's spine.

Madame Caballé's voice is more attractive in *pianissimo* than in *forte*. But the same may be said for Fiorenza Cossotto, the Adalgisa, Norma's rival for Pollione's love and Madame Caballé's rival for the love of the Metropolitan audience. The two roles are uniquely competitive and are sometimes performed by interchangeable voices; but the final scene is Norma's, and if an intermission had not been wrongly introduced into Act Two, Signora Cossotto would not have reaped the slightly larger share of the applause that she did during this artificial break. It may be that Caballé and Cossotto do not blend quite so mellifluously in the duets as do Sutherland and Horne, and certainly the intonation of the Australian is more reliable than that of her Spanish counterpart. Yet Caballé is the more believable as the opera's tragic protagonist. But what invidious comparing this is, and how churlish to criticize any performance on the level of either team.

Almost everything in the score of *Norma* is constituent to the dramatic effect, the rhythmic figuration—those leaping syncopations when Norma decides against infanticide—to the smallest detail of the instrumentation. The chorus, for example, though largely confined to tramping on and off stage, is always directly involved in the play: not for Bellini those merely atmospheric hunting, drinking, and warmaking hallooings of the time. Concerning his orchestral skill, many august opinions have already been handed down, most notably a damning one from Chief Justice Verdi. From this, however, I emphatically dissent. Admittedly the music is thinly scored. But Bellini obtains the most from instruments, and every touch of orchestral color is perfectly conceived; one thinks of his discreet and superb use of trumpets and trombones, and of the mystery that he draws from the clarinet. More important, the instrumentation is functional to the destiny of the characters. Thus the horns, though limited to the simplest of cadential figurations, are primarily employed to intensify the dramatic situation and only secondarily to gild the sonority.

Verdi was no less mistaken in his evaluation of Bellini as a poor harmonist. He may not have been startlingly adventurous, and progressions of his chords are not likely to appear in histories of harmonic innovation. But that is hardly proof of poverty; and anyway, the sense of tonality relationships manifest in the last scene of *Norma* is beyond improvement even by Verdi. Vincenzo Bellini, the great melodic ensorceller, was a master of every facet of his art.

—

One of the most pleasing concerts I have heard this season was the program of Haydn's *Harmoniemesse* and the *Mass* and *Symphony of Psalms* by Stravinsky, all three works nobly performed by Leonard Bernstein, the New York Philharmonic, and assorted solo singers and choirs. *The New York Times* duly noticed the event but unaccountably not its sensational feature, the Newark Boys Chorus. The *Times* wasted few words on the Stravinsky *Mass* but should have withheld even those few in order to mention this remarkable, wholly commendable group. Happily the audience responded where the professional did not, and the youths were applauded even as they began to file on stage, for their personableness, deportment, irresistible good looks (in smart tuxedos). They numbered about thirty, of whom two-thirds or more were blacks. Of these latter about half had elegant Afros, which, at the end of the performance, when the boys bowed from the waist, looked like marine plants as they bobbed up and down in the waves of applause.

Their parts long since memorized, the boys sang with aplomb, musical conviction, and a sense of occasion. Standing with hands folded behind their backs, they watched Mr. Bernstein for every cue, listened for and co-ordinated with the instrumentalists, sang precisely and in tune. I, for one, have never heard a better performance, and I thought the applause and the several curtain calls well deserved.

The last of the four performances was followed by a post-concert concert in the antechamber of Mr. Bernstein's dressing room, where, for a small audience that included Mr. Bernstein (in a striped Joseph's-coat-of-many-colors dressing gown), they sang jiveass and Bach, Schubert and gospel songs, all from memory and all extremely well. They did more than sing, too. In one piece a small boy banged a tambourine, while in another the whole chorus "swung and swayed." At one point it was announced that due to the illness of an accompanist a certain work would have to be performed with a substitute at the piano. This provoked a remark from the audience to the effect that the stand-in seemed to be doing very well "for a nonblack." And at that the young choristers unanimously and heartily booed the would-be ingratiator. Condescending remarks of this sort are doubtless shocking anachronisms to these truly integrated youths. In any case, when they sang a new piece dedicated to the Brotherhood of Man, they proved that thesis by the quality of the performance rather than by the preaching of the text.

The attention of the U.S. Department of State, Division of Cultural Affairs (if such a thing exists), should be drawn to the Newark Boys Chorus. What other group can surpass them musically and fraternally? And who is more fit to represent the American people abroad? Surely not the standard exportables–Van Cliburn, the Philadelphia Orchestra, the Mormon Tabernacle Choir? But move quickly, cultural diplomats, whoever you are. Some of these other acts can go on and on, but boys' voices change.

GLINKA'S OPERAS

The titles *Ivan Susanin* (*A Life for the Tsar*) and *Ruslan and Lyudmila* are known to us all, but how many of us west of the Curtain have heard, much less seen, either of these founding works not only of Russian opera but also of the special character of the Russian Nationalist School? Thanks to two new albums we can at last familiarize ourselves with the music, which is the first step in the realization of what until recently has been a documented but unexperienced chapter in our musical histories. Both albums, released by the State publisher, Mezhdunarodnaya Kniga ("International Book"), are available at the Four Continents Bookstore, 156 Fifth Avenue, New York.

The technical quality of these recordings is by no means

the worst we have had from the U.S.S.R. But the orchestral sound is one-dimensional, lacks presence, and provides little more than a vaguely defined background for the singers. A solo instrument in dialogue with a voice is kept to a low secondary level, and at times even the characteristics of instruments are indistinct, partly, no doubt, because the orchestral groups have not been separated. Nor has any attempt been made, by positioning the singers, to create the illusion of staged performances.

These singers, by the way, confirm our prejudices about Russian voices in general, namely, that while the contraltos and basses are rich in tone and wide in range, the sopranos are pinched, nasal, almost metallic, and the tenors sweet, unctuous, and uncertain on their uppers. The choruses, of whom much is required in these operas, are superb, although in a few instances they must be faulted on their intonation, possibly because of loss of contact with the orchestra.

Despite these criticisms, *Ivan Susanin* is competently performed, *Ruslan* a shade better than that. Both recordings would be valuable if only as guides to performance practice, however, for the divergencies from the scores are numerous. Changes of tempo occur, unmarked in the music; the Lesginka, for instance, should be taken at half the tempo of the Arabian dance. And where the score indicates long notes and a legato style, the recording sometimes does the opposite.

The music lover's chances of seeing either opera in the American theater being very slight, the best that can be hoped for from this discussion is some stimulation of audience interest. The Hamburg Opera revived *Ruslan and Lyudmila* a few seasons ago, staged by George Balanchine, but with only mixed success. The dance element in both operas—"Our theater is the ballet," Pushkin once remarked—is paramount. With the superior dancing of the City Ballet, in a staging that would also involve the finest talents of the City Opera, *Ruslan* would be a stellar event in Lincoln Center, south side of the mall, of course. Another indispensable requirement is an ample and superior chorus. Both works are "choral," choruses, like ballets, being a featured part of Russian opera.

Ivan Susanin, the earlier (first performed in 1836) though not less important work, in so far as can be judged from this abridged recorded version, could bog down in one or two scenes if played entire. But the final act and the Epilogue might be performed separately, and would be especially effective on television—a project for NET Opera Theater, perhaps. The ending is a five-star spectacular, its musical substance a Russian anthem sung by augmented chorus and orchestra and accompanied by a mighty ringing of bells. It is in this act, too, that Glinka reveals his full powers as a dramatic composer for the first time. That a Russian "provincial" produced this music some fifteen years before *Rigoletto* is astonishing, although of all other composers, it is the Verdi-in-Donizetti whom Glinka most often resembles. It should surprise no one to learn that Glinka wrote a set of piano variations on an aria from *Anna Bolena.*

The features of Glinka's musical personality are less clearly defined in the slower arias than in the fast ones, perhaps because of the strong dance impulse in the latter. Furthermore, quality is often inversely related to length, some of the longer pieces lacking both intensification and rhythmic variation. The most successful movements, in fact, are the Polish dances, the second-act Polonaise, the Krakowiak, the Mazurka, the Polacca. Except that the last requires a chorus, these brilliant numbers can be enucleated and performed as a ballet. Tchaikovsky was obviously inspired by them, as well as indebted to them as models of form and instrumentation.

Glinka's orchestration, a justly celebrated attraction of his music, can be only partly divined from these low-fidelity records. A predilection for the winds may be noted among the attributes of his instrumental style, along with a penchant for novelty in their use. One wonders, for instance, if the trumpet double-tonguing in the recapitulation of the Mazurka may not be the first time this effect has been employed in an opera; in any case, Glinka's orchestral originality and skill have not yet been appreciated in the West.

Since the likelihood of an American staging of *Ruslan and Lyudmila* (first performed in 1842) is somewhat greater than that of *Ivan Susanin,* I might give a brief description of the libretto, not, however, that anyone will be tempted to stage the opera for the sake of its story. The plot, from the wildest realms of fairy-tale fantasy, is long and labyrinthine, and its subject matter seems to have been drawn from such yet-to-be-created sources as Tchaikovsky ballet and Wagnerian opera. The action begins at the wedding feast of the knight Ruslan, and Lyudmila, daughter of the Grand Duke of Kiev. A minstrel predicts misfortune for the newlyweds but promises that it can be overcome by love (*cf. Tannhäuser*). The conventional "clap of thunder" follows, during which the bride is abducted by a wicked dwarf (*The Ring of the Nibelung* and *The Sleeping Beauty*). Ruslan searches for the missing heiress through an enchanted world whose flora and fauna include magic gardens and sirens (*Parsifal*), a witch (*Hansel and Gretel*), and the decapitated head (*Dantons Tod*) of a sleeping giant, a role voiced by the entire male chorus. The weather is suddenly bad in this Russian Disneyland, and the required musical storm makes effective use of ascending and descending chromatics (remarkably similar to those in the storm in *Rigoletto*). Some of the props, too, are startlingly familiar: a magic ring and a magic sword (*Siegfried*); a beard which "contains [*sic*] the dwarf's magic invincibility" and which, at the dramatic climax, is "lopped off" (*Samson*). Finally, the dwarf's spell over Lyudmila leaves her in a coma (*The Sleeping Beauty*).

All of this, at any rate, can be deduced from the booklet accompanying the records, apparently translated by an undergraduate in a crash course in heaven-knows-what English: "the pusillanimous Farlaf is scared, and his knees have turned to jelly"; "the giant's head blows furiously into Ruslan's face trying to topple him over"; "the dwarf is followed by a sumptuously clad court."

Ruslan is almost twice as long as *Ivan Susanin*. It is very slow-moving at the beginning, moreover, and not without dull patches in the first two acts. But the refreshing use of a piano as the accompanying instrument partly redeems even the minstrel's protracted aria. And the first act is memorable for two very striking musical events, the interlude following the thunderclaps and the disappearance of Lyudmila, which closely resembles the introduction to the *Pas de Deux* in *The Firebird*, both in the construction of the melody and in the way it is relayed from flute to clarinet to bassoon; and the quadruple canon(!) which leads to a scene that, both dramatically and musically, resembles Verdi at his best.

Among the opera's novelties of instrumentation are the new importance given to the bassoons in an unsupported bass line (an effect made familiar by Prokofiev); the use of muted horns, of string and harp harmonics, and of solo strings—the single viola in the prelude to Act Two, and, later in the opera, the four cellos, a combination Stravinsky was to exploit in *Oedipus Rex*. Having mentioned Stravinsky, I should add that, during the last two decades of the nineteenth century, his father sang, on different occasions, the roles of both Ruslan and Farlaf (one of Lyudmila's rejected suitors) in St. Petersburg's Mariinsky Theater.

As in *Ivan Susanin*, the dances are the highlight of the

opera (the ballet in the fourth act, not the one in the third, which is as insipid as Ponchielli's *Hours*). Introduced by a march, they include Turkish, Arabian, and Lesginkan *Danses de caractère*, and clear the way both for Borodin's Polovetsians and Broadway's *Kismet*. The impression of the Arabian dance on the composer of the *Nutcracker*, incidentally, is very evident. But dance is at the heart of Glinka's music, as I have already emphasized, and his liveliest arias and choral ensembles could be choreographed as effectively as the ballet pieces.

The same might be said of the operatic music (as of most other kinds) of Glinka's greatest admirer, Igor Stravinsky. His one-act opera *Mavra* not only is dedicated to Glinka (and Pushkin and Tchaikovsky) but in its substance is a tribute to him. Stravinsky favors and continues the Italian strain in his compatriot's musical heredity, and *Mavra* is, above all, an imitation or parody of Glinka's Russo-Italian vocal style. Specifically, the B-minor aria of Parasha, Stravinsky's heroine, may have been suggested by an aria of Lyudmila's in the same key, while the ensembles in Stravinsky's little opera, the duets, trio, and quartet, show signs of having been modeled on those in *Ruslan*. But the source of Stravinsky's most obvious borrowing from Glinka is to be found in the Chorus and Romance, numbers fourteen and fifteen, in *Ivan Susanin*, and in the Prelude to Act Five of *Ruslan*:

It is possible, too, that the idea of scoring *Mavra* for an orchestra of winds may have derived from *Ruslan*, one of whose female choruses is accompanied by winds alone. More important than that is Glinka's wind-band stage ensemble, used both by itself and as a supplement to the orchestra in the march and oriental dances. This band-music scene, one of the most stunning in *Ruslan* and the one whose tunes, after a single hearing, are the most memorable of the opera's melodies, is especially close in spirit and style to *Mavra*.

The Russian language is no longer an obstacle for American opera companies. All the same, a *Ruslan* in English would be better than none, and an English translation is unlikely to wreak any very grievous harm, unless entrusted to the author of that aforementioned booklet! The sound of the Russian language is a less integral part of the music than it is in, for example, *Pique Dame*. The first priority is to bring the opera to the stage, and this can be achieved only by an audience already devoted to the music.

It would be absurd to pretend that either *Ruslan* or *Ivan Susanin* is in the class of *Boris*, *Onegin*, or *Pique Dame*, and not only because of *their* overwhelming dramatic superiority. But our Russian repertory is hardly so prodigal that we can afford to ignore its two earliest masterpieces. The timeliness of a Glinka opera production may be indicated by the vogue in Janáček. And, with our eyes still on the clock, we should learn how to do both operas from the one man still in our midst who can teach us, George Balanchine.

PIKOVAYA DAMA AT THE MET

The Metropolitan Opera's current *Queen of Spades* demands review on at least two counts. First, though the opera is a masterpiece that belongs in the permanent repertory, it is by no means universally recognized as such. (The four lines allotted to it in Grout's long *Short History of Opera* indicate the extent to which it is still neglected.) Second, as a revival, a newly studied if not wholly new production, it serves to point up the strengths and weaknesses of the Met itself. Not that they have changed appreciably, or that symptoms of the health of the new regime are more discernible in this than in any other production. But then, the character of the Met, middling, safety-first, may be unchangeable, having been established for so long that the policy holders have come to think of their institution as a branch of "Metropolitan Life."

The visual aspects of the performance leave much to be desired. The dramatic action is so wooden that one wonders whether the director believes in the opera's stageworthiness; and the decor is impossible, in the strict sense of Byron's "[a painting] must remind me of something I have seen or think it possible to see." Which must be said both because the production aspires to literalness and because any other approach would be difficult to imagine. The plot could be transposed to another locale—ante-bellum New Orleans, say, Poe for Pushkin—but the style could not, depending as it does on a number of factors including the relationship of *dix-neuvième* frames to *dix-huitième* art, the latter by Grétry, Greuze (the ballet), and even Mozart.

Scene One is supposed to take place in the Summer Garden of Saint Petersburg, but the only prop that would support the impression that it actually does is a backdrop of the city at a peculiar angle. Of formal gardens no trace can be found: not only no statuary (except for the cast) but little vegetation, which is as scarce as it threatens to be in the defoliated American city of the future. In short, it is a street scene, but one so empty that the date of the opera might be the year of the Great Plague. This is partly accounted for by the deletion of the children's choruses (a kindergarten strike?), removing not only the infants themselves but also their nurses and governesses. Except for a basket vendor, a few "strollers," and one or two "customers" in a *Konditorei*—but what is a pastry shop doing in the ground floor of a palace?—the unpopularity of these gardens suggests a high incidence of mugging.

All of which greatly reduces the credibility of the aged Countess's visit there, an apocryphal episode introduced by the librettist, Modeste Tchaikovsky, to give dramatic shape to Pushkin's story; but a mistake, for this initial appearance of the Countess weakens her subsequent ones. She is a recluse, after all, too old for promenades in the park (except, perhaps, in a *carrosse*) and so fragile that she can be—indeed, demonstrably is—frightened to death.

Nor is this the only unfortunate divergence from Pushkin. Another is the salute to the Tsarina at the end of the ballroom scene where Her Highness's failure to materialize—which she could not be represented as doing on a Russian stage—puzzles the audience. Yet another is Lisa's fatal plunge into the canal after discovering that her lover's fidelity to money is more passionate than his fidelity to her. (Pushkin sensibly, if undramatically, married her to someone else.) The Metropolitan's staging of this scene, by the way, is more than a trifle ridiculous. The snowfall implies that the canal is frozen, and therefore that the heroine is not likely to suffer more than a bump or a broken bone. Moreover, while Lisa is warmly clothed (though too poorly for her station, which would require an ermine-trimmed coat—or bonnet, at least, like a Pope's camauro), her hotheaded lover enters hatless. Yet it was the composer, not his librettist brother, who decided that Lisa's fate must be settled so summarily (and by the same means that Tchaikovsky was to try himself only a short time later).

The staging of the ballroom scene is also incorrect. It is

dominated by an escutcheon of the imperial eagle, improbable in a private palace. Some of the male guests wear black, too, though in that era and on such an occasion, the funereal shade would have been questionable. But even the pastoral ballet unsettles one, because of the recklessness with which the dancing maidens swing their sickles. (In Soviet performances do their male partners carry hammers?) Act Three begins in a barracks long familiar to New York operagoers as Boris Godunov's apartments—except for black columns on either side of the stage, where they have been in every scene of the opera, as if the director were counting on them to impose a pictorial unity. The next scene, "By the Winter Canal" (according to the libretto), is again the "Summer Garden" not altogether disguised by snow, while the final one, which should take place in a boisterous gambling room, is as dull and forbiddingly formal as a convention of teetotaling clergymen. The only excitement is in the audience's apprehension for some fat fellows attempting to dance the prisiadka.

The oddest staging in the opera, nevertheless, is that of the Countess's ghost at the end. Instead of the apparition of a face (deadpan, of course), in a mandorla of light, and visible to the murderer alone, this specter arrives not only in full view of the whole stage but in full form as well, an animated corpus delicti, looking considerably healthier and less haggard than when alive. So far from "fleeting," moreover, this female Commendatore stays around until the very end of the opera, thus upstaging poor Herman even in his demise.

The musical performance compares favorably with the stage spectacle, less favorably with the recording of the opera on Melodiya-Angel (SRD–4104). At the performance I heard (January 12), the conductor, Kazimierz Kord, was generally too brisk, damagingly so in the prelude to Act

Three, which introduces the funeral music for the Countess. As Herman, Nicolai Gedda was uncertain both of his part and of his voice—to judge by the intensity of his concentration on Maestro Kord and by his reluctance to abandon high notes once he felt sure of them (and his rapidity in doing so when he did not). In contrast, Raina Kabaivanska's Lisa was musically secure and histrionically almost credible. As is well known, Metropolitan audiences will applaud any inanity in the scenery and staging—the snow got an especially warm hand—and interrupt or obliterate the orchestra during the slightest pause in the singing, thus betraying their uninvolvement with the work and its performance as a whole. Yet these same audiences are often discriminating in their evaluation of singers, and it seemed to me that on this occasion their response to the participants was condign.

The main novelty of the revival is the singing of the opera in Russian, and the enunciation was superior, on the whole, to that of the English in the version I heard at the old Met. Apart from the principals, whose native languages include Russian, the quality varied; Paul Franke, for example, sang a very un-Russian "*Nietschze-vo,*" but in a minor part (Tchekalinsky). In the case of the Countess, Russian is hardly more important than French. But since Regina Resnik's pronunciation was unclear only in the crucial word *tuz*—when she reveals her "winning" formula for Faro: *troika* (three), *semyorka* (seven), *tuz* (ace)—this may have been intentional.

Having learned *Pikovaya Dama* myself from one who knew it as intimately as any musician since Tchaikovsky, my views are prejudiced. They led me to expect more. The production is sadly in need of an artistic director, not simply a *metteur en scène* or conductor but someone with a knowledge of the functions of both, as well as some experience of the opera. Among other things, this artistic tyrant would have forbidden the cuts, obliged each section of the strings to articulate the same music in the same way, raised the emotional stakes in the gambling scene, demanded a slower tempo for the Sarabande, and banished that imperial eagle to a remote crag.

Having hailed the opera as a masterpiece, I must substantiate the claim. Briefly, it has a suspenseful story, roles for three believable characters, an abundance of fine arias and ensembles, a variety of choruses (street, salon, ballroom, church), ballet (trite but not protracted). It even has some good ersatz Mozart. Each act builds, moreover, and the sequence of scenes, in contrast and balance, is successful: the opera achieves both musical and dramatic momentum. Not even during that obligatory inset ballet does the composer lose his grip on the dramatic development. No less remarkable are the ways in which Tchaikovsky comes directly to the point, as in the quiet, staccato brass chords announcing the Countess's death, and in the confining of her Ghost to a single pitch. Furthermore, the score displays an admirable restraint, never lapsing into the hysterics of the late symphonies, and avoiding those abiding faults, inflation and perseveration.

—

In a week in which the White House has so exactly carbon-dated its cultural level by the choice of the *1812 Overture*, a little-known but important work by Tchaikovsky has appeared for the first time on records, somewhat offsetting the worst taste of the composer, if not that of the inaugurated. This is the *Liturgie de Saint Jean Chrysostome*, a large-scale "Russian Mass"—fifteen movements, including many litanies and antiphons, though only thirteen are recorded (Philips). The work in its entirety may not be suitable for concerts, given the limitations of the liturgical style—attributable in part to the Orthodox Church's interdiction against instruments; yet the harmonic range is probably not much narrower than it would have been had Tchaikovsky used an accompaniment. The performance is by the "Ensemble Choral Tchaïkovsky" (Paris? the album is almost deliberately mysterious, as if the group were a political front organization). The singing is out of tune, but characteristically, as Russian Church choirs are. This is not disturbing and may even be indispensable to the style, while the bottom-heavy harmonic imbalance and the wobbling of the women in the upper range seem to add authenticity. The same chorus should give us Tchaikovsky's later *Vesper Mass.* Between its proemial psalm and Katabasis (recessional), it contains a Kathisma (one of the divisions of the Psalter), a Theotokon, and a Troparion, another example of which is sung at the funeral of the Countess in *Pikovaya Dama.*

BIZET, BERLIOZ, AND *OPÉRA-COMIQUE*

That the performance of the Metropolitan Opera's new *Carmen* on Deutsche Grammophon (2809043) does not fulfill the greatest expectations for it is partly a natural consequence of the recording process itself. But patchwork seems a more accurate description than performance. The opera was recorded in ten sessions and pieced together from 261 "takes," none of them, in final form, as long as an aria. So much for continuity, even of a mechanical kind. As for larger questions, such as the aesthetics that this electronic tyranny imposes and the price it exacts in individuality and personality, these lead to some vertiginous conclusions.

The logistic requirements of taping a full-length opera are formidable. A scene is begun one day and resumed several days later, or recorded complete in a single session, only to be corrected later with a dozen inserts. Since the speeds, the sound levels, and the balances of these different takes do not match, they must be made to do so artificially, by flooding the splices with canned echo. As always, too, the technical problems are minute compared to the human ones. The Don José may be in better equilibrium next Tuesday on take six than he was last Friday on take five, when, in addition, the microphone placement was slightly different. In short, contexts are indispensable; and though the worn-and-torn, end-of-season performance of the opera in an opera house may be perfunctory, it is a *performance*, nevertheless, and the embers of the drama, fanned by the bellows of even the weariest singers, will still generate heat. A take that starts cold in the middle of a scene, on the other hand, could hardly be expected to kindle any warmth.

That this recorded "performance" wins a bronze rather than a gold medal may also be blamed on the cast. For the first time in my experience of the opera (which includes conducting it), Escamillo's entrance is unexciting, no doubt partly because his singing is so woolly. Nor is that of Micaëla consistently silken, a modest requirement since any acting talent in the role is supererogatory; compared to the dagger-flashing violence of the other characters, Micaëla is in danger of expiring from nothing more terrible than an overdose of poise. But the Carmen, who *is* vocally capable, has limited the character by portraying only a single aspect of it, the venality and vulgarity. (The tone of her rebuff to Don José can be rendered only by the vernacular: "bug off" or "get lost.") The glamorization of the heroine's "easy virtue," incidentally, contributed heavily to the initial failure of the opera, for Carmen shocked her first critics, just as, decades later, Lulu shocked hers. Not that this interpretation of the role is illegitimate; but the exclusively low-life view of the immortal gypsy robs her of her grandeur, reduces the mystery of her fatalism, and cheapens her concept of freedom—for I do not agree, as one critic has put it, that "bitchery disguised as a love of liberty is the mystery of Carmen."

The performance is an argument for opera in English–or for *Carmen* in French. The language used here, polyglot American-French, is less distracting in the arias and ensembles than in the spoken dialogues. The repeated "*des*" for "*de*" in the *Habañera* is especially noticeable (although the plural adventitiously fits the grammatical construction). And so is Carmen's failure to cross her t's, in contrast with Don José's loud and clear enunciation of *his*, albeit often in the wrong places, "*soit*," for example, coming out as "swat." But it is the unaccompanied speech which brings into the glare not only mispronunciations and mistaken accentuations but also egregiously alien tempi and rhythms. Don José talks like someone out of *Gunsmoke* who has learned his lines by rote from the New Orleans school-mistress, and his spoken exchanges with Carmen at Lillas Pastia's *posada* are pure camp, a potential hit in a different branch of the entertainment industry.

Leonard Bernstein's conducting is thoughtful, controlled, immaculate, even inspired. Its shortcomings are the consequences of these very virtues, for it misses both the high passion of the opera and much of its idiomatic flavor. Part of the trouble may be that unlike *Tristan* and *Parsifal*, for instance, *Carmen* is not a "conductor's opera," at least not to the extent that Mr. Bernstein makes it one. (Toscanini's symphonic *Traviata* is another instance in kind.) A lesser *chef d'orchestre* would be obliged to give the singers their heads, indulging them in some of their habits, good or bad. But this might also have made for a more "natural" performance, which in turn could have heightened the drama. In sum, the conducting is admirably clean, but cleanliness is not always next to godliness. (*Mozart* is.)

"The performance uses the original spoken dialogue." Thus a *New York Times* review of the recording (April 22) that is a "Flower Song" in itself ("The page sings with aching beauty as expressive countermelodies weave sinuously in and out"). Actually only a small part of the original dialogue is used—mercifully, so far as this production is concerned. But Mr. Bernstein has generally followed the Oeser edition, which quite mistakenly to my mind opens the so-called cuts (they may have been Bizet's alterations) made at the first rehearsals. Inexplicably, however, Mr. Bernstein chooses the short version of the duel scene in Act III, though the longer original is crucial to the understanding of Don José's emotional state at this point. The long version exists only in Bizet's piano score but has been competently orchestrated.

The recording is "super": opulent in sound, clear, and so close that if tambourines and castanets had contagious diseases, the listener would certainly contract them. The book accompanying the record flatters the buyer by giving the first page of the commentary in English, the second in French, the third in German. One expects the foreign-language texts simply to translate the English, as they do in the case of a companion article, *Carmen and the Met;* yet all three contain different information. The color photographs are more numerous than those in most monographs on Leonardo da Vinci, and the cost of the album, if manufactured in America, would probably have been as high without the records. But the budget for the project has already been widely publicized, often with the implication that $300,000 is too much to spend on still another edition of a permanent best-seller. Experience should have taught that this money would otherwise have gone to a worse cause rather than to a bettter one, however, and besides, the criticism ill becomes us, Deutsche Grammophon having done as much to bolster our failing musical economy as have any of the pump-priming foundations.

To go from the most popular to one of the least known of great French operas, the new Philips recording of *Benvenuto Cellini* (6707–019) is the revelation of a musical masterpiece. Whatever its merits and demerits as a dramatic composition, the score is among the richest and most original of any opera of the time. (This is not to say that *Carmen* is *un*original—its repeatability is proof of its originality—but an opera that few people avoid hearing at least once between the cradle and the urn cannot compete in this regard with a fresh discovery.) The music of *Cellini* is in fact almost bewilderingly inventive. Skeptics of Berlioz's melodic gifts not disposed to accept my high evaluation of them as displayed in this opera should turn to the duet between Teresa and Ascanio (with a monotone litany in the background, ingeniously imitated in the timpani). In rhythm, Berlioz invades the twentieth century in one passage, the orchestral accompaniment to Fieramosco's shadow swordsmanship: the meters here are 7, 7, 6, 6, 5, 5, 5, 5. Novelties of instrumental usage abound, not unexpectedly in Berlioz, and at least one of them, the obbligato for ophicleide (tuba) in Pasquarello's Cavatina, would have delighted the composer of the bombardon part in *Wozzeck* as well as softened the anti-Berlioz prejudice of the creator of the Bear's music in *Petrushka.*

The differences between *Cellini* and *Carmen* are more numerous than their similarities, but both have suffered from the inane division by which the French classify their operas as either *comique* or *grande*, a distinction based not on content and genre but solely on whether the dialogue is spoken or sung. The first productions of both operas having used the spoken form, both were originally *opéras-comiques*. Later in their careers they were fitted out with recitatives and hence converted to "*grande*," only to be restored by purists, still later, to "*comique*." (The *Cellini* recording, like the *Carmen*, has spoken dialogue.) But here comparison ends, for apart from this history, and a surface similarity in exploiting local color, most other resemblances between the operas are factitious.

Some of the neglect of *Cellini* is due to problems of dramaturgical arrangement arising from discrepancies between the original (1838) and revised (1852) versions. Since the recorded performance collates these two, and since the only available orchestra score is that of the revised edition (Vol. XXIV of the Complete Works), score readers must consult the album notes for an explanation of the sequence of pieces (or a new book, *The Music of Berlioz*, by A. E. F. Dickinson). The strongest criticism of the opera is that the individual numbers *could* be shuffled about in the first place, and that musical and dramatic succession are therefore less than vital. But Berlioz's weakness as an opera composer is precisely this: he can create scenes complete in themselves yet often fails to connect and integrate them into a unified whole.

Two other deficiencies must be mentioned as well: the unreliability of Berlioz's sense of theatrical timing—*e.g.*, the tavern scene, with its interminable discussion of wines drunk and of how to pay for them–and a lack of dimension in his characters. During most of the opera we are given Cellini the lover, a mere *buffo* part, instead of Cellini the artist. Until the last scene, in fact, when his statue of Perseus is finally cast, the great sculptor hardly seems to be concerned with his art, or indeed with anything other than the abduction of his girl friend, Teresa.

Yet these weaknesses of the work in the theater should deter no one, both because the catalogue of musical highlights is so full and because American audiences are unlikely to see a staging anyway. But if that opportunity should ever arise, their wisest attitude, it seems to me, would be that of the character Pope Clement VII in the opera itself: "*A tous péchés pleine indulgence.*"

THE *RING* AS HOUSEHOLD ORNAMENT

It should at last be possible to dislike Wagner's music for its own sake, without incurring the charge of prejudice. I, for one, am repelled by some of its grandeur, the Entrance of the Gods into Valhalla being for me about as sublime as a military parade. And I am repelled by the egotism in it, an obstacle wholly absent from the music of Bach and Mozart, Beethoven and Monteverdi; nor do I think that this reaction is influenced by the music's unfortunate historical alliances. Which is not to deny a relationship between the egotism in the music and Wagner's peculiar notions of ethics. For in contrast to those other composers who thought of themselves and their music as part of a larger moral order, the moral order of Richard Wagner was his own creation and he its self-appointed lawgiver.

Not surprisingly, it is a smaller, more limited world, morally speaking, than that of the other composers. But it is an artistically valid one, because of the power of Wagner's music. Whether moral limitations are ultimately artistic ones is a question as old as philosophy. Beyond question is Wagner's musical genius: for in *Tristan* and *Parsifal,* at least, he is the compeer of these composers, perhaps the only compeer to have succeeded them. Our own century has produced but two musico-dramatic works that can be measured against his greatest achievements, *Wozzeck* and *Pelléas,* both of which are heavily dependent on his example. But I continue to feel oppressed by that egotism and by more besides.

The complete *Der Ring des Nibelungen* is now available in two performances, one by Solti on London Records (nineteen discs, stereo), the other by Furtwängler on Angel (eighteen discs, mono only). The two recordings will bring the music to the largest audience it has ever had, especially since the Solti version is now being distributed by Time-Life Records. Most of this new audience has never been inside an opera—let alone a music-drama—house; and most of it cannot understand what the singers are saying except by following translations that may render the German, but are still some distance from English: "hast followed fain," "shameless wight," etcetera.

Apart from displaying it as a status commodity, how is the Time-Life housewife, women being the dominant culture-consuming sex, to use this largest single ornament of our musical theater? She can, of course, even without seeing Wagner's music dramas, and without cassettes, scores, or anything to watch, still listen to Wagner's very dramatic music. But the *Ring*'s famous highlights are separated by miles of very low ones, such as those interminable angry-sounding dialogues in the second act of *Die Walküre.* Imagination balks at the picture of that typical housewife foregoing an installment of *As the World Turns,* gluing herself instead to *What Can Fricka Do to Save Hunding's Honor?* and sticking it out *in toto*. Yet perhaps the *Ring* has afternoon-TV potential: certainly it does not lack the melodrama, the marital problems, and the length.

Das Rheingold easily survives in concert performance in a foreign language. It is short (two and a half hours), has symphonic continuity, and its musical argument is simple to follow. Moreover, the music is pictorial. Like a cinema soundtrack, it creates atmospheres, evokes the weird and wonderful in Nature, transports in place and time, is rich in color and contrast. It also identifies the characters; and however intricate the plot, the *dramatis personae*—gods and demigods; sublunary, subterranean, and subaqueous monsters—are always recognizable musically. No character in *Das Rheingold* is likable, not only because all of them are unloving and motivated solely by cupidity—the denizens of the heights as well as those of the depths—but also because they are as two-dimensional as creatures in an animated cartoon. Nor are our sympathies engaged by the plot, which is about as intricate as Tolkien dipped into at random. Explicatory literature abounds, of course, but however edifying to learn that the Rhine gold and the Nibelungens symbolize Capital and Capital's slaves, Wotan the Church, Fricka the State, and the Valkyries a women's emancipation league, the allegory is not audible. So, too, indexes of musical motives are of little help in dealing with those miles of truculent-sounding dialogue. Wagner's discovery of the leading motive may be as important for the *Ring* as Balzac's discovery of the reappearing character was for the *Comédie humaine*, but the utility of the device is not yet apparent in *Das Rheingold*.

Despite one's lack of involvement with its protagonists, and with the peculiar contingencies of its moral argument, *Das Rheingold* compels the attention. For one thing the development of Wagner's musical powers more than matches the development of the drama, and his growth in the course of the opera is phenomenal. That the music of the later scenes is a prodigious advance on the earlier also corresponds to the dramatic content, yet the first scene scarcely predicts the fecundity of ideas in the third. It is a natural distortion of ours to search the past for adumbrations of the contemporary, but *Das Rheingold* is particularly rewarding in this sense. Many passages might have been written by Debussy, while Alberich's renunciation of love is answered by a whoop in the horns that could have found a place in one of the early Stravinsky ballets. But it is *Wozzeck,* above all, that one hears behind the great scene-changing interludes, in Alberich's repeated-note motive, and in the mighty blows of the drum as the Giant Fasolt slays his brother.

The competition between the recordings is useful, but no definitive choice should be made between them, partly because both are valuable, partly because they are incomparable in too many ways. It would be agreeable to be able to proclaim a triumph of performance over technology in the 1953 monaural, but radically face-lifted, Furtwängler recording. Yet this is only sporadically the case. The truth is that one goes from the mono to the stereo smoothly enough, but not the other way around—just as stick-shift driving is awkward after automatic. On the whole, then, one is obliged to admit that in this music, sound may be more important than performance. (It is the opposite in the recent reissues of the Busch Quartet performances of Beethoven; but four strings are less difficult to record than a Wagnerian orchestra with its many color combinations and manifold differentiations of volume and balance.) In the range of orchestral highs and lows, too, the Angel records are inevitably more limited than the London. Thus Alberich's transformation into a mammoth serpent, a striking episode in the London recording, is an insignificant one in the Angel; Wagner expresses it by tubas alone, a still fearsome effect, though Alberich was always a creep.

It must also be admitted that the orchestral playing in the Furtwängler recording is inferior. Loge's chromatic string passages, for example, are unclear (though two of them are hardly better in Solti's reading, which is rhythmically unsteady as well, while in other places conductor and singer are in open disagreement about tempo). The very first horn phrase of the opera, from the depths of the Rhine, so to speak, has a bubble on the top note, appropriate in the circumstances, yet a reminder that the performance is not a studio product (*i.e.*, tailor-made) but a live broadcast (*i.e.*, off-the-rack and unadjustable). Naturally enough, with no intersplicing and only one time around, the ensemble is less than perfect.

This said, the singers in the monaural album, souped-up but not irritatingly so, are at a lesser disadvantage—in *Das Rheingold,* that is, for in the Solti recordings of the later operas, made over a considerable period of time, the disparities are greater. Neither *Rheingold* cast is near the ideal, yet the Angel singers—Fricka excepted, though her acoustical presence is mercifully remote—are near*er*. Flagstad, the Fricka of the London recording, is also a disappointment, and the London Wotan is wobbly, out of tune, and inclined to fall behind the beat (faults not completely corrected by his replacement in *Die Walküre,* who, at the beginning of Act II, sounds as if he had vocal Parkinson's disease). The outstanding singer in the London recording is the, as a rule, insufferably sycophantic Mime. But too much of the singing in both recordings is no better than approximate in intonation, and sometimes it is even in a different key from the orchestra, as in the case of Solti's Rhine Maidens at the end, who are already at sea, pitchwise.

The ultimate choice offered by the performances, as distinguished from the recordings, is between conductors; and finally Furtwängler's is the more consistent in conception and style. As expected, his Rhine is a less turbulent body of water than Solti's; and by comparison much else in his reading will seem phlegmatic to some. His tempi definitely are slower (the whole performance is one-eighth longer) but in a balanced scale of relationships. Thus he takes the first two-four music in Alberich's first scene in what sounds like a distinct four, *versus* Solti's brisk, rather harrying two. But he never drags, as Solti does in Erda's aria and because of which he is obliged to accelerate after it.

At the beginning of the second scene, Solti observes Wagner's articulation markings for the brass—dots on the fourth eighth note—as Furtwängler does not; but this fourth eighth comes too soon and results in an awkward hesitation before the next beat (which may be why Solti ignores the dots in the first act of *Siegfried*). Then, too, after the change to a faster tempo in the first scene with the Giants, the trombone off-beats are so late that they sound like triplets instead of eighths, a skipping effect as ill-suited to the gravity of these boulder-lifting Brobdingnagians as to that of the dramatic situation. The Giants, incidentally, are by no means the simpletons they are reputed to be, knowing far too much about themselves and their condition.

I have reserved almost no space for *Die Walküre*, partly because it is so much the more popular opera but primarily because the philosophy and the musical foundations of the *Ring* are established in *Das Rheingold*. (As well as some of the musical specifics: the music of Fasolt's "*Holda, die Freie, vertragen ist's*" is the source of one of the principal motives in *Die Walküre*.) Among the reasons for this popularity, the greater expansiveness of the music may be the most important, for the outer acts contain "love" music, missing in *Das Rheingold*, of a new breadth and sweep. Nor does it seem to count that the love is incestuous, overtly and consciously in Act I (brother and sister), covertly in Act

III, where, to judge from the length of the leave-taking and the references in it to kisses, caresses, and other details ("The drinkhorn thou fillest no more for me"), matters may have gone further between Wotan and his favorite daughter than Wagner is willing to tell. But the harem of these muscular maidens is one of Wotan's, and Wagner's, most peculiar fantasies.

Die Walküre is the *Ring*'s "human" opera. Yet no character in it, human or otherwise, is appealing—which is not to say that the Valkyrie girls are not at least fun. But whether the explanation is in those aforementioned limitations of Wagner's moral world, I cannot say, being unable to feel any community with it myself. According to Shaw, Wotan teaches Siegmund "the only power a god can teach, the power of doing without happiness." But anyone who had learned that lesson exclusively, and early on, would end up a hopeless catatonic.

And Shaw is wrong. Wotan can also teach the lesson that Wagner gives to us *through* him, that of the power of living with great music, of which the greatest in the *Ring*, so far, is this final scene in *Die Walküre*.

THE *RING*—

Thoughts on the Final Operas

Complete cycles of the *Ring*, four nights running, are rare, hence few people can have experienced the work as the entity Wagner intended, or, before the present recordings, even have heard it that way. The reasons for this infrequency are both technical and artistic. They include such impediments as the scarcity of Siegfrieds and Brünnhildes and the extraordinary physical and mental stamina required in, as well as on both sides of, the orchestra pit. But the approaching centenary of the first performance of the full deck should provoke the few companies capable of performing the operas on consecutive days to make the attempt. They can be produced separately, after all, one each season, as the Met originally planned, and retained not only in repertory but in readiness. The objective should be to provide audiences with the opportunity to immerse themselves in the *Ring* in the concentrated dose Wagner conceived, and which is his and his masterpiece's due.

That each of the operas has had to make its way individually has been a disadvantage to all except *Götterdämmerung*. *Siegfried* by itself and removed from its position in the *Ring* suffers most of all. For one thing, it is lopsidedly all-male in the first two acts (ornithological imitations excepted); but this complaint diminishes in the context and huge scale of the whole and is forgotten in the majesty of *Götterdämmerung*. If the latter is the only entirely self-sufficient *Ring* opera, this is partly because the recapitulations of previous events ("This Is Your Life") are less important and less obtrusive than in its two predecessors.

Act III of *Siegfried* and all of *Götterdämmerung* were composed after *Tristan* and *Meistersinger*, a hiatus of ten years, and they differ from the earlier operas by a stylistic change of direction. *Tristan* and *Meistersinger* were unprecedented in every way, of course, and were in no way conventionally operatic. Yet in many respects Wagner evolved through them to become a more traditional opera composer. *Das Rheingold* is a mere exposition of plots, in comparison, while *Die Walküre* and Acts I and II of *Siegfried* disregard many of opera's most familiar features.

Götterdämmerung, without sacrificing any of the symphonic fluidity of the others, utilizes older operatic components, such as duets, trios, choruses—for the Gibichung tribe has been introduced partly for choral effects: it would have been quite possible for Wagner to confine himself to Gunther, Gutrune, and Hagen, the three principals. What *Götterdämmerung* does not retain from older opera in extended amounts is precisely what is believed to be the hallmark of its vocal style, recitative. For this work, at least, his claim to have superseded recitative with "continuous melody" must be granted.

Wagner's restorations of older forms are not of course the result of any concession to antiquarian opinion but of a maturing of his powers; for however one appraises his development as a dramatist, he had grown musically, in *Tristan* and *Meistersinger*, beyond any composer since Beethoven—or, in the scope and dimension of his creations, of any composer including Beethoven. A new sense of musico-dramatic timing enters the *Ring* in its final portions; thus the Shakespearean, predawn scene between Hagen and Alberich is, in its brevity alone, unimaginable in an earlier Wagner opera. But then, despite its great length, nothing in *Götterdämmerung* is too long.

Munitions-making is the principal subject of the first act of *Siegfried*, and its climax, during which Mime's cave might be a branch of Krupp's, is the hero's forging song, an orgy of "Ho-Hei," "Ho-Ho," and again "Ho-Hei," in which some of the hero's exuberance is expressed in a fioritura from exactly the kind of opera Wagner affected to despise. Siegfried's new steel is the sword Nothung, divinely ordained and destined to shatter Wotan's spear. The musical motives representing the two weapons are the most banal in the *Ring*, however, as well as the least frequently varied in instrumentation—trumpet and trombone, respectively, perhaps for correspondence in size. But an even less attractive feature of the first act, and one that because of continuing exposure becomes still uglier in the second, is Mime. The part is too large. Wicked dwarfs are always tiresome, but this one wheedles and whines by the half hour. When Siegfried finally dispatches him with Nothung, at the end of Act II, anyone not closely following the story is likely to conclude that the hero must have acted out of outraged musical sensibilities.

Nothung's first victim, the Giant Fafnir, now a dragon, is very handily the opera's most sympathetic participant, at least until Brünnhilde appears in the last scene. (Incidentally, the beast's expressively bilious "*Pruh*" would lend itself ideally to exploitation in Alka-Seltzer commercials—"You ate it, Ralph.") The great *Ring* worm is intelligent, too, correctly deducing that his assassin has acted not on his own but at the instigation of someone else. Furthermore, offered the bargain of "his life for his money," he very sensibly decides to hold on to what he has, doubtless realizing that to accept would be to lose both. Finally, unlike his zoological betters he learns from experience and dies cursing, an unprovoked and brutal death wantonly disrupting the ecological balance. In short, Fafnir may be big, but is not very fair, game. Still, dragons are boring *à la longue,* though understandably they must live long enough to justify their logistic problems. Fafnir, the unwilling star of Act II, reluctantly awakened from his beauty sleep and singing "*Lasst mich schlaffen,*" probably voices the sentiments of a good many in the audience.

Yet both acts move with appropriate speed, despite the resumé in Act I for latecomers-by-two-operas, the scarcely disguised reason for the quiz contest between Wotan and Mime. I should mention that Wotan's music at "*Was zu wissen dir frommt*" and in the rhythm of the horns in the measure before has something of Mozart's Commendatore. Even stranger resemblances occur in Siegfried's aria about the birds, which, at first and owing in part to the instrumentation for cellos, sounds like an introduction to a Tchaikovsky *pas de deux,* or an aria by Massenet. But nowhere does the music attain anything like the poignancy of Act I of *Die Walküre,* probably for the reason that Siegfried is not a poignant character. Nor is he, until the last act of *Götterdämmerung,* a very appealing one. Heroism of the militant kind he practices is passé, today's audience preferring more diffident and even ineffectual types such as Prufrock and Monsieur Teste, Malte Laurids Brigge and Bloom. Unlike them, Siegfried "knows not fear"—until he learns it from a woman, one of Wagner's heavier ironies. But he has precious little self-awareness, too, which is meant as a virtue, and hardly any of the suspicion and savoir-faire with which natural savagery and nurturing by an evil dwarf should have endowed him. The survival of his credulity into *Götterdämmerung,* where "Siegfried's Rhine Journey" is a kind of gullible's travels, is more than a little alarming.

Like *Götterdämmerung,* the last act of *Siegfried* is more "operatic," and moments in the duet "*Heil der mutter*" are not remote from Puccini. But the color of Wagnerian love-death is present in the E-minor wind chord at Brünnhilde's awakening—the most exalted musical event in the *Ring* so far—as unmistakably as it is in any chord in *Tristan und Isolde.* The tonality and the timbre are unforgettable, moreover, both when lowered to E-flat minor at the beginning of *Götterdämmerung* and in the original key at the end of that opera when Brünnhilde's name is on the dying Siegfried's lips. It is a flash forward, in other words, in refreshing contrast to the continuous succession of flashbacks. And the other wind chords that follow, with the high sixteenth notes in the harps at the end, sound newer and nobler even today than the music in *Zarathustra* which the passage must have inspired. The sound is so gorgeous, in fact, that it discourages any inclination to ponder the absurdity of the situation, for the woman whom Siegfried seduces is his aunt. Progressing from resistance to cooperation, this extraordinary lady begins by branding the event "the day of my shame" and ends by "hurling" herself into Siegfried's arms, an encounter not only strenuous but, with all that armor, also noisy.

If *Siegfried* is the scherzo of the *Ring* symphony—and to some extent its comic movement, what with the near waltzing of the hero in Act I, to say nothing of his sideshow adventures—the final movement is tragedy on a grand scale. But the plot is terrible. Virtually on arrival in the world of ordinary mortals Siegfried succumbs to a unique form of amnesia, a consequence of his guileless acceptance of drink. (And after *Tristan und Isolde*! The magic-potion music is surely more than coincidentally the most *Tristan*esque in the score, as well as some of the most beautiful.) Siegfried's thoughts then naturally turning to women, he proposes to hand over Brünnhilde (his now forgotten bride of yesterday and of this morning's eternal-fidelity duet) to his new friend, Gunther, then to marry Gunther's sister himself, and, finally, to arrange this swinging scene by impersonating his would-be brother-in-law. Hardly less inane is Brünnhilde's assumption that Siegfried could have betrayed her entirely under his own steam, her visit with her former Valkyrie sister Waltraute having just revealed that she still possesses the residual knowledge of an ex-goddess and thus should have suspected foul play. (Waltraute's picture of Wotan, incidentally, of the philandering god in retirement suffering from melancholia, aphasia, and loss of appetite—"Holda's apples tastes he no more"—wells up no tears.) Not that anyone expects or wants *verismo* from Wagner, but this sort of thing borders on the Theater of Mistaken Identity.

For the other part, the secondary characters, the earth people, Gunther and Gutrune, are fully drawn, amazingly so considering how late in the *Ring* day—twilight—Wagner has waited to introduce them; they might have remained mere accessories of the plot. Hagen, too, for all of his melodramatics, has more stature than any other Wagnerian villain, including Fafnir, with whom he is similarly typecast (by diminished fifths) as a "heavy," and who is orchestrally even more dinosaurian.

As for the recordings, the *Götterdämmerung* is Solti's and London Records's best. The vocal performances could hardly be bettered, and the sound engineering approaches perfection. The only flaw in the album is the accompanying explanatory booklet. It is written in a peculiar blend of colloquialisms: the goddess Erda is "plainly put off her stroke by the news . . ."; Siegfried has "taken a strong pull" at the drinking horn. And archaicisms: "the mazed Brünnhilde can scarcely comprehend . . ." which sounds like the "English" versions of the libretto, with their "Knows't thou what will hap?" and "I trow 'tis forgot." And unusual grammatical forms: "pretexting his years . . ."; Wotan "riddles him something to the effect that . . ."—which refers not to a gangland killing but to a simple question-and-answer game.

The passion of Wagner's music is always physical, whether or not it also reverberates in the soul. But after *Götterdämmerung*, who could not feel himself a true Wagnerite, whether or not he aspires to being a perfect one?

OUI, J'AIME BRAHMS

New books about Brahms are rare, possibly because the biography is dull and the subject is assumed to have been exhaustively researched. Hence the publication of two monographs is something of an event. And so far from being understood, the personality of Johannes Brahms is one of the least explored among the great composers. Nor is his music so familiar as we dismissively pretend, a fact indicated by the absence of recordings of most of the *Lieder*, and the absence, or poor quality, of those of the choral music. The symphonies and concertos, the favorite piano and chamber music, and the most popular songs do not represent every aspect of his work, and the final opus, the posthumous Chorale Preludes for organ, suggests potentials that alter our estimate of him as a whole.

Any attempt to redress critical appreciation is bound to be apologetic. Brahms is patronized now, belittled for adhering to anachronistic classical procedures, a target of invidious comparisons and of avant-garde derision. That he was to some extent the spokesman-composer of the unattractive epoch and society of Bismarck's bourgeoisie—he openly exulted in the fall of France in 1870—cannot be gainsaid. But he transcends his period, and neither his life nor his art exemplifies bourgeois qualities. He has been further demeaned as an epigone, a criticism that says nothing in itself and that leads nowhere. Finally, his denigrators regard the nonetheless continuing appeal of his music as a misunderstanding, which is also true, except, as I see it, the misunderstanding is *theirs*.

Burnett James's *Brahms: A Critical Study* (Praeger) does not illustrate its argument with many musical cases. Nor is it a biographical study in any ordinary way, since it provides the merest outline for the main events. Only a small part of the book, moreover, is devoted to the Viennese years, though these were his most productive ones. But then, Mr. James eschews "pedagogic analysis of compositions" and "biography of everyday fact" in favor of "existential biography," a genre undeniably chary of "hard" information. Thus we are told that Brahms made eight trips to Italy, but not where he went or what experiences he encountered, apart from a visit to Palermo to see his dying godchild, Felix Schumann. We also learn that Brahms "had a good appreciation of the old Italian music," but not which music, a question of no small interest in his case, for he was steeped in "old" music and was an expert on, among others, Bach and Haydn, Handel and Couperin. One of his letters to Elizabet von Herzogenberg reveals that he owned "over three hundred manuscript copies of Scarlatti." But surely Scarlatti was not his *only* "old Italian"!

What this book does offer is a just appraisal of Brahms's achievement and an earnest appreciation of the qualities of his music. But the vocabulary is too remote from music to be other than mystifying. Thus the Brahmsian attributes are described as "solidity," "prudence," "sturdy moral strength and artistic rectitude," as if the composer were one of the Last Puritans. And the language is occasionally confusing as well as inapt. We read about a "half-concealed paradox" that revolves "in two confluent orbits that may touch many times but seldom quite succeed in interlocking"; which is not so much a mixed metaphor as a mixed-up one. Nor does the author always say what he means: "Why those who hailed Brahms's First Symphony as 'the Tenth' could not see that the big tune of the finale was much closer in tone and spirit to *Meistersinger* than to any part of Beethoven is beyond credulity . . ." Meaning "is incredible"?

"Just appraisals" of Brahms appear to depend on *not* seeing him as the heir of Beethoven. "Brahms is nearly always at his best and most himself when he is furthest from his great predecessor." Yes and no. Certainly his gifts are of a different order from Beethoven's and, where of the same order, of a different magnitude. But these differences must be postulated in musical terms, or, in lieu of them, by means of such categorical distinctions as that Beethoven is primarily an instrumental composer, even when writing for voices,

Brahms a vocal one, even when writing for instruments. Mr. James, however, does not define his subject's individuality with any precision, either with those or any other tools. Brahms, he says, "recharge[d] the then established forms of German music by looping back to the old medieval music and the complex polyphony of the preclassical period, and welding what he learnt there into the framework of sonata form." It is true that medieval *would* be old, though Brahms did not reach *that* far back; but "complex" is superfluous, "looping" and "welding" are execrable, and a "framework of sonata form" into which anything so vague could be grafted did not exist. Finally, what of the many instances in which Brahms does overtly use Beethoven as a model—the last movement of the Quintet, Opus 88, No. 1, for example, to say nothing of the symphonies, which, no matter how unlike Beethoven's, could not have been written without them?

The Brahms–Wagner controversy is discussed with fairness, and the heredity of twentieth-century music, Schoenberg's anyway, is correctly attributed to the two together in complementary strains. But it might have been added that in Schoenberg's case the Brahms side of the family proved to be the more enduring. Nor is this derivation always obvious, partly because Wagner's music was an entirely new experience, Brahms's an extension of old experience. Incidentally, "Wagner" *in* Brahms, in the *Alto Rhapsody*, for instance, is a subject still to be investigated, and one that might prove to be larger than would be suspected.

Compared with Mr. James's "critical study," Max Harrison's *The Lieder of Brahms* (Praeger) is factually informative almost with a vengeance. Mr. Harrison begins with origins—which scholar does not?—and histories of the musical forms and verse. He examines all conceivable influences, beginning with German folk music and including Weber, a composer seldom mentioned in this connection with Brahms. That Mr. Harrison does not refer to the obvious source of Brahms's not-very-good duet *Die Nonne und der Ritter* in Schumann's great song *Auf einer Burg* (with its stunning suspended cadence!) can only be because it *is* obvious. For Mr. Harrison is awesomely learned, at home apparently not only among the complete works of all the great composers but conversant as well with the symphonies of Kozeluch and Vanhal, the operas of Marschner, the cantatas of Andreas Romberg, the songs of Zumsteeg. In fact the main difficulty with the book is in the overwhelming number of unfamiliar (to me) titles of songs, and the referring to and comparing of the unfamiliar songs themselves, for Mr. Harrison is an inveterate comparer. This part of the denouement must remain purely theoretical, except for readers with pianos and months of leisure in which to test the comparisons on them. Nevertheless, the book is an important general essay on Brahms, Mr. Harrison always relating the *Lieder* to the other music; or perhaps one should say that he relates the other music to them, the songs being the most comprehensive, chronologically speaking, of all the forms of Brahms's art.

The musical analyses are skimpy, partly for lack of space, partly because of Mr. Harrison's comparing obsession. But if the reader can weather a few such sentences as "In Opus 3, No. 3 there is a striking move through B major–B minor–B-flat minor–B major"—is this information necessary?—he will be rewarded with new insights into the composer.

My own recommendation with respect to the *Lieder,* a much less informed one than Mr. Harrison's, is that a select few should be taken to heart, if not exactly learned *by* heart, on the principle: better an intimacy with the few than a passing acquaintance with the many. I would suggest *Herbstgefühl* for a starter, a favorite of mine though evidently not of Mr. Harrison's; autumn is Brahms's season as spring is Schumann's, and the song is drenched with loneliness and nostalgia. The songs with viola, Opus 90, could come next, especially the second, *Geistliches Wiegenlied,* then the *Lieder,* Opus 94, and, above all (but not to be heard first of all), the *Vier ernste Gesänge,* the last music Brahms was to publish. These songs are among the most affecting ever composed, and they cannot fail to seduce anyone who loves music, whatever his feelings about Brahms. Yet the question of whether they are Brahms's greatest songs involves consideration of all of his music, since he is a "song composer" in much of it. Some of the Intermezzi, for example, are songs without words (especially those in A, Opus 118, No. 2; in E-flat minor, Opus 118, No. 6; and in E flat, Opus 117, No. 1), but so are the second subjects of the symphonies, not to say entire movements, and who could deny that the whole of the beautiful first movement of the Horn Trio is anything but a song?

The enigmas of Brahms are not solved by either of these books. Little is said in them about the self-suppressor, the self-critic who destroyed his musical traces and was opposed to "complete editions" (*e.g.*, those including juvenilia), probably out of fear that some substandard work might turn up in his own. Mr. Harrison finds a duality in Brahms amounting at times to a conflict and at other times to a "fusion of opposites." This dual nature is manifest in the life no less than in the work, but in more ways, or so I think, than anyone has been willing to see. Clearly Brahms's feminine temperament was more pronounced at times than his masculine, and most pronounced of all, perhaps, when as a young man he seemed to be most in love with Clara Schumann. We are told that he "had the voice of a young girl" but do not need to be told, being able to hear for ourselves, that the bearded composer of so many *Wiegenlieder* also had the tenderness of a young mother. He was predominantly masculine (though perhaps "subdominantly" would be more pertinent in his case), yet bad manners—by all accounts he could be insufferably rude as well as forbiddingly dour—are not necessarily proof of masculinity, as his biographers suggest, but quite possibly of symptoms of repression. The most revealing evidence for this was found on the manuscripts of his music, where he scribbled the names of Viennese prostitutes in the margins. Music paper, after all, was his closest confidant.

Nor do these two books, as well as others that come to mind, begin to account for some of the mysteries of Brahms's music. Why, for example, in a lifetime of sixty-four years, were all of his orchestral pieces composed in one period of only fourteen years? And though both books propose explanations for Brahms's failure to compose an opera, neither suggests the obvious one that so inward a man was simply incapable of any kind of theatrical gesture. Rhythm, too, is ignored in the stylistic analyses, whereas Brahms's addiction to that most awkward of meters, six-four, with its middle-of-the-measure hemiola, is one of the unstudied oddities of his music. Surely these and similar questions are worthy of further discussion.

BRAHMS—

A "Reproach to the Haste of a Superficial Generation"

Thus James Huneker, writing shortly after the composer's death, though the reader will no doubt have assumed that the generation referred to is his own. As an epitaph it leaves Brahms's achievement to implication, but its signal intention is to honor his uncompromising dedication to the sovereign ideals of his art—that, perhaps, more than the music itself. Huneker may also be alluding to Brahms's self-incinerated early work, however, and to his long-delayed debut, aged forty-three, as a symphonist.

The larger part of my discussion being concerned with the symphonies, I should immediately reject the two hardest-to-kill explanations for their late birth, a supposed lack of aptitude for the orchestra, and a bundle of inhibitions owing to the existence of Beethoven's nine. Neither the shadow of Beethoven nor the orchestral medium, in which Brahms's skill was always commensurate with what he required of it, is responsible for the delay. What must have given him pause, however, was the challenge of symphonic form. As a musical architect his talents are not primarily suited to large-scale structures, and his powers of development, in the formal, sonata-movement sense, are peculiarly weak. The development sections in those four redoubtable symphonic masterpieces are the least ably sustained, and compared to Beethoven he is in this regard no symphonist at all. The four are alive and well by virtue of other qualities, above all the composer's supreme melodic gifts and unfailing harmonic instinct.

Having presumed to distinguish two of Brahms's "natural" shortcomings as a symphonist, I may as well make the most of the impertinence and add a third: his sense of timing. Not that he fails to respond to the exigencies of contrast and change, for he knows exactly when to go as well as where. The defect, looking down from Mount Beethoven, at least, is that *we* know, too. Almost every event is easily foreseeable and, compared to Beethoven's, his symphonies contain few surprises and even singularly little suspense. The timing, in short, is accommodatingly loose and the smaller units are to a remarkable extent complete.

To be incapable of composing successful works of great length, as Brahms evidently was, ought to be a built-in aesthetic virtue—though "length," of course, is a metonym: the limitation is in the substance. The substance of the *Requiem*, his largest work, is flawed, first of all, in its sentiment. This lacks a creed and therefore a focus. One would suppose that Brahms was a "fatalist," yet he appears to have been seeking a religious identity, and at one point even turned to the Koran. In relation to the church, he was a recusant, and his *Requiem*, though pious, and rich in the cultural atmosphere of religion, is a concert piece. Instead of spiritual edification it offers a spurious solemnity, and instead of universality, nationality, being not merely a *Requiem*, after all, but *Ein Deutsches Requiem*. This is not to say that a "humanist," godless Mass for the dead is a contradiction in terms but simply to suggest that it should probably not borrow the mold of the other kind. Brahms celebrates the "spirit of man" far more triumphantly in his less ambiguously secular music.

His weaknesses, in my minority opinion, are more apparent in the *Requiem* than in any other work, but since this is an unpopular view, perhaps I should enumerate them. At the start of the piece the rhythmic vitality is so low, the pulsation so weak, that, given the subject, one suspects a planned effect. Surely the gruelingly dull pace is deliberate, Brahms clearly intending to close the door from the very beginning on any question of an afterlife—or at least of a life after the *Requiem*. Nor does he provide compensatory interest. The orchestra, always a potential source of it, merely doubles the chorus, when not alternating with it, clarifying its lines, no doubt—Brahms is almost always a contrapuntal composer—but at the same time congesting the textures. This doubling, not only here but throughout the *Requiem*, is curious in that Brahms's *a cappella* music is the most difficult to sing, in the matter of pitch and intonation, before that of

Schoenberg, his direct successor as a choral composer. I wonder if anyone has *ever* heard an in-tune performance of the beautiful motet *Warum ist das Licht gegeben den Mühseligen?*

The second movement of the *Requiem,* a military dirge—relieved, but too late, by an *allegro*—temporarily clarifies the object of Brahms's worship, rendering unto the Kaiser the things that ought to be God's. But the remaining movements do little to mitigate the standards of tedium established in the first two. The fifth is turgid and the beginning of the sixth is the deadest in the *Requiem,* though the competition is admittedly stiff. The middle part of the sixth is a *vivace,* but in name only, while the ending is a fugue as mortally academic as the diploma it could have won. The final movement, with harp arpeggios in the last measures, is conventional sublimity par excellence.

To go from the worst to the best, any discussion of the symphonies is warranted only in relation to performance, for they are the most overexposed works of their class in the repertory. The canned versions being too numerous for comparison, I will comment on only one, Von Karajan's with the Berlin Philharmonic (Deutsche Grammophon), which I chose, hoping for spirited tempi, clarity, and some vestiges, at least, of a Brahmsian style. All three expectations were frustrated: the tempi are sluggish, the rhythmic diction is minimal to indistinct, and the interpretive license is grossly abused, intensification and acceleration, for instance, being equated. Brahms did not protect his symphonies with metronomic markings, trusting solely and unwisely to certain traditional but now meaninglessly elastic Italian words. Not that the music should be constrained by a metronomic beat. But a flexible tempo must be based on a steady one and the range of variation fixed. Surely Von Karajan exceeds the boundaries when, for instance, he shifts to half speed for the *tête-à-tête* between clarinet and horn in the first movement of the First Symphony, thereby investing the episode with a heavy foreboding, or some other kind of unjustified significance.

He also overplays the drama, a simple tale of elation and dejection, by pushing and pulling too strenuously on the upward swing and by releasing too completely on the downward—for Brahms was no more than "normally" depressive, it seems, and even in his lowest phase probably not inconsolable. Thus the G pedal-point in the same movement, a tautening device, introducing the form of the theme to be used in the coda, is here utterly limp. Nor are these exaggerations of mood comprehended in either the form or the style of the music, which in this performance resembles not so much the first movement of a classical symphony as a symphonic poem—a manic-depressive *Heldenleben* perhaps.

The aims of Von Karajan's style of articulation are beauty of tone and smoothness of line, and he is successful in both: the orchestral sheen is irresistible and so, to some, is the sostenuto which obtains virtually from beginning to end. But the cost in rhythmic diction is high—as well as unnecessary, the room for contrast, to say nothing of the desirability, being vast. Syncopated and accented notes are hardly separated, and in consequence the syncopated feeling sometimes disappears, which is the case from measure 249 in the finale of the First Symphony, where the "offbeats" are indistinguishable from the "ons." In the Andante movement, too—played adagio—the separation between the strings' syncopated eighths and the sixteenths following them is scarcely discernible, with resulting gains in smoothness but losses in rhythmic impetus and in that "agitation" which is standard usage for this pattern.

Von Karajan's style is better suited to the long melodies of the Second Symphony, except that his decelerations into them, given the obviousness of the goal, are too broad.

And the style runs into trouble in the finale. Compared to Beethoven's, Brahms's silences are empty, mere concessions to the respiratory process. In the latter part of the *Alto Rhapsody*, for instance, the music stops after each large phrase and then, a breath later but for no other very compelling reason, goes on. One of the pauses (measures 263–64) in the finale of this Second Symphony is an exception, being highly explosive in the Beethoven sense. And for once the music does not recommence mechanically on the beat but begins on the eighth after it; or should do so, for in Von Karajan's performance the eighth is late enough to be indistinguishable from the quarter following it, a consequence of his generally imprecise rhythmic approach.

On the same subject, I should mention that in the late 1930s Arnold Schoenberg rehearsed Brahms's Third Symphony (Schoenberg's choice) with an orchestra of Hollywood film-studio musicians, and that he conducted six full beats for every measure of the first movement, just as he had heard and seen the symphony performed in Vienna in Brahms's lifetime. The tempo proved to be too slow for the Hollywood players, accustomed to a large two-beat, which, I suppose, is Von Karajan's as well, since the strings, in that pattern, tend to start late after the eighth rests and do so in his performance, resulting at one point (measures 195–97) in a *mêlée.*

The lack of rhythmic diction in Von Karajan's reading of the Fourth Symphony is especially deleterious in the quarters-against-triplets in the first movement, causing the last notes of each group to blur. But it is the second movement that exemplifies my thesis as to the looseness of Brahms's timing. An elderly lady sitting next to me during a performance of the work in London some years ago turned in my direction after the opening horn theme and said: "That was a jolly good blow"—which she would not have been sufficiently distracted to say, nor would she have had the time to say, if the symphony were by Beethoven.

Richard Wagner, our ethnic expert among composers, dismissed Brahms as a "Jewish czardas player" and meant that to be the end of him. But he is the greatest composer of the decade after Wagner's death, a time of little greatness. Brahms was not born with the endowments of a Mozart, but if ever an artist achieved by labor and self-criticism more than he otherwise might have done, that artist was Johannes Brahms. Which, I fancy, is what Huneker meant. And Eliot, when he said of Tennyson: "He has been rewarded with the despite of an age that succeeds his own in shallowness."

TOWARD THE FLAME

To judge by the programs of younger pianists and conductors, a Scriabin revival—or resurrection, in the case of this Messianist—is under way. What, then, are the reasons for the former neglect? An unfashionable aesthetic and character of emotion? A degree of harmonic complexity or other musical obstacle not encountered in the more popular products of the same period? A difficulty in distinguishing the individuality of the voice beneath the louder and more rampant ones of Wagner and Strauss? Whatever the answers, and as a result of whatever shifts and processes, Alexander Scriabin is now in the New Wave, swimming hard with the *au courant,* and not merely swimming either, being for the moment, anyway, one of the surf riders.

Faubion Bowers's skillful and even-tempered narrative of

the life[1] is an exoneration unmarred by polemics. Mr. Bowers makes an absorbing story out of a career that had never seemed half so interesting. And while he begins well before the beginning, and seems a little slow in setting the stage, surely this is necessary with a background so unfamiliar as that of *fin de siècle* Moscow, where, to mention but one mysterious detail, "a brothel cost a man 50 kopecks an hour." (It was purely a matter of time?)

The people in the story are allowed to speak for themselves in extracts from letters and reminiscences. But where the music is concerned, this method yields a great many inconsequential interim opinions; what the reader wants is more of Mr. Bowers's own mind. He is familiar with all of the works ("every note of the music is splendid"), and many of the musical insights that he offers are valuable. But his exposition, perhaps because he deals with the compositions strictly in relation to events in the life, is richer in poetic adjectives than in musical analysis. Only two pages are devoted to the music of *The Divine Poem*, while the score of *The Poem of Ecstasy* is much less closely examined than its "poem." This is in the tradition of composers' biographies, of course, yet the music alone matters, and Scriabin, prophet of multimedia expression that he may have been, survives purely as a composer. Having mentioned his prophetic side, I should note that the book performs a useful service in unraveling Scriabin's beliefs in such forms of synaesthesia as "joint musical and literary effects" and absolute correspondences between tonality and color.

Tending to see the music as belonging to a uniquely Russian area of sympathy and understanding, Mr. Bowers does not undertake to relate it explicitly to the work of Western con-

1. *Scriabin: A Biography of the Russian Composer*, 2 vols., Kodansha International Ltd., Palo Alto and Tokyo, 1969.

temporaries. But the comparison of an excerpt from a late sonata (the *molto meno vivo* in No. 9, for instance) with Debussy and Schoenberg would have helped to orient the reader. And a comparison of *The Poem of Ecstasy* with *The Firebird* would have revealed a larger debt than is generally realized of one of the least to one of the most popular of early-twentieth-century masterpieces.

Scriabin himself provides psychiatric material of some curiosity. On the evidence of this book, his most conspicuous feature might be described as autoeroticism of the ego—if by no means only of the ego, as readers will deduce on learning that he was a compulsive hand-washer and glove-wearer. One witness reported that "his morning toilet took as much time as it takes a young girl in love," and the book's frontispiece is described as the composer's "favorite photograph of himself." To some extent the hypochondria, sadomasochism, and, depending on the visits of his afflatus, manic-depression, are related aspects of a not-all-that-repressed homosexuality. This, at any rate, is Mr. Bowers's diagnosis, and the reader will concur with it as, on page after page, Scriabin is revealed to be emotionally hermaphroditic.

A turn for the psychopathological worse in Scriabin's estimation of his own powers seems to have followed the success of *The Divine Poem.* His autointoxication and sense of omniscience increases thereafter, and in proportion as his interest in the music of the past declines. In the effusions of this period the abuse of the first person pronoun is on the scale of *Zarathustra.* The composer begins to talk about a "doctrine" and "converts," moreover, and even about the possibility of "colonizing," while in one megalomaniac raving he actually launches an appeal to follow "his" laws of time and space. It would not be in character for such a man to compose strong endings, Mr. Bowers observes, after the fact, but he does not cite the most spectacular failures in this regard: the last chord of *Prometheus;* the wildly inappropriate final chords, of which the very last is usually cut, of *The Divine Poem;* and the abrupt extinguishing, only just in time to save the self-immolating moth in the composer himself, of *Toward the Flame.*

It is hardly surprising that Scriabin's opera remained unwritten, considering that he wanted not only to "get away from the coldness of classical opera" (that old freezer *Don Giovanni?*), but to keep his opera "outside of space and time." Yet the almost total absence of vocal music in so literary-minded a musician *is* strange. The verbal annotations in the instrumental music are remarkably, if inevitably, imprecise, I should add, yet the extent to which the composer relied on them is amazing. "What a pity I did not know sooner that you were conducting the symphony," he writes on one occasion. "I would have sent you its explanatory text."

While at the Conservatory Scriabin was thought to lack talent for instrumentation and his first orchestral opus was harshly criticized in this department by Rimsky-Korsakov. Yet the domain of color was the largest and most developed in his musical imagination. And although he was a piano composer primarily, the fullest expression of his genius is in the three orchestral poems. His orchestral style, furthermore, no matter how derivative, is personal, distinctive, and surprisingly not pianistic; and, finally, it attains moments of musical power of which Rimsky never even caught a glimpse. Readers with no experience of Scriabin's orchestral works should listen to the passage in *The Divine Poem* marked "*Mystérieux, romantique, légendaire*" and recognized by the eery luminosity of the woodwind octaves; to the passage marked *più vivo,* shortly before, which is as suggestive of the sensation of caressing, a favorite Scriabin annotation, as any music this side of the "Feelies"; and, finally, to the full-orchestra sostenuto at the end of *The Poem of Ecstasy,* which *my* contemporaries think ideally suited to underscore simple sentiments evoked on wide screens, but in which younger listeners profess to find psychedelic exaltation of the kind imputed to the fungus of immortality, *ling chih.*

It remains to be said that the book is handsomely bound, boxed, printed, and that it includes ten pages of discography, *versus* fewer than ten entries in *Schwann.* On the debit side, it is expensive for a volume containing no music type. Nor are sources always specified. And some of the facts are wrong; thus Stravinsky did not accompany Rimsky-Korsakov to Paris in 1907. Lastly, the text has apparently not been proofread. Transposed letters, a sign of brain damage in children, are as common as they used to be in Swedish editions of *Fanny Hill,* nor is the *sense* always resolved by the context: a "guardian angle" (p. 217), after all, could as well mean a secret ploy as a seraph.

SCRIABIN CENTENARY

Unlike that of Gustav Mahler, the musical personality of Alexander Scriabin—he was poet, preacher, prophet as well as composer—has not been automatically delineated by time. The years have made the music accessible, however, and the boom in Scriabin performances and recordings at this hundredth anniversary is rivaling the boom in Sufi saints. Time, if anything, has identified the composer with the Huysmans era and the *première-guerre,* confirming the verdict of the substantially cooler decades, artistically speaking, between the wars when his febrile music was relegated to whichever closet stores old hats. By now, more than a half century after his death, a clearly recognizable profile of the music should have emerged. That it has not may indicate that the blur and indistinctness of outline are permanent, that Scriabin's musical character is destined to remain in some degree amorphous. Yet in spite of this, the composer is still very much an active force.

The problem of disentangling Scriabin from other composers, owing in part to his confusing musical genealogy, is emphasized in the symphonic works. Criticized in his early years as an incompetent orchestrator, he later drew heavily on the scores of Debussy and Richard Strauss. Even while working on his last orchestral opus, *Prometheus,* he kept *La Mer* and *Ein Heldenleben* by his side, which helps to explain why the music seems to shift at times from the one composer to the other. Yet despite the borrowing, Scriabin had an original orchestral imagination. And now that his tone poems are entering the repertory, these remarks may be concentrated on *Prometheus,* his flawed orchestral masterpiece, of which three new recordings have appeared where none existed a little more than a year ago. The new albums of the complete piano sonatas will also be noticed, but principally for the vantage they offer of the orchestral work. *Prometheus* is the color portrait, the piano music the black and white. The dimensions of the one in color are larger, but the outlines of the black and white are more sharply drawn, and Scriabin's musical identity may have been more fully realized in the last sonatas than anywhere else.

The three versions of the "Poem of Fire" offer no choice, the Maazel-Ashkenazy[1] outclassing the other two[2] in every

1. London Records (No. 6732).

2. Philadelphia Orchestra, Victor LSC-3214; Dallas Symphony, Candide 31039.

department, especially Ashkenazy's. The AWOL Soviet pianist respects Scriabin's scale of dynamics and shapes his frilly figurations with rhythmic exactitude; whatever one thinks of the music, Ashkenazy's performance is exciting. In contrast, the piano in the Philadelphia album is rarely played *piano*, let alone *pianissimo*, and in the final passages the instrument is so loud that microphone placement must be blamed, along with sound engineers who believe that large orchestral works are recorded primarily for hi-fi addicts to test their equipment. One would have thought the predictable Ormandy faults, homogenization for one, might have been turned to advantage in this music, and that his famous *sirop de grenadine* would have been exactly the right ingredient in the Scriabin dessert. But rhythmic precision is required and not forthcoming, at times the sumptuous old orchestra sounding as if it were merely cutting bar lines. Oddly, and for better or worse, in Ormandy's hands the "Poem of Fire" suggests Ravel, in Maazel's, Richard Strauss.

The peculiarly Scriabinesque contributions to the orchestration are the flammiferous ornaments, the trills, tremolos, arpeggios, glissandos, appoggiaturas, and other musical sequins with which the score glitters like some imperial Fabergé jewel. This decor almost buries the ideas, but in some cases possibly for the better. They range in quality from bits of cocktail-hour piano music to passages of striking beauty (*e.g.*, the four measures before [30]). But the score is also a short thesaurus of film situation-music. The brooding motive at the beginning, for example, might have been composed by any of several French, German, or Russian composers of the decade before and is perfect stuff for a super-epic, while the solo violin music between [53] and [54] would serve for the scene in which Chaplin gives the rose to the blind girl.

Despite this farrago, both raw and overcooked, the piece has unity and, for most of the way, propulsion. Scriabin achieves this largely by simple repetitions of motives—though repetition is also one of his weaknesses—and by means of a basic chord, from which the intervals of those motives are derived. The chord is arbitrary both in itself and in Scriabin's use of it, but it is a viable substitute for the "key centers" that had been dissolved by the new music of the time, and it enabled Scriabin to disregard the old boundaries of consonance and dissonance. The chord is obviously limited but limitation is the beginning of art, and in this case it helps to establish the unity. Nor does it matter that Scriabin's harmonic devices are synthetic: all harmonic systems *are*. What does matter is that in this piece they are successful.

Regrettably, the piece itself is not. Scriabin rarely composed a satisfactory ending—the last two piano sonatas are notable exceptions—partly because his free-flying musical fantasy might come down anywhere or nowhere. But here he reaches out for a large idea—and reaches too far, as well as too egotistically; I see no other way of describing Scriabin's contempt for the aesthetic virtue of economy, for he suddenly caps the composition with a large chorus and organ. Not finding a musical idea within his resources, he can think only in terms of expanding means. But the result ruins what until this point was his orchestral masterpiece. Whereas the timbres of *Prometheus* have been delicate and iridescent, the color of the chorus is monochromatic and vulgar. And the chorus has the further effect of truncating rather than of concluding the piece. True, the melodic and other material had already begun to outwear its welcome, but another ending in the same amount of time might have erased or offset that impression. As it is, the chorus jolts, even on repeated hearings, a sudden reminder that the worst is still to come. The last pages are sadly below the level of the music as a whole, and the final chord can never be forgotten quickly enough.

The non-score-reading listener is unaware of two attributes, immaterial to the appreciation of the music but clues to

Scriabin's world, aesthetic and otherwise. First, verbal directions occur every few measures, "*avec un intense désir,*" for example, and "*impérieux,*" and "*avec défi.*" Difficult as it is to believe that Scriabin thought the understanding of his music depended on such graffiti, that seems nevertheless to be the case. One of these silly exclamations is "*sublime,*" which provokes the counterexclamation that *sublime* is as *sublime* does.

Second, the top line of the score is reserved for a mysterious, unheard and unseen, "keyboard of light." Notated in single pitches or two-tone chords, within the range of an octave, it is sustained throughout in ghostly harmony with the orchestra, sometimes silently doubling motives. Scriabin, who believed in absolute correspondences between musical pitches and colors, intended this "keyboard of light" to fuse the visual and auditory senses.

Believing that music was not enough, Scriabin had a great need to go beyond it, to mix it with extramusical sensations. That he could not accept his art as a sufficient end in itself may indicate that it was a form of erotic excitement for him—autoerotic, to be sure, for this hyperaesthete depended on colors, perfumes, and other sensual stimuli himself, and was always in search of a new *delectatio nervosa.* In short, he believed that the "final ecstasy" he sought was in the enhancing of the effect of music through the involvement of the other senses. This of course is the exact opposite of Goethe's "The senses are *too* numerous, bringing disorder into enjoyment. If I *see* you, I wish I were deaf, if I *hear* you, I wish I were blind." One shudders to think of what Scriabin might have demanded of his listeners with the resources of *our* drug culture. Aphrodisiac suppositories? It seems to me, in any case, that if one wants something beyond music, music is not what one wants.

Returning to the black-and-white Scriabin, both albums of

the complete sonatas can be recommended. The Ponti performance[3] is more frenetic than the Szidon[4] and Szidon applies too much pedal at times, as, for example, at the beginning of Sonata No. 10. But each performer conceives the music so differently that a fair comparison would require a lengthy analysis. It seems to me more useful instead to point out that however satisfying to the purchaser, "complete works" can rarely be digested whole and in chronological order. The Scriabin sonatas thus taken from beginning to end might prove to be the composer's own strongest antidote.

To many listeners, Scriabin's Never-Never Land is still remote and exotic country. One approach to it could be to listen repeatedly to Sonatas Nos. 9 and 10. The last pages of No. 10, in particular, contain some very impressive music, in which, for once, the inspiration is sustained as well as the exaltation. The very end sounds like *Des Pas sur la neige* but the fragmentation on the next-to-last page approaches music that is more "modern" than Scriabin's *or* Debussy's. In any case, this sonata, together with No. 9, succeeds in a way that the early ones—partly because of their observance of the classical concept of recapitulation—do not, nor is the listener's involvement ever frustrated.

3. Vox (SVBX-5461).

4. Deutsche Grammophon, 2707053.

A RACHMANINOFF CENTENARY PROGRAM

A PRELUDE (Minor Key)

One night in July 1942 Igor Stravinsky had already gone to bed when footsteps sounded on the stairs leading to his front door. He opened it to a tall, shy man who apologized in Russian for the lateness of the hour, saying he had been told that Stravinsky worked until midnight. The composer of *The Firebird* then recognized his visitor as the composer of *the Prelude* and asked him in. Rachmaninoff had come to invite Stravinsky to dinner—promising that music would not be discussed—and to present him with the gift of a jar of natural honey, representative, it would seem, of Rachmaninoff's gifts to the world. He had heard, correctly enough, that Stravinsky liked honey—in edible, of course, and not thickly mellifluous aural, forms. On July 22 Stravinsky went to the dinner and on August 8 returned the hospitality at his own home, the last time the compatriot-colleagues were to meet. The following March, while changing trains in Chicago, Stravinsky caught sight of a newspaper headline announcing Rachmaninoff's death.

Five years later Stravinsky's opinion of Rachmaninoff's music, as told to this reviewer, did not taste of honey. Yet whatever the effect on his judgment then, the reviewer's only prejudice now is in a fleeting nostalgia for that utopia of hopeless melancholy which the Second Concerto induces in adolescents of all ages.

I—SONGS

The features of Rachmaninoff's musical personality first emerge in the songs, but so do the limitations, concerning which no more need be said than that the songs of Opus 4 (1893) and of Opus 34 (1912) are hardly distinguishable by date of composition. But then, apart from the half-dozen works of his final two decades, chronology in Rachmaninoff scarcely matters. What *does,* in the songs, is the vocal gender, women's voices on the whole being preferable. Nicolai Gedda's tenor, in any case, is too flat to sustain a seventeen-song album (Angel S-36917), flat not as in pitch but as in champagne—and I mean flat, not "still" (champagne *nature*). The *Vocalise* sung by a tenor—by Gedda, anyway—is unbearable, the endless "aaaaaah . . ." a nightmare of a doctor's tongue depressor sticking in the throat.

Moreover, Gedda's falsetto, at least as resorted to in *At My Window,* sounds like a different voice rather than a mere change of organ stop in the same one. Nor is the rapport between the tenor and his accompanist, Alexis Weissenberg, all that could be desired in rhythm and dynamics. And, finally, the album's selection of songs fails to include any out-of-the-way piece, such as the composer's setting of his letter to Stanislavsky, which would have made more of Rachmaninoff's limited variety.

II—AN ORCHESTRAL INTERLUDE

Rachmaninoff's mastery of a dense chromatic idiom and its utilization in the orchestra is evident in the *Isle of the Dead*

(1907), though not in the murky recording by Svetlanov (Melodiya/Angel SR-40019). Whereas in the score the strands of the instrumental fabric are interwoven but distinct, the conductor homogenizes them as if with a Hollywood orchestrator's spray can. The piece is well constructed. Its flaws, the climaxes, are those of the period, most orchestral climaxes for a half century after Wagner being scarcely disguised imitations of *Tristan.* The *Isle of the Dead* precedes the orchestral work of Scriabin that it most resembles, the *Poem of Ecstasy;* but Scriabin's hysteria is more modern than Rachmaninoff's despair, and Scriabin, the more difficult composer, is also, in all likelihood, the greater. Yet the beginning of the final Largo in the *Isle of the Dead*—the *Dies Irae,* cushioned by tremolos—resembles nothing so much as *The Firebird.*

III—TWO CONCERTOS

The most recent recordings that I have heard of the Concertos, those by Ashkenazy, Previn, and the London Symphony (London CSA-2311), are as performances no challenge to Rachmaninoff's own, which is a small victory for superior music-making over superior technology. The weak opening movement of the First Concerto sinks the work as a whole. (Incidentally, one passage is marked "*non allegro.*" Wide license, indeed!) Still, the movement at least begins like a concerto—Grieg's, in fact—and it contains ingredients of the composer's mature style. The cadenza, its lowest ebb, is not worth the lesson it teaches: if you have absolutely nothing to say, it may be best not to call attention to the fact. Not only is the second movement better music but it also settles, in Rachmaninoff's favor, the question of whether he or Scriabin composed better Chopin. But the high point of the opus is the E-flat section in the third movement, unfortunately marred by Ashkenazy, who bangs the octave in measure five of the solo-piano episode, thereby losing the line.

A large part of the Second Concerto's effect comes from seeing it performed. It is the epitome of the popular idea of the piano concerto, and its soloist—pounding chords, splashing arpeggios, rocking and rolling betwixt seat and keyboard—must be seen to be heard. The success of the work could never have been established by recordings alone, despite the towering stack of them. That the opening chords were not meant to be "broken" is obvious; in fact one suspects the composer of writing them this way on purpose to thin out his competition among the Concerto's performers. (Lacking Rachmaninoff's huge hand-spread, Ashkenazy "breaks" the chords.) The Concerto is almost all "theme," and between thematic expositions, mere time-killing—by improvisation in the first movement and by a slow-down *doppio movimento* device in the last. I might add that the viola melody in the last movement, doubled all the way by oboe, would have benefited from a change of color at the halfway point.

IV—VARIATIONS

If the *Rhapsody on a Theme by Paganini* is the best of Rachmaninoff's later works, this may be because he was happier composing variations than wrestling with sonata form. Most important, he discovered new terrain in the *Rhapsody*—new to him at any rate—proving that he was still capable of invention and stylistic renovation, and this despite the failure of other late works. Variation XVII displays a marvelous transparency between piano and orchestra, though in this respect the entire score is limpidity itself. The musical level, in everything except volume, is less evenly sustained, however, and it falls off sharply from the tutti of Variation XVIII to the end. Variation XVIII is sweet; but that quality is not necessarily a shortcoming, and in the piano alone, before the string octaves, the confectionery is by no means indigestible. Variation XIX promises a return to the higher caliber of the earlier variations, but it does not deliver, and a flashy ending dilutes the impact of the *Rhapsody* as a whole.

It has been said that Variation IX imitates a train, and that Rachmaninoff, not always so dour as he looked, was spoofing a sound track to *The Perils of Pauline.* Certainly he did not lack experience of trains. (Once as he boarded one for yet another concert tour, an admirer asked him when he would return home and was told: "This *is* my home.") He is also known to have been fond of automobiles, and hence of the money that buys them. Surely he must have been aware that Variation XVIII would bring in that commodity.

V—SYMPHONIES

The First Symphony is rightfully unknown; it is music of no personality, suitable only for an audience with time on its hands. The Second is no less rightfully popular, at least by the token of personality: it is rich in the composer's stock-in-trade. But the time scale of the music is much the same. The Ormandy recording (Columbia D3S 813) attempts to telescope it by means of numerous cuts—approved by the composer, for all I know, but wrongly so: the music cannot be tightened and some "marking time" is essential to its dimensions.

To me the Third Symphony is the most puzzling of all Rachmaninoff's works. The all too evident effort to modernize his language is misguided in this case, and after the first movement, with its seductive opening theme, the music becomes bombastic. For all the composer's striving, the second movement attains no more of the recognizable character of Rachmaninoff's music at its best than does the second movement of the First Symphony, composed more than thirty years before. A "Foreword" to the score refers to the composer's belief in the opus and adds that "[Rachmaninoff's] faith has been borne out by the constant popularity of his works in the midst of ever-changing fads." (As distinguished from unchanging fads?) But that popularity will never extend to this stillborn and hard-to-bear symphony.

—

None of the centenary tributes that I have read has even mentioned what seems to me most important, Rachmaninoff's failure as a composer in his mature years, when he virtually stopped composing and lived on his talents as a performer. Those talents place him among the great pianists of all time. But a pianist, even a very good one, is far less precious than a creative musician who actually has something to say in his art. Rachmaninoff had that gift of saying, and perhaps his creativity need not have ended. He was a "heart" man who survived into a "heartless" era but nevertheless might have found ways of developing. I know of no more bleak and gloomy score than that of his Fourth Concerto—it is sadder than his song *By a Fresh Grave*—and one cannot listen to it without thinking of the agony it must have cost him. But he himself can hardly have been unconscious of his tragedy as a composer, and it may even help to explain that gift in the night to the younger colleague whose demon of creativity would never allow *him* to stop composing. Thus when we applaud the talent that Rachmaninoff fulfilled in his Second Concerto, we should appreciate as well the struggle of the composer of the Fourth.

VIRGIL THOMSON BY VIRGIL THOMSON

This self-portrait by the ranking critic-composer is indispensable to anyone concerned with the contemporary musical scene and how it got that way. To others it can be recommended for its skillful characterizations of the intellectual moods in Paris and New York between the wars, and its distinctions between fashions and main lines of development. As a chronicle of that period it is one of the most readable in existence, for, unlike many writers of indispensable books, Mr. Thomson is consistently perspicuous, always fluent, and nearly always engaging.

Autobiographers differ from their book simulacrums because of the exigencies of artistic selection as well as the discrepancies between their own and other people's versions of themselves. Hence their "I am" is a convention for "I portray myself as," a convention the reader generally accepts. The reader might question it at times, however, in connection with the character analysis served up in this book. The author does portray himself as—and, I am convinced, is in fact—an independent, one who has made his own way both in life and in art. He also shows himself to be intellectually *mondain* and vain about his reputation among "the knowing ones." Nowhere does he record a serious self-doubt or inner trial, whether or not he was beset by them. He stands at the opposite pole in this from, say, Maurice Sachs, who traveled in some of the same, or overlapping, circles. But neither is Mr. Thomson ever really intimate, and though he is neither expected nor required to be, the reader nevertheless feels that the author has much more about him than he is willing to give in a book.

What Mr. Thomson does give is a well-balanced view of a career in relation to its time. This widens his book's appeal and vendibility, of course, but the absence of the inner picture is not entirely explained by that. Neither is it entirely a matter of choice. Certain features of the face we are shown are too obvious to be taken at face value: the display of self-confidence, for example, and the air of having known all along that one need only bide one's time and keep the pedestal polished. And the descriptions of virtues, skills, successes, supported by steady dollops of outside opinion (Christian Bérard: "Virgil speaks the truth"). And last, but far from least, the determination to avoid false modesty: "I remained for two decades quite possibly the finest choral conductor of them all . . ."; "I wrote the best exam on orchestration ever seen . . ."; "The title essay for my next book is probably the best statement now in print of the whole experience of hearing music . . ." As I said, some of these features are exhibited a little too obviously, as if the author badly needed to believe them.

Mr. Thomson can be disarmingly frank ("I thought perhaps my presence in a post [the *Herald Tribune*] so prominent might stimulate the performance of my works"), but for calculated effects. Adverse judgments of his work are quoted for effects, too, unless I have misunderstood the feelings they aroused in him. For in truth he is fervidly touchy about the neglect of his music, as are all composers. Otherwise the body temperature of the book is cool. No argument is blurred by passion, no episode soured by angry or indignant notes. The more surprising, therefore, Mr. Thomson's periodic bouts of "frustration grippe." He is never down for long, though, this lucky-starred one who always "lands on his feet," as he remarks of himself after his safe exodus from wartime France. Do I make him sound overbearing? If so, blame the clumsiness of my language. *His* language not only saves him from the imputation but is felicity itself, even when most mannered and gay: "I practiced up a fine prelude and fugue"; "Harlem was full of lovely people. So was the WPA. The times were for sweetness and joy in work" —which reminds the reader of the Japanese commandant in *The Bridge on the River Kwai.*

In many autobiographies the reader is tempted to skip the family background. To do that here, eliminating the hero's early days in Arcadian Missouri, would be to rob Mr. Thomson's discovery of Paris of its contrasting force (and, incidentally, to remove the setting of the book's best quip, from Thomson *mère* on first hearing John Cage's prepared piano: "It's pretty but *I* never would have thought of doing it"). Paris discovered, the story centers there, then moves back and forth to and from New York, while the author, comparing the two cities, is at his epigrammatic best. Some of his pictures are enlarged for detail with excerpts from his own newsletters of the time, and all are enlivened with thumbnail portraits. That of Gertrude Stein is the most vivid, and a new view of her is exposed, and an old score settled, simply by printing her correspondence concerning the financial arrangements of their collaboration. At no time during these negotiations did Miss Stein risk the Stein style, one notes, and though the prose parses as it rarely does elsewhere, the woman behind it shows herself to be as hard as nails.

The reader encounters a number of aesthetic formulations along the way. Mr. Thomson invokes a "spontaneity which can be original if it comes from self-containment." He believes, too, that "if a text is set correctly for the sound of it, the meaning will take care of itself." As a film composer—for Mr. Thomson is a man of parts—he subscribes to the theory that "landscape should be rendered through the music of its people." But what he divulges of his own composing procedures is less satisfactory and not always plausible ("I let the piece write itself"). The statement that he selects chords "for their tensile strength" is unobjectionable, so far as it goes (which is nowhere), but the claim that his "skill was to be employed not for protecting composers who had invested in the dissonant manner . . ." explains nothing at all. *Whose* dissonant manner? (there are many) and were these investors in need of Mr. Thomson's protection? And what are we to make of the following? "Before I could lay out the score I had to decide what instruments to use." Well, yes, goodness me, you certainly *would* have to do that. Finally, while the world awaits Mr. Thomson's new opera, *Lord Byron,* readers will be disappointed to find no hint concerning the substitutes for the hymn-tune harmonies which were the charm of his first two efforts in that form.

The roundup chapters ramble a bit, tidying odds and ends, but the very last one comments pertinently and wisely on the current scene, and it concludes with an intelligent barometric forecast. Mr. Thomson argues the need for both a comparative musicology and a musical sociology, a "clarification of music's varied roles in our civilization." And he enters an eloquent plea for the "recognition of art and artists as national wealth." Who, we suggest, could more ably serve a bureau of the arts in furthering these aims than Virgil Thomson himself? And not only serve but adorn, for though he compares himself, in his freshman days at the *Trib,* to a "stormy petrel," he was then and still is a bird of some very fine plumage.

BOULEZ—

Teacher at the Philharmonic

Enfant terrible to grand old man and not yet fifty, Pierre Boulez is already modern music's Establishment figure. Moreover, having recently had his reign at the Philharmonic extended for a three-year term, and long before the expiration of the present one, he is certain to retain the title. His position as chief conductor of the BBC, head of the Centre des Etudes de la Musique Contemporaine in Paris, and his guest appearances at every point on the musical compass, as well as the Philharmonic's continuing endorsement, acknowledge him as at least the most energetic, if not influential, musician alive. Not by any means the world's most popular conductor, he is, nevertheless, as composer-conductor, the one musician who has succeeded in imposing a doctrine and a style on his age. His equipment, therefore—skills, aims, musical credo—is worthy of examination, not only to explain his preeminence but also to indicate what New York and assorted far-flung musical outposts may expect in the next decade.

Boulez may not be the only musician with a solid progressive philosophy, one that synthesizes both the highest values and the innovatory techniques of his greatest twentieth-century predecessors; but he *is* the only musician with the gifts, the mastery, and the authoritarian assurance to impose it. A man with a mission, then, the most remarkable aspect of his phenomenal career is fidelity to the convictions of his youth. In the past two decades he has mellowed, grown more tolerant—doubtless because of his experience as a conductor—of other kinds of music than those with which he is identified and for which he has been the chief propagandist. But essentially he stands where he did in 1948. This may be admirable, and certainly it provides the basis for his spectacular success. Yet such consistency has built-in limitations, which ought to be recognized by Boulez himself and by the public, neither he nor they being very certain of what *he* ultimately wants.

A missionary is a teacher. Boulez has created and is expanding the educator's role for himself, establishing it as a respectable function of public musical life. If a systematic learning process takes place between conductor and orchestra, the latter is seldom conscious of it, the involvement of the players, as a rule, amounting instead to a combination of begrudging cooperation and acceptance of mesmeric domination. It is the same in Boulez's case, except that his orchestras, knowingly or otherwise, are always "in school," pursuing goals beyond, as well as including, the immediate performance. For Boulez tirelessly trains, cultivates, inculcates, not only the musician but the listener. He is the New York Philharmonic's, and its audience's, glorified French *professeur*—very responsive, incidentally, to the American appetite for the condescension of Europeans.

Oddly, Boulez the composer is hardly an influence at all, though that elusive personage should not be written off. After setting up, nearly thirty years ago, as a creative musician primarily, he now seems unlikely to make much of a mark as such. No one can be more aware of this than Boulez himself, which explains both his inability to complete works-in-progress and his desperation to "keep up" (shown in the influence of Stockhausen in the disastrous *Poésie pour pouvoir* of 1958, no less than in the "*explosante/fixe* . . ." of

1973). Still, Boulez's decision to divide himself between the study and the podium is a loss for the former not outweighed by the success of the latter. No living composer approaches him in the invention of beguiling instrumental colors, and his *Pli Selon Pli* contains some of the finest passages in recent music. But it is unlikely now that Boulez will ever renounce his career as superconductor and accept the solitude in which masterpieces are written. And at approximately his age, after all, Gustav Mahler and Alban Berg had already composed almost all of their music. Yet Boulez the composer is the vital force behind Boulez the teacher-conductor and prophet-crusader.

What kind of conductor is Boulez? How, for instance, does he compare to Bernstein, Solti, Maazel, none of whom brings an exclusive, not to say deterministic, philosophy to the job? First, assuming that their faculties—sense of tempo, pitch, color, volume—are equally acute though qualitatively different, Boulez is the professional musician's conductor. He knows instruments better than the others, can tell the cimbalom player how to restring his box of wires to facilitate complexities, or show the violist a more effective fingering for a harmonic. Second, he is more fastidious about articulation. Third, he has the keenest ear for balance in the equilibrating of the various components of the orchestra. Finally, he draws the most refined colors from an orchestra. It follows that his performances are clean, clear, intelligent, supremely controlled.

In the totality of what one seeks and expects when listening to a Beethoven symphony, however, these undeniable virtues become more than a little negative. A modicum of sloppiness, some discreet opacity, a moment and more of "abandon," even an occasional surrender of intellect to feeling are tolerable in any rendition that is deeply moving. The Boulez X-ray performance is ideally suited to contemporary music and is best of all in music of approximately the same age as its performer. Here the spirit can be left to itself. Fidelity to the letter is the prime requisite, and no one understands the orthography of new music, or is better able to decode it, than Boulez. His comprehension is in advance of that of most of its composers, in fact, for which reason he is not above "improving" their scores—by playing them faster, for example—much as Stokowski doctored the new music of another era with hormone injections to the orchestrations. Not all composers appreciate this kind of help, and in the case of a contemporary classic such as the Schoenberg *Serenade*, where Boulez disregards the rhythmic relationship between Variations I and II, he should be challenged as firmly as purists once challenged his hoary colleague for the liberties he took with Bach.

But Boulez's command over contemporary music far outstrips his ability to throw light—infrared, in his case, of course—on the music of the eighteenth and early nineteenth centuries, or even to give better than average performances of it. Would it not be preferable, then, for him to confine himself to the late nineteenth and twentieth? Could not a special position be created for him, one designed to utilize his talents at their optimum, an international orchestra, for instance, its every member selected by Boulez himself, not only for virtuosity and musicianship but also for predisposition to his aims?

The New York Philharmonic is hardly such an institution, nor should it be turned into a forum for untried new music. Thus Boulez is not its best choice of conductor. He would debate these points by claiming that our symphony orchestras have been stultifying as museums for familiar antiquities. But the argument is false, for the great music of the past can have as much life as that of the music of today if given it in performance. In addition, contemporary masterpieces are too few in number to constitute more than a handful of programs. Strauss, Debussy, Mahler, Ravel, early Stravinsky are now as much a part of the standard repertory as Tchaikovsky and Brahms. What remains, by Boulez's own criteria, are Schoenberg, Berg, Webern, whose combined orchestral works fill no more than three or four programs; Bartók (for whose weakest pieces Boulez has a curious partiality); Varèse (whose *oeuvre* is quantitatively tiny); probably one or two works by Messiaen; and possibly Carter's Concerto for Orchestra. But a major orchestra cannot sustain very many seasons on so slender a menu, much as these composers deserve repetition—the only method of entering the repertory—and much as some new and little-known ones merit more exposure than they have so far enjoyed.

This year, however, Boulez has suspended his regimen of contemporary music. His programs are indistinguishable from those of any number of other conductors, including Kostelanetz (the *Prelude and Liebestod*, excerpts from *Meistersinger*, the *Rosamunde* Overture and Ballet Music, *Till Eulenspiegel*, the *Valses Nobles et Sentimentales*). He offers music by Schütz, Telemann, Bach, Haydn, Mozart, Beethoven, Berlioz, Brahms, Mahler, Scriabin, but the only moderns on his programs are Stravinsky, Bartók, Schoenberg, Webern, an early piece by Stockhausen, a premiere by Berio, and two American works–a skimpy showing for a champion of the new who promised to revolutionize Ye Olde Philharmonic. No philosophy of any kind, no structure, no design is manifest in these programs, and in truth not even any character. Lorin Maazel would conduct them as well, and, in the "pop" pieces, rather better. It would therefore be absurd to pretend that the Philharmonic has entered a New Era. What *has* happened is that the other conductors have caught up with Boulez on the contemporary staples while he is trying to catch up with them on the war-horses. Meanwhile, the times have caught up with everybody: compared to the rich choice of music available to the Philharmonic subscriber on records, these programs are inexcusably dull.

Which raises larger questions concerning the future of philharmonic orchestras in general, the scope of symphonic repertory, and the suitability of the community orchestra as a laboratory (to say nothing of the willingness of its patrons to lend their ears as guinea pigs)—all subjects for still more foolish foundation-sponsored research grants. Meanwhile, what is the best course for the New York Philharmonic, and if Boulez is not its ideal navigator, who would be? Unquestionably the orchestra of a great musical capital must excel in every aspect of its art. The obvious choice, then, is the former captain, Leonard Bernstein. No less progressive than the Boulez of the present season, Bernstein can also "send up" masterpieces as different as *Messiah*, Verdi's *Requiem*, Stravinsky's *Oedipus Rex*, all very remote from Boulez's temperament and tastes. As for Haydn, Mozart, and Beethoven, if no conductor can ever completely satisfy in music of such cosmic proportions, Boulez can rarely even please. His specialties, that exquisite transparency, for one, are irrelevant in this music. Moreover, the phrasing of it seems to elude him, a difficulty not posed by Wagner and his successors, whose instrumentation obviates the problem. Still another impediment to Boulez's ambition to be an all-around conductor is his lesser competence in the domain of vocal music. His performance of *Parsifal*, for example, a revelation orchestrally, is marred by mistakes in vocal casting. Uncannily exacting as he is with instruments, he has not yet developed an expertise with choral ensembles.

What Boulez *can* do, and better than anyone else, is teach. More illuminating than most of his concerts in New

York this season was his public dissection of two student compositions at Juilliard. Turning the stage into a musical Theatricum Anatomicum, he gave precisely the criticisms young composers too rarely receive in the classroom. New Music's most learned and experienced practitioner proceeded directly to the point in exposing faults of construction and other weaknesses. The critic was biased, of course. Boulez likes complex textures and musical rebuses, and not finding them in new works, he tends to recommend an increase in the density. But thank Boulez for intelligent bias!

In sum, the exposure of young musicians to Boulez as teacher, critic, composer, performer is an invaluable experience. For most of those sufficiently old and affluent to own Philharmonic subscriptions, however, he has little to offer, while they, in turn, are wasting his time and his genius.

BOULEZ IN THE LEMON AND LIMELIGHT

Even had it been favorable, few could survive the publicity to which Pierre Boulez has recently been subjected. Moreover, the most critical pieces, "The Iceberg Conducteth" by Stephen Rubin (*The New York Times Magazine,* March 25) and the Profile by Peter Heyworth in *The New Yorker,* March 24 and 31, seem to have been timed for Boulez's birthday. Saved for it, in the case of the Profile. This study, since it reflects nothing of the present mood in New York, was no doubt commissioned long ago, and is therefore at a disadvantage when compared with the work of Mr. Rubin, who reports from the very locker rooms of the Philharmonic and draws his conclusion—that "the general discontent [is] not with Boulez the music director but with Boulez the conductor"—directly from the orchestra members. The main source of the Profile, on the other hand, is Mr. Boulez, who, I think, does more harm to himself with his own words than all the critics do to him with theirs.

The following contribution will be limited to a discussion of Mr. Heyworth's Profile, my purpose being simply to amplify his account of part of the background. The eminent English critic repeatedly refers to Igor Stravinsky, at one point stating that "of all the composers who have emerged since the war, Boulez, both as a man and as a musician, was for years the closest to Stravinsky." This may be true.[1] But the phrasing suggests a deeper and longer relationship than actually existed, its active years reducing to two. Besides, Mr. Heyworth presents only one side of the story, and that in a drastically abridged version. "Stravinsky and Boulez had first met at a party in Virgil Thomson's apartment in New York in 1952," Mr. Heyworth says, so far correctly. But he continues with a mistaken assumption: "It is inconceivable that [Stravinsky] should have been unaware of Boulez's assaults on his neoclassic music."

What *is* inconceivable is that Stravinsky would have attended the party if he *had* been aware of these assaults. Although acutely conscious of the French reaction against his music at the end of the Second World War, he had read none of its polemics, except for one critique by René Leibowitz. Hence Stravinsky's shock in March 1966 when a friend in Paris sent a copy of *Relevés d'apprenti*, a collection of Boulez's early articles, and Stravinsky discovered what

1. Elliott Carter was far closer for a far longer time, but it is arguable whether he emerged since the war.

Boulez had written about him.[2] Nor did it matter that these writings antedated the friendship. Stravinsky never forgave an attack on his music from any quarter, and if he had seen Boulez's early writings at the time they were published, no association between the two composers would ever have existed. *Relevés d'apprenti* was the underlying provocation for all of Stravinsky's later criticisms of Boulez, as well as Stravinsky's final "public withdrawal" of his "earlier 'extravagant advocacy.' "

Stravinsky's first encounter with Boulez's music took place in Baden-Baden, in October 1951, when he heard a tape of *Polyphonie X* made at its premiere in Donaueschingen shortly before. The "nose-thumbing force" of the work is what impressed the composer of *The Rite of Spring*, who may have been reminded of his own 1913 premiere, for *Polyphonie X* was at times all but drowned out by laughter, shouts, hoots, and whistling. The following year, on May 7, in Paris, at a concert in which Boulez and Messiaen played a part of the former's *Structures*, Stravinsky was again intrigued, if only, as he said, by "the arrogance of the music."[3] Then five months after that, in Hollywood, Stravinsky assisted at several rehearsals of *Polyphonie X* and even made an analysis of the score. But between December 1952, the date of Mr. Thomson's party, and November 1956, when

2. Next to Boulez's name on the title page of the book, Stravinsky has written: "*Les rares mots de sa dialectique m'épatent de moins en moins. Pourvu qu'il n'arrive pas la même chose avec sa musique.* Istr." A clipping from *Le Monde*, March 29, calling the book "*les écrits du plus grand musicien et penseur de la musique d'aujourd'hui,*" is attached to the cover of Stravinsky's copy, the words "*plus grand*" and "*penseur*" having been underscored by him in red.

3. On May 23, 1952, Stravinsky attended a concert of Musique Concrète in the Salle de l'Ancien Conservatoire, at which he heard Boulez's *Etude à un son.* At the same concert another piece by Boulez, *Etude II,* was performed, but Stravinsky had departed at the first intermission.

Boulez called on Stravinsky in a Munich hospital, the two composers were not in touch. A few weeks after the Munich visit, Stravinsky, passing through Paris, supervised recordings of two of his works for Boulez's "Domaine Musical."

The close relationship began that day and flourished three months later when Boulez came to Los Angeles to conduct his *Le Marteau sans maître* at a Monday Evening Concert. Staying in the Tropicana motel, a few blocks from the Stravinskys, Boulez was with them constantly, and had soon captivated the older composer with new musical ideas and a rare intelligence, quickness, and sense of humor. Boulez was fully cognizant of his conquest, of course, and when he delayed beginning the *Marteau* at the concert some twenty minutes until Stravinsky's mislaid score of the work had been found, it was apparent to some that the only audience which mattered was Stravinsky. (The vividness of these and other details in the mind of your reviewer is explained by the coincidence that he shared the podium with Mr. Boulez that evening, which, incidentally, was also the occasion of Boulez's American debut as a concert conductor.)

The scene then switches back to Paris, seven months later, where "[Boulez] achieved his greatest coup when he persuaded Stravinsky himself to conduct the first European performance of his most recent work, *Agon,* at the Domaine Musical . . ." Mr. Heyworth adds: "Today Boulez likes to quote a remark attributed to Lenin that 'not every compromise is a concession,' and it was during this period when he [Boulez] served as impresario of the Domaine Musical that his once intransigent character began to accept the need for compromise." So the coup was actually a compromise! (At the time many of Stravinsky's friends felt that *he* was the compromised party, and they blamed his participation on the influence of your reviewer.) What Mr. Heyworth neglects to say, however, is that the orchestra which played *Agon* was that of the Southwest German Radio, that it had been meticulously rehearsed by Hans Rosbaud, and that, in effect, the concert was simply a German import.

The event was such a success that Boulez invited Stravinsky to Paris again the following year to conduct *Threni,* but this time with an important difference: the participants were to be recruited locally. This would have been a shaky arrangement even if Boulez had fulfilled his obligations to rehearse the piece. That he did not find time to do so can be attributed to a work that he was late in finishing for the Donaueschingen Festival. In consequence, *Threni* was so badly sung and played that it was received with jeers by the audience. And when at the end of the performance Boulez tried to maneuver Stravinsky into taking a bow, the humiliated composer curtly refused, swearing that he would never conduct in Paris again, a promise that he kept.[4]

Still another blow—a coup of a different kind!—awaited Stravinsky that same night when he learned that *Rencontres avec Pierre Boulez* (a new book by Stravinsky's archenemy Antoine Goléa) had been sold in the foyer during the concert. But luckily, Mrs. Stravinsky spirited these *Rencontres* away before her husband could see even the first page of the text, a description of one of Boulez's "assaults" on Stravinsky's neoclassic music. On all counts, then, the Paris *Threni* was a disaster, and it was the true cause of the rift between Stravinsky and Boulez. Strangely enough, Mr. Heyworth does not even mention the episode, noting only that "in the middle sixties, relations grew less cordial and after 1967 there was no further contact between the two men." But from the time of the *Threni* fiasco, "contact" was slight indeed.

By the early sixties, too, Boulez's recordings of *Renard, Les Noces,* and *The Rite of Spring* had so infuriated Stravinsky, because of their "arbitrary tempi," that he refused to attend a program of these three works conducted by Boulez

4. Stravinsky wrote in his diary: "My concert (*Threni*) at Pleyel (unhappiest concert in my life!)."

at the Paris Opéra, June 5, 1965. The following day the two musicians did dine together, with friends, but it was their next-to-last meeting,[5] and Stravinsky reported afterward that he was appalled by Boulez's talk, which had been exclusively about conducting and not at all about composing. True, Stravinsky had been expressing disappointment in Boulez as a composer as far back as the Third Piano Sonata, which Stravinsky heard Boulez perform in Baden-Baden, and the Mallarmé *Improvisations* (1958). But the story of this disillusionment must await the translation and publication of Stravinsky's correspondence with a Russian friend.

Mr. Heyworth quotes Boulez, in a debate with Rolf Liebermann, belittling all twentieth-century operas except Berg's. Yet the esteemed critic does not seem to see that Stravinsky took this as an affront to *his* operas or that Boulez's remarks naturally added some ice to the cold war. Mr. Heyworth further ignores Boulez's abuse in 1967 of Stravinsky's "Webern-influenced" music—the same kind of music, in that sense, that Boulez had invited Stravinsky to Paris to conduct not long before. Even more surprising is Mr. Heyworth's questioning of Stravinsky's criticisms of Boulez's first recording of *The Rite of Spring*. (I might add that his second recording provoked still more vehement objections from its composer, as the many people who listened to it with him can testify.) Mr. Heyworth would be the first to agree with those criticisms in anyone else's performance.

As for his general assessment of Boulez, surely Mr. Heyworth has overly handicapped himself in attempting to view the whole of post-World War II music through the eyes of a single exponent. Thus Mr. Heyworth says, "In a truly Napoleonic act of leadership and daring [Boulez]

5. The last one was in Stravinsky's home in Hollywood in May 1967. On October 5 of that year, Boulez wrote to Stravinsky asking him to protest the imprisonment of the Korean composer Ysang Yun, a request with which Stravinsky complied.

was to bring his generation to and through serialism, the most devastating musical purge to which music has ever been subjected." But at the time to which Mr. Heyworth is referring, few "serial composers" would have acknowledged Boulez as their "leader." Nor was he. Moreover, the remainder of the statement is an imponderable. How, for instance, can Boulez's "musical purge" be compared with the "musical purge" of the Council of Trent? Mr. Heyworth asserts, too, that "Boulez was the first to perceive [the] implications [of Webern's achievement] for the future." Yet René Leibowitz had awakened musicians to the potentialities of Webern long before Boulez discovered him—which I mention because Leibowitz has never received due credit for this.

Mr. Heyworth tries to explain Webern analogically. His "substitution of intervals for themes was a step as momentous as any in musical history, directly comparable to the beginnings of abstract art, for what are themes if not the equivalents of objects and human figures?" But beginnings of abstract art are the beginnings of art, period. And, one wonders, when are successions of intervals *not* themes, and by what means are the two distinguished in, for example, the *Grosse Fuge*? Furthermore, why is a tone row *not* an "object" while a theme *is* one? And how, in this footnote to the *Dehumanization of Art,* can themes be equated with human figures?

A conviction of Boulez's youth, to which he is still faithful, is that Webern is one of the cornerstones of contemporary music. Messiaen may be another. "Through his study of Hindu rhythms and the pre-1914 music of Stravinsky [Messiaen] had come to see that rhythm . . . which had traditionally played a supporting role in Western music, might be subjected to rational discipline . . . and so could become a primary, even an autonomous element in composition . . ." Thus Mr. Heyworth. But let me say that whatever the advantages of "autonomy" and "rational discipline," the rhythmic element is as "primary" in Beethoven as it ever is in Messiaen.

It is to Mr. Heyworth's considerable credit that he manages to follow the bewildering trail of Boulez's discardings and retrievals, the progressive renouncings (and denouncings) of almost every development that he has ever embraced, and the equally progressive reembracings of almost every development that he has ever renounced (and denounced). In this cycle, electronic music has been thrown out and taken in again, opera banished but welcomed back piecemeal (the pieces being those that Boulez has been invited to conduct), composer after composer, from Berlioz to Berg, jettisoned but later hauled aboard. The one admissible position seems to be that which Boulez happens to hold at the moment; which may be understandable since he says that he has been thinking about "how I might construct a musical language from scratch." From *scratch?* But can he really believe that it is either possible or desirable to "scratch" the language developed by Bach, Mozart, Beethoven, Wagner in favor of a new one, even if invented by a Boulez?

SOLTI, CHICAGO, SCHOENBERG

It is not unusual in America to hear great music played by good orchestras led by more or less competent conductors. But to hear a masterpiece performed by a great orchestra under the guidance of a superb musician *and* in a perfect hall is rare indeed. One is especially appreciative of the last of these conditions after a season in New York's Philharmonic Hall, where at least some of the problems of the resident orchestra can be blamed on the uncongenial house it is obliged to call home, and where the perennial acoustical improvements seem to do little more than change the distortions and increase the impression of amplification. Entering Chicago's agreeably old-fashioned and unimproved Orchestra Hall recently, before a rehearsal of *Erwartung*, I heard some of the Chicago Symphony's string-bass players practicing one of that work's most difficult passages. Astonished by the true timbre, full tone, and clear pitch of the instruments, I could only deplore the contrast with the hormone-injected sound of the basses—and other instruments—in New York's cultural amusement park.

Erwartung, as rehearsed in Chicago, may be approaching realization of Schoenberg's vision of the work for the first time since it was composed (1909). Technically the players could have mastered the music long ago, of course. What the orchestra needed was Georg Solti, who has inspired it with a new keenness of ensemble as well as with a new dedication to the music—that of Arnold Schoenberg being not merely tolerated but obviously enjoyed.

The conductor himself, whom I consider to be without peer, has not yet assimilated every detail in Schoenberg's great monodrama, nor even all of the larger features. He strode over the great climax at measure 329, for instance, without the slightest reining in for the *molto ritenuto*. (Oddly, though, while overlooking some of the written tempo-controls, Solti added a few of his own, including a *ritenuto* in measure 317 that destroyed the idea of the continuing triplets.) Clearly he was learning the music as he rehearsed it, both in the sense of what should be done with it and of the way to do it; this, however, is not to label his performance a failure, perfection in this music being unattainable, success relative. The principal weakness was that rates of speed and time values in *Erwartung* change more quickly and frequently than Solti allowed. But he is our greatest Wagnerian, and Schoenberg's super-Wagnerian masterpiece lies very close to the conductor's temperament, which, if not identical to Schoenberg's, is nevertheless in the same magnetic field. At long last that almost unbearable nervous intensity of Schoenberg's music may have found an emotionally consanguineous interpreter.

"Richard Wagner wanted a different kind of movement. He overthrew the physiological presupposition of previous music. Swimming, floating—no longer walking and dancing. Wagner seeks deliberately to break all evenness of time." *Also sprach* Nietzsche, who went on to predict that the Wagnerian tendency would lead to a "complete degeneration of rhythmic feeling." This accurately describes the mayhem of *Erwartung*, at least as Nietschze would have heard it, for Schoenberg extends the Wagnerian conception in this—but not only this—regard, perhaps as far as it can be made to go.

Solti inevitably revealed himself as well as the music he rehearsed. Let me say at once that the orchestra worked "for" and not "under" him—"under," to me, suggesting an army of players beneath a field marshal's baton. They freely asked his help, even to the extent of requesting a change of beat pattern when he conducted a succession of complex six-four measures in large twos. No doubt the twos were correct, but, without subdivision, music so profusely detailed can be cumbersome. Solti acknowledged the difficulty and graciously complied, switching to a full six-beat, though sacrificing his tempo, line, and phrasing to do so. The new pattern clarified the rhythmic design, however, and enabled each section of the orchestra to hear the other. (I cannot understand why he *did* subdivide, unasked, the horn solo at measures 169–70, which does not need small units.)

Solti was as efficient and effective in rehearsal as any conductor I have ever observed. Going directly to the essential, he knew what must be explained as opposed to what the players would correct by themselves on a second or third reading. His elucidations involved an amount of singing—if that is the word for the eerie falsetto with which, whenever possible, he gave the actual pitch rather than the note at the octave or double-octave below. Above all, he never rehearsed out of context and was careful to reassemble any troublesome measure that he took apart. After laboring for five minutes to obtain the exact degree of *pianissimo* in measure 153, and another three minutes to shape the *ponticello* arpeggios in measure 274, he played through, not once but four or five times, the passages in which these effects occur, then placed them in still broader contexts of forty or fifty measures. It seemed to me that at the end of the rehearsal everyone in the orchestra had a sense of the piece as a whole.

Special mention should be made of Solti's sensitivity to Schoenberg's colors, those sudden jagged brass chords, twirling woodwind figures, scarcely audible flurries of string notes, and, above all, the final chromatic orchestral shiver without which Wozzeck might have drowned accompanied by a different kind of music. But the conductor was also remarkably attentive to articulation—although the trombones should slur, not tongue, in measure 344. And to balance—although the *leitmotiv* in the strings, three measures from the end, was obliterated by the trumpets and upper woodwinds. And to intonation—although he failed to correct some inaccurate pitches by the soprano soloist, Anja Silja.

But perhaps I should have begun with Miss Silja, for the orchestra merely sets the stage, the center of which, both literally—in the opera house, where *Erwartung* belongs—and musically, is dominated by the singer. *Erwartung's* protagonist must be an artist of uncommon talents, musical and thespian, it being a *tour de force* to perform the part at all. Miss Silja seems to possess the qualifications (I say this only on the strength of her reputation in the role of Lulu, for I have not yet seen her as an actress). I suspect, nevertheless, that she would play the part of Schoenberg's heroine, which demands bodily movement, no less compellingly than she sings it. Her voice, in any case, is ideally suited to the role, in quality and color, range and power, and she has mastered the music's highly inflected style. None of these resources was employed to anything like full capacity in the run-through that I heard, but that counts for little, an orchestral rehearsal never being a test of a singer.

What a pity that the Metropolitan Opera does not offer us this *Erwartung*, with Silja on the stage and Solti, the pendulum, in the pit! A work for the theater, and one of the greatest in our century, it loses a great deal in concert performance. (For one thing, the dramatic timing depends on the division into scenes, and these, of course, are imperceptible in concert performances.) What an opportunity, too, for our leading opera company actually to lead. Even better, 1974 is Schoenberg's centenary. How fitting in every sense for New York to celebrate the event with what would be, in effect, his local operatic debut!

Schoenberg does not lack interpreters, at the moment, and he may be even better off in this regard than Mozart, who is the more difficult composer in that his music requires historical stylistic interpretation. Turning from *Erwartung* to the *Jupiter* Symphony, Solti reduced the number of strings to about half, but he remained particularly alert to disequilibriums between wind and string volumes. Most of his rehearsal time was devoted to articulation. Let me try to illustrate the importance of this with a single example. The second movement begins with a melody in the violins that can be made to sound very different, in stress and accentuation, according to the bowing. The music starts on the first beat of the measure, with a dotted two-note figure. This leads to a third note, longer and stronger, on the second beat, which in turn leads through two rapid passing notes to the first beat of the next measure and the end of the phrase. If played on a single up-bow, those first two notes of the first measure will give the feeling of an upbeat. The third note can then be played by a down-bow, giving it natural emphasis and a downbeat feeling. Pedantry? Perhaps, yet this art of bowing determines not only the scansion and respiration of the music but also its texture, as the texture of a rug is composed of warp and weft threads.

Solti shaped every phrase of the movement in this manner, then addressed himself to questions of note lengths, for these can be neither precisely indicated by notation nor automatically "felt." Finally, he adjusted the vibrato—from none to too much to just right—and played the movement through. Afterward, searching for reasons why this performance was the most satisfying I had ever heard, I attributed some of the credit to the perfect tempo (to my senses), and some to the transformation of every note of "rhythmic figuration" and "accompaniment" into melody. That the "structure" was clear, the rhythmic movement never mechanical, the sentiment free of exaggeration goes without saying. Solti's secret was in that melodic pervasiveness. I have since learned that the performance was recorded, and if the results can compare with those that I heard in Orchestra Hall, this should be the finest *Jupiter* in package form.

Congratulations to Chicago, by no means the Second City, philharmonically speaking.

MOSES AND AARON AT THE PARIS OPÉRA

Moses and Aaron, Schoenberg's largest twelve-tone work, was composed between May 1930 and March 1932. Although the opera as planned is incomplete, the ending as it stands is in no way truncated, the unwritten third act, to judge from the libretto, containing little promise of further dramatic development. Yet Schoenberg's failure to compose music for all of his text has been attributed not to unresolvable difficulties in the subject but to the threat of Hitler, a credible hypothesis but a difficult one to prove since the composer could very well have stopped where he did because of a philosophical and artistic impasse. After all, the dilemma of the Moses of the opera—has "the Kingdom of God become words or syllables?" (in the language of the King James Version)—became the philosophical and typological problem of Schoenberg's and of our age.

The opera has also been accepted as an expression of its composer's religious beliefs, an interpretation that Schoenberg's correspondence of the time tends to confirm. After the Hitler years, however, these beliefs changed, to the extent that if the composition had been begun in 1945, Schoenberg, whose sympathies by then were Zionist, might have found more to embrace in Aaron's activist philosophy than in Moses' idealist one.

The first complete performance—in March 1954, nearly three years after the composer's death—was not staged. Partly because of this a mistaken belief emerged that the opera was not theatrical and could as well be presented in concert form. The initial staging, in Zurich in 1957, was followed by others in Berlin, London, Boston (Sarah Caldwell), Düsseldorf, Vienna, and now Paris, which last, more than all the others, should establish the work in the international repertory.

French is obviously the wrong language. When Covent Garden gave the opera in English George Steiner objected that "[Schoenberg's German] words are not less 'fully composed, musicalized' than the music," and French, of course, as sound and prosody, is that much more remote again from the original. Yet despite all handicaps the French translation not only preserved a high proportion of Schoenberg's rhythmic values but was in some instances superior to the English. Moses' "*Ich kann denken/aber nicht reden*," for example, is hardly the same as "thought is easy/speech is laborious," which also happens to be the opposite of the truth. "*Capable de penser/incapable de parler*" does convey the sense, at least, though it seems to suggest that Moses suffers from a speech defect. The meaning is vital, moreover, being no less than the dramatic theme of the opera reduced to the simplest form.

Much is to be said in extenuation of the Opéra's decision to produce the work in French. Dr. Steiner's argument against the necessity of translation was that "the story of Exodus is known to everyone and . . . a brief outline would have given an English-speaking audience all the help it wants." But Dr. Steiner was speaking for himself. Most of us require more help than that and of a less elevated kind than he provides: "The twelve-tone system is related in point of sensibility and psychological context to the imaginative radicalism . . . of Cantor's mathematics or Wittgenstein's epistemology." (How, one might ask?)

An audience accustomed not to understand the foreign language of an opera—having accepted the claims of "cultural unity" and the integrity of verbal and musical rhythms and sounds—is more likely to tolerate that language when sung than when spoken. In *Moses and Aaron,* however, speaking voices are crucial. And though Exodus is indeed well known, and though a synopsis of Schoenberg's libretto should take no more than a minute or two to read, the opera lasts an hour and a half, during which the audience's perception at every level depends on understanding not only the story but the words. (For this reason Schoenberg, in his later American years, began to favor translations—even of *Pierrot lunaire,* in which the words contribute as much to the color of the music as do the instrumental timbres.) I daresay that if *Moses and Aaron* had been performed in German at the Opéra, an exodus of quite general proportions would have occurred within a quarter of an hour.

Nor is the verbal argument easily inferable from the action, some of the main events of which take place offstage, and, as in the case of the Flight from Egypt, between the acts. The essential drama is internal, its action a philosophical debate the staging of which should embody and give dramatic representation to the principal ideas. This is not to say that the opera lacks theatrical spectacle; on the contrary, its longest scene, that of the Golden Calf, is on the scale of, and even looks something like, the Triumphal March from *Aida* combined with the Bacchanale from *Tannhäuser*. Furthermore, the work uses traditional operatic structures and models: its principals, for example, both individually and as a pair, are indebted for some of their features to Wotan and Loge, while the Sacrificial Virgins are descendants, musically speaking, of Wagner's Flower Maidens. The dramaturgical form, too, respects customary divisions of scenes and their subdivisions—solos, ensembles, choruses, interludes. Finally, the shape of the whole is symmetrical, Moses' inner journey returning him to his starting point, a perfect ending even though not the one Schoenberg intended.

Schoenberg also exploits many kinds of conventions, ranging from simple matters of style, such as the use of *ostinati* in the dances, to musical imagery on the order of the Bach cantatas. Thus, Moses ponders the nature of the "Omnipresent but Invisible One" on a single repeated note, while Aaron articulates his abiding thought—"He has chosen us folk before all other people"—on the twelve pitches of the series. (One per tribe, no doubt.) The symbolism has another stratum, too, in that the brothers voice their minds simultaneously, as they do while exposing their articles of belief in the opera's first scene, thus implying that the two prophets are projections of different sides of the same divided self, as well as separate persons.

Revelation in the Old Testament is aural—the *Word* of God, not His Image. (In the New Testament it is visual—Logos, the Word Incarnate—which must be one of the most profound distinctions between Judaism and Christianity.) Idolatry is visual, and Schoenberg's Moses, unlike the scriptural one, rejects as idolatrous every visual manifestation of God, including the Pillar of Fire, that "God-sent signal," as Aaron calls it. The Burning Bush itself, the theophany that marks the entrance into history of the Israelites as a nation and entrusts its destiny to Moses, only succeeds in filling the Moses of the opera with negative vibes. Aaron, of course, relies on the visual. Thus when Moses returns from Sinai—which the Talmud defines as "the mountain from which hostility [*sinah*] to idolatry descended"[1]—destroys the Golden Calf, and cries out to his errant brother asking what he has done, Aaron vainly replies: "I worked marvels for eyes and ears to witness."

The God of Schoenberg's Moses is "inconceivable" as well as invisible, however, a paradox that engaged conceptualizing, semeiotic-minded French critics far more than the

1. But see Rashi on Shabbos 89a.

opera itself or its performance. The theological background was discussed on television by the Grand Rabbi of Paris, and, from another perspective, the Dominican scholar François Refoulé gave the opinion (*Le Monde,* September 29) that Schoenberg's God resembled the deity of neo-Platonic philosophy more than He did the One of Abraham and Jacob. Moses' final speech denouncing Aaron, his mouthpiece, as "an image, too, false, as an image must be" reminded Father Refoulé of Plotinus, for whom "*le concept formé par l'entendement pour cerner la divinité est encore une idole.*"

All of which assumes that the Moses and Aaron of the opera *are* their namesakes in the Bible, that Schoenberg *is* speaking through them in the first person, and, in short, that the composer has not exercised artistic prerogatives. But the truth is that for Schoenberg, as for the rest of us, Exodus was a departure. The prophets in the opera are very different from their biblical counterparts. At the same time, the opera's Aaron is to some extent the biblical Moses' "rib," Schoenberg having formed the second-born from the first much as Eve was created from Adam. Furthermore, in addition to transplanting a share of Moses' inner qualities into his brother, Schoenberg credits the prodigies which Moses works in Exodus to Aaron—a great stroke of dramatic verisimilitude on the composer's part, for Aaron is a "natural" charlatan.

Thus reconstituted, the brothers become prototypes of the Mosaic and the Aaronic—of the mystic and the politician, for example, as well as of innumerable variants. And it follows that the opera itself might be classified as Aaronic, since Moses does not believe that the Word of his inconceivable God *can* be transmitted to a misunderstanding people even by oral means. Aaron, on the other hand, might be identified with Zionism—"Israel endures," he sings in the final scene —and certainly his ends-justifying-means philosophy is more likely to appeal to pragmatists today than is Moses' almost perversely pure transcendentalism, for the new Moses, without his Aaronic side, loves cogitation and contemplation more than he loves the people.

Schoenberg translates the theological into the musico-dramatic, and Moses' paradox into the human tragedy of isolation. The tragedy is without catharsis for him, though his people, and the audience, experience it in the orgies inspired by the Golden Calf. The ideological oppositions between the brothers—represented by a variety of musical devices but primarily by having Moses speak and Aaron sing—are never resolved, and the opera concludes, as it began, in Moses' dualities: thought versus speech (the Word of God versus the interpretation of the Word), the spiritual versus the material, a purely spiritual religion versus a religion for the people.

Of all the stagings that the opera has had, the one at the Paris Opéra was least likely to be rated X. Even so, the orgies should have been still more drastically curtailed. The eventual solution to the staging of this scene must involve cinematography, Schoenberg's requirements being either too difficult to meet ("processions of camels") or downright impossible ("four virgins"). The opera was composed in the era of the Hollywood biblical extravaganza, and it is not farfetched to suppose that Schoenberg envisioned some of the camera stunts of the De Mille epic. What other explanation *can* account for stage directions that require the slinging about of entrails and the sloshing of blood, and which instruct people to "leap into the fire and run burning across the stage"?[2] But only once did the audience even wince; this

2. Fire reveling is, of course, forbidden to the Jews as one of the 613 commandments. See Leviticus 18:21 and Deuteronomy 18:10 (New English Version)—"Let no one be found among you who makes his son or daughter pass through fire . . ."—as well as the Gemora Sanhedrin 64a–b.

was at the slaughter of those "virgins," and the cause was the crudeness of the descriptive musical effect, a stab from the horns and an "expiring" glissando of the violins, rather than the scenic "horrors."

Schoenberg acknowledged his remoteness from the art of the dance and his inability to imagine suitable choreographic movements for the Golden Calf tableau. This helps to account for but does not excuse a nondescript and amateurish procession around the idol, and a ballet of knife-flashing butchers reminding one of Caucasian swordsmen. The "naked" girls were at least professional dancers, but of the Folies-Bergère kind, to judge by their movements and evident discomfort in wearing more clothing than during regular working hours. (The Inspecteur des Moeurs, splitting a pubic hair, had at first demanded *rasoirs*—shades of the punishment for female collaborationists!) At a certain point, when a mass of bodies *à la* Bouguereau was piled against the Golden Calf, the top torso dangling just out of plucking range, one felt that paroxysms of laughter were being held back only by Schoenberg's music. The other crowd scenes were cramped, leaving no elbow room for the people to vacillate between the two leaders in deed as well as in thought. But the music requires an unusually large chorus, and one section of it was already stationed in the orchestra pit.

The production was bizarre in other ways, too. Whereas the blackout in the first scene was a piece of successful symbolism—in the sense of Tolstoy's "Power of Darkness," that awareness of the lack of understanding of words is the beginning of knowledge—the second scene, owing to a solar-shaped disc of background light, and to a tilted surface on which the two prophets groped like astronauts reacting to the change of gravity, might, for no logical reason, have been on the moon. The same set, glaringly lighted and unmistakably intended to represent a Middle East desert, served for the rest of the opera. But this was a major mistake, implying as it did that the deliverance from captivity, the issue at the end of the first act, must have failed and that the Israelites are still on the wrong side of the Red Sea. Another drawback was that a hillock in Act One had to make do for Mt. Sinai in Act Two, therefore, through familiarity, weakening the effect of Moses' descent at the end of the opera. Either a mountain should have been made out of this molehill or the scenery relandscaped, but a change was needed, if only to indicate the passage of time.

The costumes and props were hardly less peculiar. Exodus is explicit: "fine-twined linen," "gold, blue, purple, and scarlet" garments, "wreathen chains fastened in . . . ouches of gold."[3] This is not to say that the drama should be furnished realistically. But, with the exception of a Father Time Moses, the production at the Opéra *was* pseudo-biblical, pictorially speaking, an illustrated Sunday School *New* Testament. And the Moses not only was out of place in his New Year's party costume, but was grievously miscast as well, and in consequence vociferously and cruelly booed by the knowing young. An actor instead of a musician, he was unable to negotiate the rhythms and pitch-inflections, to say nothing of the one all-important phrase, "Purify thy thinking," that the score requires him to sing. Finally, he was also the wrong actor. Quite apart from the inaptness of Comédie-Française as a substitute for *Sprechstimme,* he was never a commanding presence, and, so far from being lacerated by that conflict between "*penser*" and "*parler,*" much of the time he seemed merely befuddled.

As for the props, the Tablets of the Law were remarkably frangible—no doubt to indicate the ease with which the actual Commandments are broken—while Moses' rod in serpent form could neither slither nor coil, being rigidly jointed. If the Golden Calf failed to impress, however, the fault—

3. These materials were for the high priest and his son, of course, not for Moses.

gilt?—is that of the Opéra itself. The animal might have come straight out of the woodwork, or been carved or melted down from it; and, whatever the idol's actual size, it was cowed by the Opéra. One imagines that in Texas baubles of this kind, but solid twenty-four-carat ones, are awarded for prize-winning livestock.

Not much was said in Paris about the music—or for that matter ever has been said, except for analyses of Schoenberg's system of combining pitches. But something more elementary is needed, including an introduction to Schoenberg's sound. This can be found in works of approximately the same period, such as the *a cappella* choruses and especially the *Accompaniment to a Cinematographic Scene*, which resembles the opera not only in instrumentation and rhythmic and melodic style but also in nervous intensity, that *in extremis* which is Schoenberg's normal state. Yet the music of *Moses* is theatrical before all else, and however technically ingenious the whispered double-fugue choral Interlude, its most remarkable aspects are its function in the dramatic architecture and its theatrical prescience—for it anticipates electronic music and multiple speakers by two decades, and so strikingly that a performance *with* these means would hardly seem an anachronism.

The program booklet included a mini-thematic guide with motives for the "Burning Bush," the "Desert," and the "Israelites," as well as for "Hope" and "Joy." One wonders whether the last two were recognized as such. True, their interval structure trades to a degree on clichés for these emotions in older music, though how much, if any, of this heredity survives in Schoenberg's new contexts is disputable. So is the question of the "emotional range" of Schoenberg's music, which one apologist has equated with that of Beethoven's. But surely the emotions themselves are too different to compare, and it would be a futile exercise to look for semblances of those of Beethoven in the language Schoenberg has evolved to dramatize the passions of Moses and Aaron.

The *languages* of the two composers are comparable, however, since they can be broken down into quantifiable elements and the linguistic limitations determined. Thus the instrumental combinations in the Schoenberg opera are infinitely greater than are those in a Mozart opera, yet Schoenberg's superior sound spectrum lacks the simple power of strong contrasts that Mozart is able to wield by means of his harmonic system, turning a mood around with a simple shift of key or even a single pivot note in a modulation; Schoenberg, whose harmonic language includes none of these same functions, must set each event in motion by vastly more complex means. Which is not an invidious value statement, however, but simply a differentiation. If Schoenberg's new language cannot give musical form to a Cherubino, it also is not required to, Schoenberg's world not having bred such a character. His protagonists are an anguished prophet and a troubled people, and he evokes them in music of dazzling invention and an utterly new emotion.

Judged strictly by theatrical standards, *Moses and Aaron* must be counted as less of a triumph for Rolf Liebermann's new régime at the Paris Opéra than was the recent Solti-Strehler *Marriage of Figaro.* But it would be difficult to imagine a more satisfying realization of Mozart's *liaisons dangereuses* (until, that is, the opera suddenly falls into commedia dell'arte). Having established the true hatred "below-stairs" in the first scene, Strehler did not continue to look for presentiments of the Revolution under every bed. He did look *in* a few of them, however, for signs of the moral and sexual revolutions that had been taking place inside the Protected World since the Regency and Marivaux, and found them, with more novelty in the person of Cherubino than in that of the inconstant husband. What Cherubino wants, according to Strehler, is to "*coucher avec n'importe qui.*" The words do not say this, of course, but the music does. Moreover, the sex appeal in the music is far more potent than words could ever be—to say nothing of such exhibitions as the orgies in *Moses and Aaron.*

M. Liebermann's achievement in mounting two productions of such high quality at the Opéra must be measured against a background of artistic paralysis and a foreground of artistically pernicious chauvinism: M. Liebermann has been abused for "internationalizing" the nation's first theater, though it is doubtful that the Schoenberg opera could have been presented otherwise. As it was, Paris was treated to probably the finest musical performance (Solti) that this most difficult (whatever else) of twentieth-century operas has ever had.

This revives the question of when Schoenberg's masterpiece might be expected to reach the stage in New York. Neither of the local companies has announced it for the composer's centenary. Yet by any criteria it deserves precedence over the Delius and Britten, Henze and Ginastera operas that have been included in the recent repertories. This is not because of the centenary, of course, or even for the reason that Schoenberg's opera, though composed such a long way back, is still such a long way ahead. The mandate for it is its superiority, *Moses and Aaron* being one of the handful of twentieth-century operas with contemporary musical and dramatic power.

THE BOOM IN *BHOOP* AND OTHER RAGS

Musicologists tell us that classical Indian music cannot be separated from a philosophy and a "way of life," a way that few Westerners will ever live. But some scholars are jealous of their scholarship and unwilling to concede the validity of an artistic experience that is independent of it. The conclusion of this listener, however, is that Indian music in general, the northern raga in particular, can be enjoyed, and intensely, even without the support of an education in Indian cultures.

Although the scholars are correct, on the whole, in contending that the art of the raga cannot be approached in the terms of Western music, similarities are not lacking. The physical properties, after all—the pitches—are the same. And no matter how different their qualities and measurements, the music of both cultures is comprised of intervals (melodic and harmonic), rhythms, timbres, dynamics, and scales (including one identical to one of ours; two kinds of North Indian scales, the heptatonic and the diatonic, are called *thāt,* a subject demanding a book to itself). Furthermore, the music of both is modal, though only up to a certain date on the European side, and in comparable senses. In our century, too, still closer parallels can be drawn between the *alaap* of a raga and a twelve-tone series, above all in strictness of note order (in some ragas only). Correspondences exist in usage as well. Just as ragas and Vedic chants are associated with particular phases of the day and, in many cases, seasons of the year, so Western liturgical music is designated for the canonical hours and for observances of the church calendar. In both cultures, moreover, the music is said to reflect the changing moods of the twenty-four-hour cycle, matins, for example, contrasting with vespers and complines, according to conventions both musical and humorous—in the medieval, physiological sense.

Precisely here, however, the argument of the scholars seems to me incontrovertible: it is extremely difficult for an uninitiated Western ear to tell the time of day by the "mood" of a raga. Thus, *Bilawal,* a morning piece, is described by an Indian musicologist as "spritely and joyous," while *Sarang,* a composition for midday, is said by the same author to express the "benign grandeur" of that hour. But, for this listener, these captions could be equally relevant, or irrelevant, the other way around. For which reason it may behoove us to avoid any attempt to identify the expressiveness of Indian music (or of any other, for that matter) with words. In fact, we can listen to the music only aesthetically, as so-called pure music—the medium without the message, as it were.

The technical intricacies of the raga are formidable, as is amply demonstrated in the (to me) impenetrable chapters on rhythm in C. S. Ayyar's *Grammar of South Indian* (*Karnatic*) *Music.* Stated as simply as possible, the raga is pre-eminently a melodic form. Rhythm, therefore, is another of its dimensions. A harmonic one is added by the "drone" instrument that accompanies the melody, sustaining the tonic note throughout and creating two-note chords with it; or repeating the tonic at frequent intervals, thereby fulfilling a rhythmic function as well as a "tonal" one. Owing to acoustical phenomena—overtones—triads and seventh chords (and perhaps other harmonic mirages) can also be heard, yet the music is never "harmonic" in the European sense. The drone instrument, moreover, is on a secondary dynamic plane, in spite of which this immovable element is the most objectionable feature of the music to Western listeners, who hear nothing more in it than monotony. It is a stronger objection than the complaints about the limitation of the miniaturist form, the absence of a sense of meter, and the lack of harmonic depth, modulatory relief, range of coloration, and, in short, variety. Nevertheless, the tension of the melody derives in large part from its intervallic relationships with the tonic of the drone.

The notation of Indian music is as different from ours as Hindi is from English, and transcription is a Himalayan obstacle. Of the solutions familiar to me, that of N. A. Jairazbhoy seems to be the closest to what I hear in the music, or perhaps I should say the least misleading. Jairazbhoy has not been able satisfactorily to indicate tempi and their many fluctuations, but where other transcribers attempt to force the music into the typography and the comparatively rigid and limited rhythmic quantities of Western notation, Jairazbhoy dispenses with the Western metrical system and its simple note-value ratios. His notation is pictographic to some extent, size indicating importance. He divides the music into large and small notes, which are emphasized in both duration and dynamics, the large notes being those of the Aroha and Avoroha, the ascending and descending scales on which the raga is based. The small notes are the modifiers, the elaborations and the ornaments whose relationship to the large notes is also pictographic, placement indicating both speed and phrasing. These small notes might be compared to appoggiaturas and other embellishments in European baroque music, except that the latter are vastly less important. (Although the melodic notes in many a slow movement by Handel, for example, are little more than focal points for ornamentation, we endure wholly unornamented "executions" of them; but to perform the large notes of a raga without the small would be unthinkable.) In fact, the genius of the raga, the subtlety, the art—that which distinguishes one piece from another—is in its small notes.

One must go to the music itself. From the recordings now available I have chosen two, each representing a different type, the best and the worst. To begin with the latter, Odeon-EMI's *Classical Music of India* is little more than a potpourri of popular examples, and a demonstration of instruments and instrumental virtuosity. (One of the pieces includes a brief passage for voice, but this sounds like another instrument.) The record contains seven ragas, employing some ten different instruments including the shehnai (a kind of oboe); the sitar (the plucked string instrument with movable frets whose fame is exceeded only by Lord Krishna's flute); the sarod, the sarangi, and the Kashmir Valley santoor, three other members of the string family. All of the performers are spellbinding virtuosi, able to raise ropes, no doubt, and to charm reptiles. The sitars are played by Ravi Shankar and Vilayat Khan, the flute by Ghosh, and the shehnai by—golly!—Bismillah Khan. The two woodwinds play at much greater speeds, as well as with greater feats of trilling, articulation, and intonational control than are ever heard from the corresponding instruments in the West, and if the record is delectable for this virtuosity alone, that, perhaps, is its aim. But the emphasis is so markedly on instrumental colors and resources that it distracts from composition and form. The record is a mere showcase, therefore, a "commercial," and the heavy exploitation of drums and of *accelerandi* indicates that it has been tailored for the Western market, "souped up," so to speak, for that American curry restaurant.

Only one piece, *Lalit*, would *not* find a suitable home on a TV variety show. But *Lalit* is the jewel of the record, partly because of the marvelously whining high register of the sarangi. The most popular opus on the record, however, is *Bhoop,* the well-known evening raga. First of all it utilizes the greatest number of instruments playing together. Second, it embodies such prevalent attributes of "oriental" as "daintiness" and "enchantment."

The other record, which I recommend highly, is available as part of Jairazbhoy's book *The Rags of Northern Indian Music: Their Structure and Evolution* (Wesleyan University Press, 1971), which is one of the best on the subject. It contains eight ragas, all performed by a sitar and the drone instrument. The playing time is not more than twenty-five minutes, partly, no doubt, because of the absence of color relief, but primarily, I suspect, because the record has been made to fit the size of the book.

A concentrated audition of a single raga at one sitting may be more efficacious for an understanding of the form and appreciation of the musical qualities than an extended survey of the genre. Begin with *Rag Suha,* for example. Here the neophyte's first impression may well be one of monotony of sound (especially the sliding from note to note) and repetition of contents. But if he listens more than once, the logic of the whole will begin to appear to him. He should then be able to discern the points of tension and repose, the nuances of phrasing, the linear structure, and finally the musical concepts.

Having familiarized himself with the division of the form and the punctuations of the drone instrument, he will find the music a dramatic experience, more so probably than it is for the Indian. Our hypothetical listener could then go on to *Rag Darbari,* which, sampled first, might have discouraged him by its weirdness of intonation. But with exposure, the microtonal ragas will become the most attractive to him, that which sounds out of tune on first hearing becoming, on later ones, perfectly, satisfyingly *in* tune. On exposure, too, the neophyte will also begin to savor the rhythmic irregularity of the drone notes, the symmetry and balance between the beginning and the end in the use of the low tessitura, and the nimbleness of the small notes.

In addition to the Jairazbhoy, two other recent books may be recommended: Alain Daniélou's *Northern Indian Music* (Praeger, 1969) and *Indian Music* by Peggy Holroyde (Allen and Unwin, 1972). Transcriptions of ragas, together with their analyses, fill more than two-thirds of Alain Daniélou's pages. He includes the Aroha and Avoroha for each piece, as well as the tuning of the instrument, the type of mode and scale, the sonant and consonant, the time in the daily cycle at which the raga is to be played, and the identifications of the musical symbols. As an instance of the latter, dawn, from the absence of the sun to the first glimmer of light, is represented by F–F sharp–F, a sequence of notes symbolizing critical moments in other contexts as well. These correlations between notes and natural events, as well as between notes and human emotions, seem so literal to this listener that he wonders if even the most learned Indian can be conscious of them, and if so, to what extent it enhances his musical pleasure. The remainder of the book provides a concise history and technical description of the music, too concise, perhaps, for general readers, much of the material being condensed to chart form.

Miss Holroyde's book is on an altogether different level from the other two, displaying both the faults and the advantages of popularization. Chief among the latter is readability, in the sense that the text does not start off with a defeating technical terminology. Miss Holroyde, instead, begins with a lightweight introduction to Hindu philosophy—and later, Hindu-Muslim philosophy, for the Peacock Throne was a great musical patron. Miss Holroyde offers philosophical comments of her own, however, many of them either breathtakingly platitudinous ("truth remains constant, but its facets are many-sided") or downright dubious ("we understand what we know"). She is further addicted to meaningless comparisons with Western music. (Meaning*ful* ones do exist, as, for example, between the rhythmic style of Jhala and that of Bach.) Thus, she says that the form of the dhrupad, thanks to a certain composer of the Mogul period, is "capable of conveying thoughts and emotions as moving as the Bach *B-Minor Mass.*" Perhaps. But these are incalculables, or non-probatives, and the effect of such remarks is unenlightening at best, totally misleading at worst. Yet this book supplies a fund of information and will hold the attention of the general reader.

Five minutes' experience of the music itself, however, is worth hours of reading about it. A direct experience of a radically remote art may produce culture shock or awe but it can also "mind-expand." Apart from that, the Hindu catalog of the horrors of which "the man that hath no music in himself" is capable, does not go so far as Shakespeare's. But the Hindu doubts whether the liberation of the soul (*moksha*) is even conceivable without music.

MUSIC OF FOUR AFRICAN CULTURES

Lovers of Bach, Mozart, Wagner, are probably not the most likely customers for the records singled out below. Yet devotees of the European classics can find much that is rewarding in these "concerts" from four African countries, representing several kinds of music. The listener's range of musical experience will inevitably be expanded and his awareness of radically alien societies will be intensified. And whatever the artistic and intellectual effects, as little as a half hour's exposure to any of this unfamiliar music is enough to demolish one's image of oneself as a global villager.

The music is contained in the following albums: *La Messe à Yaoundé* (Arion 30 B 147); *Danses et Chants Bédouins de Tunisie* (Le Chant du Monde LDX 4341); *Chants et Danses de Madagascar* (Le Chant du Monde LDX 74456); *Musique Traditionnelle d'Ethiopie* (Collection Musée de l'Homme, Disque Vogue, CLVLX-164). These are in the best sense commercial recordings, produced by ethnomusicologists and anthropologists but aimed at a larger audience than that of scholars. The technical quality of the discs is variable, but with this material that is a minor consideration.

To describe all of the obstacles to appreciation would defeat my intentions. Yet certain of the difficulties are so formidable that the listener should have at least some idea of what he should *not* expect to grasp. Obviously he will be unable to follow the usages of a musical language he does not understand, to apprehend the form, follow the design, trace the development in a piece that seems both endless and inchoate. Even to say this much, however, seems to imply that I am referring to "pure music" rather than to music with complex and comparatively inaccessible cultural contexts and belief systems. The twelve *maqāmāt* (modes) in Muslim music, for instance, are associated with the zodiac, yet we can hardly be expected to perceive this relationship when we are unable even to identify the modes.

Lacking the necessary cultural criteria, the knowledge of the music's role in the community's ritualistic and social life, we are reduced to inadequate aesthetic evaluations. What these amount to are mere opinions, derived from impressions of arts so remote, born of sensibilities so foreign, that we are forced to convey our reactions through totally inapt comparisons. Initially the surface qualities of the music are the only ones we are equipped to explore. These include, in addition to the timbres of voices and instruments, rhythms, scales, intervals, and such devices as canonic imitation, for polyphony is by no means a rare concept.

Even while exhorting the listener to attune himself to this exotic music, one must caution him to do so in moderation. Unlike the raga, a unique and comparatively rigid art form, refined over centuries and the expression of a high civilization, this African music is heterogeneous and primitive, and a few minutes of it at a time can be quite enough. Furthermore, the listener may find only one pleasing piece on an entire record. Yet he should cherish the record for that piece alone.

In the case of these four albums, to proceed from the nearest culture to the one farthest removed is to go from the least to the most exciting. Thus *The Mass of Yaoundé* interests us primarily for the example it provides of the transition from colonialism to autonomy. (Yaoundé is the capital of the young republic of Cameroon.) The *Mass* is also valuable as a product of the new policies of the Vatican, its Roman Catholic liturgy having been not merely adapted by the native congregation but completely transformed. This Yaoundé *Mass* is still colonial, then, but in a new sense: it preserves the message of the missionary but little of his ceremonial structures. Vestiges of the European service are apparent, from Gregorian chant to parish church bells. But the indigenous ingredients are preponderant and more important, so it seems, than the underlying form. No doubt this impression is due, at least in part, to the heavy accompaniment of percussion instruments: various shapes of goat-skin drums; orbicular gourds; hollowed tree trunks; balaphons (a kind of marimba); perforated metal sheets that would have delighted Edgard Varèse; and the mvet, a bamboo pole with five calabash resonators which look like chamber pots but emit sounds similar to those of a harp.

The most memorable and startling feature of the Yaoundé *Mass* is the *oyenga,* an ululation more hyena than human, outbursts of which occur in the *Offertory* and again in the *Elevation.* Otherwise, the atmospheric noises—twitters of birds, spectators' coughs—command more attention than the music, as well as put the listener directly in the scene. Aided by photographs, especially of female millinery—bunches of bananas, baskets, raffia plumes—this actuality gives the album its main appeal.

The music of *Bedouin Dances and Songs from Tunisia* is technically intricate. It has modal variety (the *mazmoum,* the *ardhaoui,* the *M'haïersika*), all Arab music being composed of rhythmic, intervalic, and melodic modes (or matrices).[1] These are difficult to identify, above all in the domain of rhythm, which involves cycles of time units as well as beat patterns, but the Westerner is scarcely able to distinguish wedding from funeral music, let alone songs of supplication from those of thanksgiving.

The singing, in unison and octaves, is often monotonous, and the recording unhelpfully fades in and out from one piece to another with no definite beginnings and endings (if, indeed, "closed forms" exist), thus leaving the un-Oriented ear without a sense of shape. The instrumental music seems to me richer than the vocal, no matter how unpromising my description of this Bedouin "orchestra": a bagpipe; a zokra (oboe); a gasba (a flute, more gas than "bah"); a na'i (another flute, whose escaping air makes a sound of frying); and a rabab (a two-string "violin").

1. See *La Musique arabe,* by Salah El Mahdi, Paris, 1973.

By contrast, the *Songs and Dances of Madagascar* is both accessible and congenial. And the music is not only recognizably happy but infectiously so: the shouting, cachinnations, and explosions of high spirits, in one section, will remind Americans of cowboys in a rodeo. In addition to photographs of the musicians and their instruments, the record jacket includes a map of musico-geographic zones. This identifies fifty-two instruments by picture code, locating them, like knives and forks in the *Guide Michelin,* in the regions where they are played. The map also classifies the contents of the album as "popular," "classical-Oriental," "music of primitive ritual function," and "*résultances de* melting pot." Concerning this mysterious final category, little is said except that it flourishes in Madagascar's "intermediary zones." Yet this is the most striking music on the record because of close resemblances to antecedents in eighteenth-century France, a provenance further emphasized by the sonority and articulation of one of the island's most popular instruments, a species of zither called the valiha valo. (According to a new book on the Seychelles, incidentally, *Contredanses* from the same period and country are still performed there, too.)

For this listener, however, the *Traditional Music of Ethiopia* is the prize record of all, the best of its selections having an extraordinary dignity, attributable to some extent to that aura of the biblical world still attaching to the land of the "Solomonic dynasty," however dubious its family credentials. As a general background, let me recommend W. H. C. Frend's new history, *The Rise of the Monophysite Movement* (Cambridge University Press). This gives an account of the way in which a debate over a linguistic interpretation of a point of theology divided the world of Justinian according to the philosophical and cultural traditions of each land; the Monophysite heresy, which formed a separate church in Ethiopia, began at that time and continues to the present.

The musical representation of this Church on the record is unfortunately limited to a disappointing excerpt from the Christmas service. The prayers of the Falashas, a Judaic sect, are stronger stuff, partly because the unison voices are an excruciating microtone apart. (Though perhaps that is the way they are supposed to be; the Zuñi Indians, after all, chant in major seconds.) The outstanding specimen of religious music in the collection is neither of these, however, but a song of circumcision, in which a drone of voices serves as a background to a celebrant whose ministrations are pierced by a bloodcurdling, lycanthropic, super-Ginsbergian howl.

According to the blurb, the album "gives some idea of the immense variety of Ethiopian music." If by immense variety is meant the inclusion of songs of work, love, war, jesting, and the fact of the music's having been recorded in seventeen different places, some of them more than a thousand miles apart, the claim is true. Otherwise the one-time listener might find no more in any of it than a weird and skull-drilling sameness. *The Harp of David,* for instance, rendered by a rasping bass voice and buzzing lyre, raises a suspicion that one's turntable has been set at the wrong speed, while a flute ensemble from Ghidolé, and probably from a Cushitic-speaking tribe, leads one to think that the recording equipment must have been defective. Yet on repeated hearings both pieces are hypnotic.

Apart from these leaky flutes, the principal instruments are the toum (a kind of marimba) and the masenqo (an alto-range stringed instrument, played with astonishing nimbleness and alacrity). The vocal music is more impressive: a camel driver's song, with "ha-li-la" refrains; an Amharic war song, delivered out of the side of the mouth in tobacco-salesman style; a joking song in which someone, *primus inter pares,* "burps" during the short and sudden silences in what might be a drunken orgy, a tricky feat since the pauses are irregular. In another piece an even stranger vocal effect is evidently intended to imitate frogs. Much more attractive is a canonic duet, a love song for treble voices, plangently joined in two places by another voice disguised as a wild cock crowing.

But the term "attractive" exposes the superficiality of a commentary based on aesthetic criteria alone. (Do these people even have a word in their languages for "aesthetic"?) In the absence of other touchstones, we are obliged to regard this music as we do all museum culture. But why is museum music less valid than museum painting, sculpture, crafts, and artifacts, at least those from remote times and places? Whatever the answer, one denominator is common to all: these artists were unaware that art was what they were making.

STRAVINSKY'S *SVADEBKA*—

An Introduction

I—AVANT-PROPOS

Svadebka[1] (*Les Noces*) ranks high in the by no means crowded company of indisputable contemporary masterpieces. That it does not immediately come to mind as such can be attributable to cultural and linguistic barriers and to the inadequacy, partly from the same cause, of performances. For *Svadebka* can be sung only in Russian, both because the sounds of the words are part of the music, and because their

1. "Little Wedding," a diminutive form of *svadba*, "wedding."

rhythms are inseparable from the musical design. A translation that satisfied the quantitative and accentual formulas of the original could retain no approximation of its literal sense. Which is the reason that Stravinsky, who was not rigidly averse to changing sense for sound's sake, abandoned an English version on which he had labored himself in the fall of 1959 and again in December 1965.

But performances are infrequent as well as inadequate. The four pianos and large number of percussion instruments that comprise the *Svadebka* ensemble are not included in the standard instrumentation of symphony orchestras and other performing units. Then, too, the piece by itself is long enough for only half a program, while the few possible companion works, using many of the same instruments–Varèse's *Ionisation,* Bartók's Sonata for Two Pianos and Percussion, Antheil's *Ballet Mécanique* (an arrant plagiarism hailed as an apostolic successor at the time)—derive from it as instrumental example.

As a result of the obstacles of language and culture, audiences do not share in the full meaning of the work, hearing it as a piece of "pure" music; which, of course, and as Stravinsky would say, *is* its ultimate meaning. But Stravinsky notwithstanding, *Svadebka* is a dramatic work, composed for the stage, and informed with more meanings on the way to that ultimate one than any other opus by the composer. The drama is his own, moreover, and he is responsible for the choice of the subject, the form of the stage spectacle, the ordonnance of the text. *Svadebka* is in fact the only theatrical work by him, apart from the much slighter *Renard,* that combines music with a text in his mother tongue, the only work in which ritual, symbol, meaning on every level are part of his direct cultural heredity.

It is also, of all Stravinsky's works, the one that underwent the most extensive metamorphoses, and that not only occupied his mind during the longest time but may have, in aggregate, taken the most time. (A later Russia would have awarded him a Stakhanovite medal for his industry alone, if that Russia had recognized *Svadebka.*) The reasons for the long gestation are, first, that Stravinsky several times suspended work to compose other music, which, each time, left him greatly changed. And, second, that he *was* creating something entirely new, both musically—its heterophonic vocal-instrumental style is unique in our music—and in theatrical combination and genre, an amalgam of ballet and dramatic cantata that he was himself unable to describe. "Russian Choreographic Scenes," his subtitle on the final score, does not even mention that the subject is a village wedding and that the scenes or tableaux are four: at the Bride's (the ritual plaiting of her tresses); at the Groom's (the ritual curling of his locks); the departure of the Bride for the church; the wedding feast.

The aims of the present essay[2] necessarily differ from those of the guidebook that the author is preparing to the facsimile edition of the manuscript scores and sketches and from which it has been extracted. The sketches themselves are a study in the processes of growth and refinement that can illuminate not only part of the path of Stravinsky's working mind but also the embryology of the musical mind as a whole. Even with sketches and scores in hand, however, one is limited in the verbal means for this explication to such pedantic tasks as suggesting comparisons between the sketches and the final score, and attempting to explain how changes in instrumentation have effected changes in musical substance.

2. Read at Emerson Hall, Harvard University, August 8, 1972.

II—CALENDAR

On September 9, 1913, Stravinsky, his wife, three children, and nurse Sofia Dmitrievna[3] left Russia at Alexandrov, the border station, en route from their summer home in Ustilug to their temporary winter one in Clarens. In Warsaw, where he had obtained the necessary exit visas the day before, Stravinsky was joined by his friend and co-librettist of *The Nightingale,* Stepan Mitussov. Having resumed work on the opera after his return to Russia from Paris at the beginning of July, Stravinsky completed the mechanical Nightingale's music on August 1, and, three weeks later, the true Nightingale's aria which precedes this *japonaiserie.* But another project had been taking shape in his imagination that must also have been discussed during that stopover in Warsaw. For it was Mitussov who, two months earlier, had supplied the manuscript for a song that occurs, virtually as he transcribed it, in the Fourth Tableau of *Svadebka.*

Stravinsky could not have turned his full mind to the new opus until *The Nightingale* was completed six months later. But he was thinking, and even talking, about it: a letter from Prokofiev to Miaskovsky[4] repeats a rumor that plans were afoot to mount it as early as the autumn of 1914. Work on the libretto probably began during May and June. Stravinsky wrote no music then, in any case, or since the completion of the first of the "Three Pieces for String Quartet" on April 25, and it is unlikely that he was idle as a composer during those two months, ceaselessly occupied as he was in the far less interesting world of music outside his own head. His notebooks of the time are filled with Russian popular verse, songs,

3. Sofia Dmitrievna Velisovskaya (d. 1917) was a relative of Stravinsky's first wife, as well as her nurse.

4. *Miaskovsky: Correspondence,* Moscow, 1969.

and *chastushkas* (folk rhymes), most of them capped with his scansion marks.

The need for additional texts, in any event, was the principal reason for a hurried trip to Ustilug and Kiev between July 2—on which date he completed the second of the string quartet pieces, in Leysin—and July 14—when he was safely back there working on the final one.[5] Believing that war was imminent—this was a few days after Sarajevo—he went first to Ustilug to salvage some personal possessions, then to Kiev, where he stayed at the home of his father-in-law, 28 Annenskaya Street, and where he acquired a volume of wedding songs published (in 1911) as a supplement to *Pyesni sobrannye P. I. Kireevskim*–"songs collected by P.[eter] V.[asilievitch] Kireevsky." The songs in this volume served as the main source of the *Svadebka* libretto.[6] (Kireevsky, who died

5. He was probably in Salvan (Switzerland) on July 13. A cable addressed to him there on that date from Diaghilev, in London, expresses the hope that "*Svadebka suit son chemin.*" On the fourteenth, he wrote to Alexandre Benois proposing collaboration based on something from *Koz'ma Prutkov,* a copy of which Stravinsky had brought back from Kiev. (It will be recalled that in *ca.* 1901 Stravinsky had composed "many comic songs" to the words of *Koz'ma Prutkov,* according to the composer's letter to Timofeyev, March 13, 1908.) Benois scotched this notion in a letter to Stravinsky, July 23. See Stravinsky: *Memories and Commentaries,* Doubleday, New York, 1960. Also see B. H. Monter's *Koz'ma Prutkov: The Art of Parody,* Mouton, The Hague, 1972.

6. The *only* source, apart from three lines in Tereshchenko's *Byt russkago naroda* (vol. II, p. 332, 1848 edition, used at [93]), and apart from Stravinsky himself, for the author of the unidentified lines, the neologisms, and the many amendments and modifications of the Kireevsky originals can only be the composer. I should also mention that one song used in *Svadebka,* "*Yagoda s yagodoi zakatilocya!*" ("A berry with a berry tumbled down!"), was set down by Pushkin and entrusted by him to Kireevsky. It comes from the vicinity of Mikhailovskoe. But Stravinsky was always entertained by the thought that an *original* line by Pushkin might be in the *Svadebka* libretto. The poet wrote to Kireevsky when giving his copies of folk songs to the collection, "One day as a pastime try to discover which ones are sung by the people and which I wrote

in 1856, was a great Slavophile who compiled some twelve volumes of Russian folk songs, drawing on the work of many other collectors, including Pushkin.)

Once back in Switzerland, the song cycle *Pribaoutki*—on texts from Afanasiev,[7] the source, a few years later, of *Histoire du Soldat*—came first. During this time, however, and during a sojourn in Florence with Diaghilev in September, a version of the libretto was pieced together. And by November Stravinsky had drafted some, possibly most of the music of the First Tableau; or so I deduce from a sketch, dated that month for the section at [21], though the date merely refers to a succession of intervals on the same page that Stravinsky's then seven-year-old elder son had sung (whistled? hummed?), and that his father, with the immemorial pride of the parent in the prodigies of its offspring, had written down. On November 15 Stravinsky composed a Polka. Surprisingly remote from *Svadebka,* it was the first of the *Three Easy Pieces* from which the whole of his so-called neoclassicism has been said to stem. Whatever the truth of that, one part of his amazingly compartmented mind—in which *Renard* and *Svadebka* were incubating at the same time with no tangling of stylistic lines—was always several steps ahead.

At the beginning of January 1915, Stravinsky moved to the hôtel Victoria in Château-d'Oex, where, except for brief

---

myself." (*Works,* vol. III, Moscow, 1957, p. 536.) Stravinsky might have said the same of some of the musical material.

At one time Stravinsky also planned to borrow a line (at least) from Sakharov's *Pyesni russkago naroda,* so marked by him in his father's bound volumes of the 1838 edition (Song 229, p. 331). His father, who had one of the largest private libraries in Russia, owned a number of Kireevsky's volumes, and Stravinsky was familiar with them when he was young.

7. See A. Afanasiev, *Russian Fairy Tales,* translated by Norbert Guterman, commentary by Roman Jakobson, Pantheon Books, New York, 1945.

trips, he remained until March. One night in a funicular near Clarens, he found himself with two deeply inebriated Vaudois for fellow passengers, one of whom sang a tipsy tune while the other interjected an accompaniment of hiccoughs. Stravinsky composed a hocket imitating this debauched duet, perhaps the only *real* hocket ever written, though the name has been given to a style of two centuries of European music. He made capital use of it in the Fourth Tableau of *Svadebka*, increasing the suggestion of drunkenness appropriate to the wedding feast by shifting the music from thesis to arsis, and then, in a powerful unifying stroke, identifying the hocket rhythm with the motive of the Groom, Khvétis Pamfilievitch, which dominates the ending of the work. It hardly needs to be said that what was actually heard in the funicular must have been very different from the constructions it inspired in *Svadebka*. But the incident is typical. Stravinsky was able to hear, and often noted down, the music in the rhythms and intervals of machinery, in street noises, in hurdy-gurdies and carrousels—and in troubadours, intoxicated or otherwise, such as these Vaudois.

On another excursion (January 28), this time to Geneva, Stravinsky dined with Ernest Ansermet in Maxim's Restaurant, where he happened to hear a cimbalom—which may not have provoked him to say "Eureka" though that is what he thought. *Svadebka*'s original subtitle was "Songs and Dances on Russian Folk Themes, for voices, woodwinds, brass, percussion, plucked and bowed instruments." The plucked instruments were to have included balalaikas, *guzlas*, guitars, but these were replaced in the first scores by a harpsichord—a "plucked" instrument, after all—and a quintet of strings playing pizzicato. The cimbalom, which is not plucked but hammered with wood or padded sticks, nevertheless provided exactly the articulation Stravinsky required as well as a harder and more resonant sound than the jangly balalaika of his native land. It is a large-size dulcimer[8]—the biblical instrument, pictured on the Nineveh tablets, uncertainly invoked in *Ulysses* ("like no voice of strings or reeds or whatdoyoucallthem dulcimers"), and partly described in Pepys's diary, May 23, 1662: "Here among the Fidlers I first saw a dulcimore played on, with sticks knocking on the strings, and is very pretty."

That night in Geneva the player[9] favored the composer—not knowing that it *was* the composer—with a demonstration of the instrument, and as a result Stravinsky purchased one for himself and had it sent to Château-d'Oex, where he immediately added it to the orchestra of *Svadebka.* He taught himself to play it, moreover, drawing a chart of its thirty-five strings and notating the instrument's fifty-three pitches on them at the places where they are produced on the actual strings. At first the instrument is indicated in his manuscripts by its Russian name, "tympanon," which is the name employed by its master maker and master player—its Stradivarius as well as its Paganini—Pantaléon Hebenstreit, whose patron had been Louis XIV. (Pantaléon's only surviving tympanon, made in 1705, was among the effects of Pantaléon's descendant Sacha Votichenko at the time of his death in 1971 in Scottsdale, Arizona—surely one of the odder cultural properties to have turned up in that state since the Lon-

8. A trapezoidal zither with metal strings that are struck with a light hammer. According to Plutarch's treatise on music, the verses of Homer were sung at the public games to music composed by Terpander of Lesbos and accompanied by a zither.

9. Aladar Rácz, whose account of the meeting ("I played a Serbian kolo . . . Stravinsky wore a monocle, a red tie, a green waistcoat"), and, later, of Stravinsky purchasing a cimbalom (he "prepared the flour-paste, and cleaned the rusty strings himself"), is published in the *Hungarian Book Review* for May–August 1972, together with some memoirs by Rácz's widow. Both accounts contain chronological and other inaccuracies, however, as shown by a letter to Stravinsky, dated January 29, 1915, from his friend Adrien Bovy.

don Bridge.) In the next five years the cimbalom was never far from Stravinsky's instrumental palette, but he was obliged to abandon it after that because too few players could read and play *his* music. Yet it remained a favorite instrument, and that most genial of his works, *Renard,* cannot be performed without it.

Two weeks later (February 15), Stravinsky was in Rome, playing *The Rite of Spring* (four-hands with Alfredo Casella, in a salon of the Grand Hotel), for a small audience invited by Diaghilev and including Rodin.[10] At this time, *Svadebka* was unveiled privately for Diaghilev (see his letter of March 8 to Stravinsky in Château-d'Oex) and Prokofiev,[11] who heard further portions of it in the hotel Continental, Milan, on April 1, and—Diaghilev alone—in Montreux at the end of April. But the only creative digression from *Svadebka* between April and the end of the year was the composition of that miniature masterpiece of musical catnip, the *Berceuses du Chat,* the first phrase of which so resembles the first phrase of the soprano in *Svadebka* that the one could have suggested the other—and perhaps did, sketches for both being found on the same page. On January 4, 1916, however, in ever more straitened

10. Returning to Switzerland, Stravinsky described his Roman sojourn in a note to his mother sent from Milan, February 18: "I embrace you and Grusha and send uncounted kisses from Italy, where I have spent ten excellent days. I was at Diaghilev's in Rome. They put on my *Petrushka* at the Augusteum with smashing success. I took an innumerable amount of bows from the box. Our ambassador Krupyensky was present; I was introduced to him and spoke with him during the entire intermission. After that many lengthy productions continued in the corridors. All the Italian futurists were at hand and greeted me noisily; Marinetti came specially from Milan for this."

11. Stravinsky to Prokofiev, May 12, 1915: "Some one told me that a note about my *Svadebka* appeared in the *Stock Exchange News,* and a rather well done one—was it from you? I would be grateful if you send the note (it appeared, so they informed me, at the end of March or the beginning of April, our style)."

circumstances because of the war, Stravinsky accepted a commission to compose a chamber opera. This supervention was *Renard,* some of which had been written a year before; it could hardly have been a happier one, but *Svadebka* was shelved for seven more months.

Returning to it after that, Stravinsky was again and almost constantly interrupted, by the excerpting and reorchestrating of a symphonic poem from *The Nightingale* (completed April 7, 1917); by the composition of several short pieces including the *Etude for Pianola*[12] (completed September 10, 1917); by four changes of residence; by frequent travels (three trips to Spain in 1916 in addition to quite regular visits to Paris, Milan, Rome); by endless questions relating to the performance and publication of his ever more famous works, and by *pourparlers* concerning commissions for future ones. For example, he had been asked, through Léon Bakst, to compose incidental music for Gide's *Cléopâtre.*[13] Replying to Bakst, in Paris, from Morges, July 30, 1917, Stravinsky telegraphed: "*Notions du réalisme et synthétisme pour la mise en scène ne m'explique[nt] rien. Attends Gide pour comprendre*"—and the demand for the concrete is so characteristically expressed that the message could have come from any year of Stravinsky's life, 1970 as well as 1917, *mutatis mutandis* in the matter of the authors.

In April, 1917, Stravinsky played virtually the whole of *Svadebka* for Diaghilev, then living in Ouchy, after which Diaghilev wept by all accounts including Stravinsky's. A month

12. The instrument was used for rehearsals of the Diaghilev Ballets as early as 1912. In the fall of that year Diaghilev proposed that *The Rite of Spring* be "recorded" on it for Nijinsky's rehearsals. An extremely interesting letter from Ansermet to Stravinsky, June 12, 1919, deals with some of the mechanical problems of the Etude.

13. Stravinsky's diary for August 1917 includes a scheme for this. The project was not closed until December when Ida Rubinstein rejected Stravinsky's conditions.

later (May 30) the *New York Herald* quoted the composer as expecting "to finish *Les Noces Villageoises* this summer." Yet the sketch-score was not completed until October 11, a delay that is in some measure attributable to three shocks: the death of his beloved childhood nurse Bertha ("Bilibousch," "Bertoshka") Essert[14] (April 28), the death of his younger brother Gury (August 3), and the death of "his" Russia.

For though Stravinsky welcomed the Revolution during its first convulsions—telegraphing to his mother and brother at 6 Khroukov Canal, Petrograd, March 20, 1917: "*Toutes mes pensées avec vous dans ces inoubliables jours de bonheur qui traverse*[*nt*] *notre chère Russie libérée . . .*"—Stravinsky became a Ukrainian revanchist soon after that (even writing to Swiss newspapers on the subject), and then, and more lastingly, an anti-Bolshevik, denouncing "Lénine" (in the same *Herald* interview) as a "fanatic." He quickly foresaw the consequences to himself of the sundering from Russia, in any case, and realized that his voluntary exile was over and that the involuntary one had begun. The lament in the epithalamium at the end of *Svadebka* is as much for the loss of Holy Mother Russia as for the virginity of Nastasia Timofeyevna, Stravinsky's stage Bride.

The instrumentation was not yet finished on October 11, however, nor was it to be for another five and a half years. Writing more than a year later (November 19, 1918) to Otto Kling, of the English music publishers J. and W. Chester Ltd., Stravinsky refers to the score as if it were complete, but he was trying to secure a contract at the time.[15] In a letter of April 6, 1919, to Gustav Gustavovich Struve of the temporarily defunct *Editions Russes de Musique,* he refers to

14. Born 1845.

15. Stravinsky's contract with Diaghilev for the performances was negotiated for him by Ansermet in London in June 1919.

Svadebka as "a cantata or oratorio, or I do not know what, for four soloists and an instrumental ensemble that I am in too great a hurry to describe." But this ensemble, for which the music is fully scored to the end of the Second Tableau, is described in a letter of July 23, 1919, to Ernest Ansermet:

I do not know what to do with the "*Noces*." It is ridiculous to stage this "*divertissement*"—for it is not a ballet—without decors, although the decors would not represent anything—being there simply for decoration and *not* to represent anything—with pianola, harmonium, 2 cimbaloms, percussion, singers, and conductor on the stage, together with the dancers . . .

The addition of the percussion was inspired by *Histoire du Soldat*, composed the year before: together with the pianola and cimbaloms, it shows Stravinsky well on the way to the *martellato* ensemble of the final score. He wrote to Kling again on November 23:

. . . as for the "*Noces*" you must put in the contract that it is to be described on *affiches* and in programs not as a "ballet" but as a "*divertissement.*" Here is the complete title of the work: "*Les Noces* (village scenes): *divertissement* in two parts with soloists and chorus and an ensemble of several instruments."

The contract was signed on December 7. But *Pulcinella*, the Concertino for String Quartet, the *Symphonies of Wind Instruments*, *Mavra*, and numerous smaller pieces were composed before Stravinsky could return to and complete the instrumentation. Still another letter to Kling (Paris, May 26, 1921) reveals the composer surrendering to the problem of synchronizing live instrumentalists with the machinery of the pianola:

As for the "*Noces*," I am in effect completely reworking the instrumentation for a new ensemble of winds, percussion, and one or two parts for piano. I think that this new ensemble will suit us as well as the former version which includes mechanical instruments, something that could create all kinds of difficulties for you.

Winds or percussion, "sounding brass or a tinkling cymbal"? But apart from the winds he is nearing the final stage and perhaps the most original orchestra in twentieth-century music. The volume of sound is still small, evidently, and in fact the third and fourth pianos were not added, nor the arsenal of percussion instruments expanded to include heavy armaments, until the final score. Thus after beginning with an orchestra that, vast and varied as it was, virtually excluded percussion instruments, he ended with one of percussion only, and in the process arrived at the category of the actual orchestra of a Russian peasant wedding; for percussion instruments–pots and pans as well as drums, tambourines, cymbals —were bashed, hammered, clapped together, rattled, and rung throughout the ceremony and celebration, to drive away evil spirits.

Typesetting the Russian text created new and unforeseen difficulties. Writing to London from Biarritz, August 29, 1921, Stravinsky advised his publisher that

[although] the [proof] page that you sent to me is good . . . I ask you to draw the attention of your proof-readers to the Russian text. Literally not a single word is comprehensible. It is an agglomeration of letters with no sense. You must have a proof-reader who knows Russian. Unfortunately I will not have the time to rewrite the whole Russian text in the proofs—and, anyway, it is perfectly clearly written in the manuscript you have. Try to find a Russian proof-reader; so many Russians are without work at the moment.

On October 3, Stravinsky informed a London newspaper that *The Village Wedding* was finished. But he meant the two-hand piano score, the final proofs of which did not come for another seven months, during which he composed the one-act opera *Mavra*. The full score was finally completed on April 6, 1923, in Monaco, where the ballet—or *divertissement*—was already in rehearsal. The first performance took place June 13, at the Gaieté-Lyrique in Paris, a full decade after the work was conceived.

III—A NOTE ON THE SKETCHES

Graphic analysis, in the case of *Svadebka,* is helpful as a guide to chronology, for as a rule Stravinsky's Russian script is printed, rather than cursive, on the more mature and final sketches. (I should add that he drew most of the staves with his own stylus—a roulette, like a tiny, five-furrowed plough, invented and patented by himself, though the idea may have come from the rastral, a five-nib pen used to rule music paper in the eighteenth century. I should add, too, that he used transparent colored inks in some of the *Svadebka* sketches to facilitate reading abbreviated scores; if trumpets and oboes alternate on one line, for example, the music of the former might be orange, of the latter, green.) What the sketches reveal, above all, is that in the beginning was the word. In the very act of copying a text, Stravinsky added musical notations, setting a line of verse to a melody or motivic fragment, or giving it unpitched rhythmic values, or designating intervals or chords that had occurred to him in conjunction with it.

Stravinsky is at an opposite extreme in this from, say, Janáček, who, so he confessed, discovered "the musical motives and tempos adopted to demonstrating [the emotions] by declaiming a text aloud and then observing the inflections in my voice." Stravinsky's inspiration in his vocal works came directly from the sounds and rhythms of syllables and words, while structures of poems often suggested musical structures, wordless ones included, such as the imitation of a Russian Alexandrine by Pushkin in *Apollo*.[16] And it is also clear from the sketches that Stravinsky's musical rhythms and stresses are far more commonly suggested by the text than imposed upon it, and that his own claims to the contrary are greatly exaggerated.

In this manner the earliest of the musical notations sprouting directly from texts were used in the Fourth Tableau, which was the last one composed. (The first notation for the Fourth Tableau, the song contributed by Stepan Mitussov, occurs at about the halfway point.) But in more than one instance notations found on the same sketch page are widely separated in the final composition. Still, once having found his beginning, Stravinsky seems to have composed from beginning to end, though of course not measure for measure exactly as in the published score. (The chronology can be determined by sketches evincing instrumental improvements from one draft to the next.)

I should add that the sketches oblige all of us who have written about *Svadebka* to eat underdone crow, the largest helping of which is the reward of my own unwisdom. My recantation, moreover, must go all the way back to a statement, published somewhere in my first year of working with Stravinsky, to the effect that music and sound-image were simultaneous and inalterable occurrences in his imagination. This may be true in the case of some of his music—how would anyone know?—but is monumentally *un*true in that of *Svadebka*, in which the sonority is continually and, in the end, totally transformed.

16. Not that Stravinsky's musical imagination was dependent on words, of course. In November 1947, after completing the scenario of *The Rake's Progress* with Auden, the composer immediately wrote the string-quartet Prelude to the Graveyard Scene, being inspired by its *subject* even before receiving the libretto.

IV—A NOTE ON DERIVATIONS

Stravinsky would never concede that the question of thematic origins was of the slightest importance, and though he was interested in ethnomusicology in his Russian period,[17] the subject bored him later in life and he would not discuss it. Yet it is no exaggeration to say that all of the melodic material in *Svadebka* is closely related to folk and church music. What I cannot say for certain is how much was actually modeled and how much was "innate"—a combination of memory and of a phenomenal stylistic intuition. I suspect that nearly all of it originated in Stravinsky's imagination. Musicologists have triumphantly traced the phrase at two measures before [3]:

to

which is from Rimsky-Korsakov's *Polnoe sobranoe sochinenii* (1871). But Stravinsky's sketches reveal that he began with an E-minor triad and even further from Rimsky's example than from his own final version.[18]

Writing in 1931, Béla Bartók observed that

17. From a letter to his mother, February 23, 1916: "Musichka, Museecha, Please send as quickly as possible (you'll find them at Jurgenson's) the folk songs of the Caucasian peoples recorded on the phonograph. Don't take anything but phonographed ones. Besides, if Jurgenson has any other songs phonographed, send them also. Don't forget that I have the first edition of *Great Russian Songs in Folk Harmonization* (phonographed by Linevaya). Are there no other editions?"

18. Which is not to deny the many borrowings from the collections of Rimsky and others, including the opening of *The Rite of Spring,* from

Stravinsky never indicates the source of his themes, no doubt because he wants to imply his indifference to the question. He has claimed the right to use any musical material in his works that he considers useful; and said that, once used, it becomes in some way truly his own. For lack of documents, I am unable to determine which are the themes he has invented himself, in his "Russian" period, and which he has borrowed from popular songs. But one thing is certain: if among Stravinsky's themes there exist some which are his own invention, they are extremely clever and extremely faithful imitations of popular songs. Moreover, it is remarkable that in his "Russian" period . . . the composer hardly ever uses melodies with closed structures, divided into two or three or more verses, but rather motives of two or three measures, repeating them in *ostinato*. These primitive, brief, and often repeated motives are very characteristic of a certain aspect of Russian music . . . [*La Revue Musicale*, 1955].

In one instance, however, it is possible to follow Stravinsky as he consciously transforms received material, for the music

A. Yūshkenich's *Melodju ludowe litewskie*, part 1, No. 157, Cracow, 1900. The *Firebird* melodies

are quoted here from Rimsky's *100 Russian Folk Songs*, Opus 24, numbers 79 and 21 respectively. Incidentally, the following tune—No. 486 from a book of *Old Irish Folk Music and Songs* (a book that Stravinsky had purchased during his first days in London at the end of January 1913)—was copied by him at the time of *Svadebka* and used, creatively disguised, in the March from the *Eight Easy Pieces*:

at [50]–[53] is derived entirely (and the music after [53] partly) from the Fifth Tone of the Quamennyi Chant,[19] which is sung at the beginning of the Sunday Dogmatik in the Russian Orthodox Service. Here is a fragment of the Chant:

which, after several intermediate stages, including experiments with triplet notation (a symbol for the Trinity at least as old as Philippe de Vitry), Stravinsky altered to

Another fragment of the Chant

is merely transposed and extended by Stravinsky to

while still another phrase of the Chant

he converts to:

19. From the Oktoëchos of "Book of Eight Tones." (Stravinsky no longer possessed his nineteenth-century copy of this Greek book when

This last became the duet for the two priestlike basses (*cf.* [50]), which is as close as Stravinsky ever came to a representation of the Orthodox service on the stage,[20] for the singers are unaccompanied, following the Church rule, and they are the only unaccompanied voices in *Svadebka.* Yet the entire Second Tableau, with, at the end, a *basso ostinato* (A–C–A–C sharp) imitating a great church bell, is "ecclesiastical" music.

The critical bibliography is slender. The chapter on "Wedding Ceremonials and Chants" in Sokolov's *Russian Folklore* (Macmillan, 1950, for the American Council of Learned Societies, pp. 203–23) is indispensable for the background, nor does it go too *far* back. So is Birkan's "On the poetic text of *Les Noces,*" in *Muzika,* Moscow, 1966, and *Russian Folk Poetic Creativity,* Uchpedgiz, Moscow, 1956, p. 239. But the monograph "Igor Stravinsky's '*Les Noces,*' an outline by Victor Belaiev" (Oxford University Press, 1928) is worth-

I met him, but he was given an Italian translation of the *Ottoeco* in the early 1950s, by the Byzantine monastery at Grottaferrata.) Russian ecclesiastical chant, which derives from the Byzantine, is based on a system of eight *echoi.* These are the Byzantine modes, as distinguished from *tonoi,* the Greek modes, and each of them possesses different melodic formulas. Thus the Sticheron (Psalm tropes), Troparion (hymns sung between the verses of the Psalms), and Irmos (a Byzantine strophic chant) are sung to eight different "Tones" (same sense as in Gregorian Chant), each of which includes three versions for the Sticheron, three for the Troparion, and three for the Irmos. Each, moreover, changes every week at Sunday matins. The Fifth Tone of Sticheron, the one Stravinsky chose, is sung after the matin Psalm, "Lord, I cried unto Thee," and it occurs during the part of the service in which typological parallels are drawn between Old and New Testament prophecies.

20. He was appalled by a project of Diaghilev to exploit the "theater" of the Church, its gorgeous robes, golden orarions, etcetera, in a ballet.

less as musical analysis ("The melos of *Les Noces* . . . springs, as it were, from a single melodic germ which is presented in the opening bars") and misleading in most other respects.

The only other essay worth the mention is in *Kniga o Stravinskom*—"Book About Stravinsky" (Triton, Leningrad, 1929, pp. 181–215) by Igor Glebov (pseudonym of Boris Asafiev), English translation by Richard French, 1972. Stravinsky repudiated Glebov's essay in its entirety, and his copy of the book is profusely underlined, strewn with question marks, decorated with marginal rubrics. "What well-thought-out nonsense," he writes at one place. And at others: "What good is all this stupid literature?" and "I am shocked by these pages." When Glebov writes, "We must not forget that *Svadebka* is an incarnation of the ancient cult of birth and multiplication," Stravinsky underscores the "We must not forget" and adds: "Better forget, for this has nothing to do with it." At the end, the composer writes: "Dear friend" (he had known Glebov before the Revolution), "this is entirely your own concoction. *Svadebka* is something other than a symphony of Russian songs in a Russian style."

When apprehensible at all, Glebov's analysis of the melodic content in terms of "intonations," and of the rhythmic structure in terms of numbers of measures, is irrelevant. Unfortunately, too, his better insights are substantiated with false arguments; thus, he understands the rhythmic mechanization as style but has obviously never heard of the proportional system on which it is based. He compares *Svadebka* to *The Rite of Spring*, almost inevitably at that time when even non-Russians *not* making a case for the superiority of the composer's "Russian" works were raising the specter of Antaeus. (By the mid-twenties even dug-in Stravinskyans began to fear that without Russia the wells of the composer's inspiration were in danger of drying up.)

But the two pieces can be more fruitfully compared for

their differences than for their similarities. *The Rite* is a succession of dance movements, each, to a degree, complete in itself, and each manifesting a classical outline of a first section, middle section, recapitulation. *Svadebka,* on the other hand, is nonstop; its materials are exposed in fragmentary as well as complete form, as a name is evoked by its initials (*pars pro toto*); and it depends on fusings, interweavings, trellises of cross-connection. Hence the unities of the two pieces are of a very different order. And finally, no matter how much new ground is staked out in *The Rite,* its antecedents—in the Russian "Five," in Debussy—are apparent. *Svadebka,* however, is all new.[21]

Yet Glebov's essay is worth reading for the "anthropological background," the rituals and cultural traditions (of exogamous marriage, for one) or, in a word, for everything which Stravinsky took for granted but of which Western audiences are largely unaware. Glebov's emphasis is often wrong; thus he exaggerates the role of the *skomorokh*[22] and misunderstands both the irony and the religion, greatly overdoing the pagan underground, for instance. Nor is he of any help with the text, even failing to mention Kireevsky. His terminology, too—"psalmody," "clausula"—is anachronistic and inapt. Yet he is the only commentator who understands the vital element of lamentation. In addition, his hints—that the *druzhka's* music resembles the music of Russian village street criers, that the Matchmaker may be compared to Nekrasov's character of that name—are invaluable for non-Russians.

21. Glebov's likening it to Vecchi's *Amfiparnasso* (1594)—*cf.* Casella's little monograph on Stravinsky (1926)—is farfetched but may have been suggested by Stravinsky himself, who was fond of throwing out false trails of this kind.

22. An entertainer who performed at country fairs, singing, dancing, clowning, juggling.

And finally, *Svadebka* was new when Glebov wrote, yet he saw its originality and its true stature more clearly than any other critic of his time—or of ours. This is doubly remarkable when one remembers that he was writing in a country that had begun to shut down against its greatest composer. In fact the book was banned in the U.S.S.R., despite Glebov's patriotic—or, better, telluric—invocation to Stravinsky at the end of this chapter: "Our musical age is the age of Stravinsky; *Svadebka* could have been composed only by a composer of a country in which the elemental power of communion with Nature [has] not yet been lost by the bourgeoisie." The tone, though a little overwrought, is not unlike that of Turgenev's deathbed letter to Tolstoy: "Great writer of the Russian land . . ."

V — THE SCENARIO

Stravinsky composed the libretto—selected, colligated, and edited it—from Kireevsky's collection of songs. But the first version was much longer than the final one, for Stravinsky had originally planned to dramatize the complete wedding ritual, and not to begin with the plaiting of the Bride's hair, where the score now starts. His first draft of the scenario is as follows:

SVADEBKA
Fantasy in 3 Acts and 5 Scenes

ACT I
The Inspection

ACT II
Scene 1
The Bargain
  a. At the Bride's
  b. At the Groom's (An Incantation Against Sorcery—see page 49 [in Kireevsky])

Scene 2
  a. Devichnik (The Bride's Party)
     [Dyevishnik = Maiden's Day, the day before the wedding]
  b. The Girls Take Her to the Bath

Scene 3
In the Bride's House Before the Departure for the Church

ACT III
The Beautiful Table

I have not been able to determine at what point Stravinsky scrapped this more comprehensive scheme and abandoned the preliminary matchmaking scenes, the *devichnik,* and the ritual dunking[23] of the Bride. The final version, in any case, reduces this plan to four scenes: Act II, Scene 1, a and b, Scene 3, and Act III; and it changes the content of Act II, Scene 1, b, abandoning the Incantation in favor of more barbering. The reduction in size was accompanied by a drastic change in genre. Whether or not *Svadebka* was closer to opera in Stravinsky's mind than to the "ballet cantata" it finally became, he appears to have begun with musical characteriza-

23. His sketches contain a note to the effect that "among the songs collected by Pushkin, see pages 54–60 [Kireevsky]"; references are found to "dancing in the bath"; and a reminder to "See 'Customs, Songs, Rituals, etc.' in the Province of Pskov, pages 48–54 [Kireevsky]," which refers to the same thing. I should add also that the sketches contain several reminders to look up words in Vladimir Dal's *Explanatory Dictionary of the Living Great Russian Language.*

Professor Harkins remarks that at [52] "Stravinsky has retained the Pskov Dialect use of *ch* for standard Russian *ts* in *chérkov* for *tsérkov* ('church') but corrects it elsewhere in the same quotation (*potselovát,* for Pskov *pochelovát,* 'to kiss'). The apparent inconsistency is probably to be explained by the fact that the non-standard form *chérkov* is relatively more comprehensible, particularly in combination with *sobor,* 'cathedral,' than is *pochelovát.*"

tions, in a conventional operatic way, fitting out the *druzhka* (best man), for instance, with a hunting-horn fanfare—in his secondary role of master of ceremonies, the *druzhka* evidently blew a horn—which, transformed beyond recognition except for rhythm, became the music of the bass voice at [53].

In the final form of the work, roles of this kind do not exist but have been replaced by voices, none of which is more than loosely identified with the stage characters. Thus the Bride and Groom may seem to be "sung" by, respectively, soprano and tenor; yet no direct identification exists and the same two voices also "speak" for the Bride and her mother (see [21]). Even the Groom's final love song is "impersonated" for him by the bass.

The change in genre led to greater abstraction in the stage movement, too. Thus none of the four final scenes is actually "depicted," "enacted," or even narrated; by this time Stravinsky had renounced the use of narrative, substituting a collage of verse. In effect, *Svadebka* is a verse play for voices speaking out of turn. And as for the stage action, the choreography was conceived as an extension of music: this is to say that gesture and movement were to be stylized according to the rhythmic patterns of the music and not in imitation of popular or ethnographic dances.

As in *The Rite of Spring*, Stravinsky began with stage pictures in mind, even depending on them. But when the music had been completed he began to pare the stage directions away and actually to forget them, until no picture existed but only music. Many of his stage directions in *Svadebka* are quotations from Kireevsky. The following are from the sketches, all later than the scenario above, and intended for the four-tableaux final score, though only one of them appears there even in part. The first is a syndyasmic epigraph from Kireevsky that Stravinsky appended to an early draft of the full score:

Two rivers flow together
Two matchmakers come together,
They think about the ashblond braid,
How will we unplait this ashblond braid?
How will we part the braid in two?[24]

First Tableau

The father and mother meet the Bride with an icon, when she comes home from the bath. After the blessing, the Bridesmaids seat the Bride on a bench at the table, and place a dish before her, next to which they place a comb. Each Bridesmaid approaches the Bride, takes a comb from the table, combs her tresses, replaces the comb on the table and leaves some money in the dish. [Kireevsky, p. 241.]

Second Tableau

The Groom's train enters. The cart is drawn by village women from the opposite side of the stage from that on which the Bride's cart entered. In the cart are the Groom and his father and mother and best men. The mother is combing his locks.

The mother combs Khvétis's locks, moistening the comb in *kvas*.

At the end of the Tableau, Stravinsky marks the measure in which

The Groom's train prepares for departure . . .

24. Plaited hair is "a fetish which Freud places at the origin of weaning (institutionally assigned to women). The braid replaces the missing penis . . . so that 'cutting off the braid,' whether on the level of play . . . or whether as social aggression among the ancient Chinese, for whom the pigtail was the phallic perquisite of the masters and the Manchu invaders, is an act of castration." Roland Barthes (*Erté*).

and the measures during which

The Groom's train departs slowly, in their carts.

Third Tableau

Enter the Bride's cart (from the same side of the stage as in the First Tableau), all glittering with icons and mirrors. The characters (the same as in the First Tableau) are also dressed in sparkling clothes.

Fourth Tableau

The backdrop is raised revealing a large room in a Russian *izba.* It is almost entirely filled by a table, around which a large number of people are seated. They eat and drink. A door is open at the back showing a large bed covered by an enormous eiderdown.

In the wedding parlor stands a table. On a table is a *karavay* [very large loaf of bread] with various wondrous decorations: the figure of a little man, a little bird, etcetera. This *karavay* is surrounded by other, smaller *karavays*, and by honey cakes, cookies, sweetmeats. The table is made of wood. The mead is strong. The newlyweds eat the *karavay* first. The *karavay* signifies the marital union.

Svadebka ends with the following song, during which the *druzhka* and the *svaha* [female Matchmaker] lead the young couple to bed. When the *druzhka* and the *svaha* have put them to bed and left them, the parents of Khvétis and Nastasia close the door, place four chairs in front of it, and sit on them. The act is over. The curtain falls slowly. The music continues throughout. At the very end a solo voice [tenor] sings, in a saccharine, or oily, voice, drawing out the words:

"*Uzh i dushka, zhanushka Nastas'jushka,*
Pozhivem my x toboju xoroshenichka,
Shtoby ljudi nam zavdyvali."

Finally, here is Stravinsky's last statement about the staging of *Svadebka,* an introduction composed while he was correcting the second proofs of the piano score:

> "THE VILLAGE WEDDING"
> Russian Scenes in 2 Parts
> with songs and music

The protagonists of the piece are ballet dancers, and the singers (chorus and soloists) are in the orchestra pit. The director is asked to follow this strictly, as well as all indications in the score as to the changing of scenery, entrances, etcetera. On the other hand he may exercise complete freedom with regard to the stage composition, which does not affect the drama and which in no way interferes with the faithful rendering of the Russian costumes. The author is himself inspired with complete freedom.

The decor of the first three tableaux consists of a simple backdrop, which must evoke, at the same time, the interior of an *izba* and a village street. At the beginning of the Second Part, this drop is raised without interrupting the action.

The word "*Svat,*" being untranslatable, has been retained in the French version. In the Russian countryside, the "*Svat*" is the person charged, in some official capacity, with conducting the marriage service, a male Matchmaker, in other words. He is, naturally, one of the most important guests at the wedding ceremony.

STRAVINSKY—

Relevance and Problems of Biography[1]

Reviewing a recent life of Wagner, W. H. Auden writes that "on principle, I object to biographies of artists, since I do not believe that knowledge of their private lives sheds any significant light on their works . . . However, the story of Wagner's life is absolutely fascinating, and it would be so if he had never written a note."

But if Wagner had never written a note, would he have had that life? And, apart from the doubtful assumption that we read an artist's biography primarily for illumination of his work, is it always true that nothing "significant" about the art is revealed from study of the life? (I am thinking about Joyce and other authors of disguised autobiography.) Further, can it be taken for granted that public and private are always separable? They are not, at any rate, in the case of Igor Stravinsky.

A celebrated artist for more than sixty years, Stravinsky has left an immense, perhaps immeasurable, public biography. This can be found in newspaper files, in recorded talk, and on film[2] in the cities in which he performed, attended performances, and toured as a private yet always inescapably

1. Read at Goldwin Smith Hall, Cornell University, March 29, 1973, and at Breasted Hall, University of Chicago, April 10, 1973.

2. Films of Stravinsky conducting survive from as early as the 1920s, but his first sound film was a telecast concert, January 13, 1954, WGN, Chicago.

public person. Some of this public view of him blends into the private. It does not do so in a taped public interview such as he gave at the University of Cincinnati in 1965, for he was conscious of himself and the audience in his every remark. But the several reels of his talk made by Columbia Records in the 1960s contain glimpses of the private Stravinsky, since he was unaware that the machines had been left on when he was *not* conducting, and that in effect he had been Watergated.

The same can be said of at least some of the more than two hundred hours of film which CBS took of him in 1965, as well as of footage, official and unofficial, from the U.S.S.R. and other countries, by cameramen known and unknown, professional and amateur, including members of the orchestras he conducted.[3] No one can say to what extent Stravinsky may have been conscious of the lens, but it must be conceded that the line between public and private is difficult to draw. No less apparently, the forms of biography have changed. Ideally, Stravinsky's should be issued in cassettes with accompanying album notes.

But the intersection of public and private goes beyond these electronic encroachments. Stravinsky's art was directly altered by public events—unlike, for example, Wagner's, whose external career may have been disrupted by the Dresden Revolution of 1848 but whose music does not seem to have been affected either in its course of development or in substance. The Russian Revolution, on the other hand, changed both the direction and content of Stravinsky's work, first of all by depriving him of his mother tongue as the language of his vocal music, Russian being impractical for him

3. A violist in the Los Angeles Philharmonic, Mr. Philip Kahgan, has films of Stravinsky conducting in 1937; a tuba player in the New York Philharmonic, Mr. Sam Butterfield, has films of him rehearsing the *Symphony of Psalms* in 1966; etcetera.

in his life as an exile. What is more, this deprivation occurred just as he had begun to explore new possibilities of combining syllables and words with music, experiments that could not be pursued in the Latin, French, English, and Hebrew texts of the post-Russia years, despite his contentions that his approach was the same in these other languages as it had been in Russian.

The Revolution of 1917 had indirect effects on Stravinsky's music. For one thing, the accidents of Russian birth and American residence and the failure of these two governments to sign the Berne Copyright Convention cheated him of the largest part of the income from his works. To try to remedy this, he rearranged most of his "Russian" music for copyright purposes, often giving as much time to this task as he did to composing new music. On August 17, 1920, for instance, he informed a publisher: "I have spent six months (October, November, December 1918, and January, February, March 1919) composing [the new *Firebird* Suite]." As a further result of the same copyright predicament, Stravinsky was forced to earn a living as a conductor. He enjoyed conducting his music and hoped to establish performing traditions by doing so, but to play Tchaikovsky's Second Symphony more than two dozen times, largely for money, was another matter, and it kept him from composing. During the Second World War, when his European royalties were nonexistent and his ASCAP payments were in three figures, Stravinsky was better known in America as a conductor than as a composer.

During the forties, too, the kind of commission that Stravinsky sought and often accepted reflects these straitened financial circumstances. In pursuit of a popular, paying success, or an acceptable film, for which he would write a do-it-once-and-retire score, he was forever chasing wild geese, among them Paul Whiteman, Billy Rose, Woody Herman, and even Sam Goldwyn. His most spectacular flops in this sense—the 1940 *Tango*, for one (Stravinsky's "last tango," mercifully!)—were in fact openly aimed at the commercial market. As a result, the Stravinsky *Köchelverzeichnis* contains too many tiny, if always genial, masterpieces-for-money—the *Preludium, Circus Polka, Norwegian Moods, Scherzo à la Russe, Babel*—and too few larger works, or works born purely of inner necessity.

I do not wish to add to the history-of-what-might-have-been, yet it is at least arguable that circumstances did send Stravinsky's genius along some very strange detours. In contrast one thinks of the no less impecunious composer of the early *Ring* operas piling up the creations of *his* inner world even without prospects of their performance—though neither the artistic dimensions nor the ethical systems of the two musicians are comparable, Stravinsky having been a firm believer in earning his own way and in paying his own bills.

Let me proceed to the "problems" of my title as they confront Stravinsky's biographers. First and most troubling, does anyone have the moral right to use Stravinsky's own materials for a biography he would not have wanted? In 1965, moving to a new home, he marked the two largest packets of his personal correspondence: TO BE DESTROYED AFTER MY DEATH. But since he was in his mid-eighties at the time, why did he not carry out this destruction himself, if that were what he really wanted? The answer, I believe, is that he *did* intend to read and destroy the letters; forced to postpone doing so, however, he was determined to prevent anyone else from seeing them in the eventuality that his own opportunity never came. He inscribed these testamentary instructions on a day when he had been destroying letters and papers by the bushel. Moreover, during the sixteen years before that, I had often seen him read and burn old correspondence. It seems clear that he wished to preserve nothing personal in his so-called archives, and that, if the occasion had arisen, he would have made an *auto-da-fé* of them.

So far from condoning any "personal" biography, if

Stravinsky had allowed himself to think about it, he would surely have specified in his will that none be written. Further, I am bound to admit that he would have agreed with Mr. Auden on the *ir*relevance of biography. Several lives of the composer were published during his lifetime, after all, and none of them, in his opinion, was of the slightest use in relation to his art. It is hardly surprising, therefore, that his autobiography is one of the least "personal" books of its kind ever written—*viz.*, the unique reference in it to his first wife, the simple statement that he married her. I am convinced, incidentally, that his principal motive in writing this book was to bring in money, and that the formation of his artistic creed and the correction of facts about his life were less important.[4] That the book signally failed to accomplish even the financial objective, always ranking high as a worst seller, is patently due to this avoidance of the personal.

The moral question becomes more vexing to biographers when they learn that Stravinsky had no control over the microfilming of his "archives" and that he died without approving the materials that were photographed. This was the result of a series of mishaps. In October 1967 the Stravinskys invited their friend Pierre Suvchinsky to visit them in Hollywood, Suvchinsky's company always having had a salutary effect on the composer. But Suvchinsky's arrival was followed by a letter from Stravinsky's London publisher, Boosey and Hawkes, giving to themselves the exclusive rights to publish his "archives," naming Suvchinsky as editor, and requesting Stravinsky's agreement.

That he signed this paper—consenting, unrecompensed except for far distant and insubstantial royalties, to the exploitation of the documents of his lifetime—is a measure of his desire to help his old friend. The failure to consider other

4. Many of the latter are mistaken, including the date of the first performance of *The Rite of Spring*.

consequences and contingencies is explained by the circumstance that an acute circulatory ailment had meanwhile put Stravinsky in the hospital. Whether in spite or because of that, the microfilming began immediately, at first under Suvchinsky's guidance, then, after he returned to Paris, under no one's, since Mrs. Stravinsky and I spent our days with the patient.

Quite apart from the questionable, and now permanent, invasion of Stravinsky's privacy, the results of the microfilming are lamentable. Unsupervised in their work, the photographers copied not only priceless papers but also useless catalogues, programs of concerts in no way related to Stravinsky, and, in short, everything in the *omnium gatherum* of the storage area. At the other extreme, lacking a definition of "archives," the photographers neglected to reproduce photographs (which in Stravinsky's case often contain as much information as letters), ignored the contents of his libraries, and even failed to copy his piano and conducting scores. Stravinsky being a continual rewriter, for whom every performance yielded new revisions, these musical scores are rich in annotations that should have been preserved in a variorum edition. But none was photographed, and during the dismantling of the composer's library in 1970 many items disappeared. I hardly need to add that the microfilmers also overlooked his library of music by other composers, some of it with comments in his hand.

It remains to be said that despite contractual arrangements Stravinsky never believed that his private papers would be published; for the same reason, or personality trait, he rarely alluded to his death. This also explains why, in Zürich in October 1968, he signed a new agreement to pay Suvchinsky's salary (with no contribution from the publisher); and why, a month later, in Paris, after meeting separately with rival factions within the publishing company, Stravinsky still took no interest in the project except in so far as the plans had now been expanded to include a collected and corrected edition of his complete works.

At present the archives have not yet been disposed of (given to a university or public library) because of an impasse between the publishers and the fiduciaries, the former holding to their piratical letters of agreement, the latter contesting them on ethical grounds. From the standpoint of the outsider and musician, the worst of this is not only that the archives themselves will continue to be inaccessible, but also that collation with materials from other sources is impossible. Stravinsky possessed few documents dealing with the years before 1911, and not many more for the period between that year and 1914, when he was already thirty-two. Obviously this first third of his life, whether or not it included his greatest compositions, was as important in the formative sense as it is in anyone else's. But the history of these years can be completed only by the cooperation of individuals and organizations in many countries, the Soviet Union above all. Most of the composer's early letters are there, along with his early manuscripts (of works known and unknown) and all of his family's papers. Clearly a full exchange with the U.S.S.R. must take place before any biographical study can be considered.

Stravinsky's 1962 visit to Russia was a turning point in the musical life of his homeland, although at the time it was widely regarded as merely another in the composer's pattern of reversals. Hosts and guest alike had been pouring abuse on each other for forty years, and, by the date of the trip, neither side had recanted. Officially, Stravinsky was still the U.S.S.R.'s arch symbol of capitalist decadence, and as late as the late fifties his Harvard lecture on Soviet music was considered too "reactionary" even to be published in France. A rapprochement seemed improbable, to say the least. Yet the visit took place. And now, only two years after Stravinsky's death, his music is played and recorded in the U.S.S.R., and his early compositions, his letters, and biographies and analyses of his work are published with ever greater momentum. The return of the native in 1962 provided the impetus, but the change in the last two years has been greater than in the preceding eight. In short, a historical switch has occurred, not comparable to Constantine's conversion of the Empire, perhaps, but certainly to the cessation of persecution before it.

The following selection from the list of Soviet publications begins with two that Stravinsky himself knew, the volume of *Soviet Music* (Moscow, 1966) containing his letters to N. Roerich, and the monograph *Stravinsky's Early Ballets* (Moscow, 1967) by Vershinina. The composer read the former in a fever of rediscovery, the latter with mixed emotions, for while its very existence was a proof of the growing popularity of his music in the U.S.S.R., the naïveté of the explications and the rudimentary errors annoyed him.[5] I should add that Russian recognition meant more to him than that of the rest of the world, a fact I myself failed to realize until 1962. Coming to the Stravinsky household in 1948, I did not perceive the degree of its Russianness and have only recently discovered that as late as 1947, the year 1 B.C., the language, friends, habits of life of the home were almost exclusively Russian. It follows that I was also unaware of the extent to which my American views, language, and attitudes were displacing their Russian ones. And, finally, I did not see that Stravinsky's constantly expressed antipathy to most things Russian was a question of protesting too much.

5. On page 137, Vershinina refers to a "suite" from *The Rite of Spring*, and its wide performance during the years 1914–21 when the ballet was not staged. Stravinsky has underscored this, and corrected it in the margin to "the whole ballet." Also, on page 140, he has changed Vershinina's comment on the reception of Nijinsky's choreography of *The Rite* from "not just" to "*un*just."

Among present and forthcoming Soviet publications the following are especially important:

1. *Creative Formative Years of I. F. Stravinsky* by V. Smirnov (Muzyka, Leningrad, 1970). This book contains a facsimile of a Piano Scherzo, composed in 1902.
2. *Storm Cloud,* a romance for voice and piano, words by Pushkin, composed in 1902. The manuscript, in the Leningrad State Library, is not yet published.
3. Piano Sonata in F-Sharp Minor, composed in 1903–4 (Moscow, 1973).
4. *F. Stravinsky: Essays, Letters, Memoirs,* compiled and annotated by L. Kutatladze, edited by A. Gozenpude (Muzyka, Leningrad, 1972). The book contains letters to F. I. Stravinsky (father of the composer) from Borodin, Stassov, Rimsky-Korsakov, Anatoly Tchaikovsky, Chaliapin, Cui—and the teen-age Igor Stravinsky.
5. *Igor Stravinsky: Documents and Materials,* edited and annotated by Igor Blazhkov[6] (Soviet Composer, Moscow,

6. Conductor, spokesman, and intermediary with musicians in the West, Blazhkov has been one of the most active forces on behalf of Stravinsky's music in the U.S.S.R. Blazhkov first made himself known to Stravinsky in 1959 with a letter which the composer answered on January 26, 1960. Blazhkov then wrote requesting scores, and on June 28 of that year Stravinsky responded by sending copies of the piano scores of *Jeu de Cartes* and *Le Baiser de la Fée,* a vocal score of *Le Rossignol,* and full scores of *Orpheus,* the *Divertimento,* and *Agon.* In 1963, Blazhkov sent a book of *lubok* (primitive Russian graphic art of the eighteenth and nineteenth centuries), which Stravinsky acknowledged in a letter on June 20. Blazhkov's most recent project has been the reconstruction of the text of *Histoire du Soldat* from the original sources in Afanasiev (and replacing Ramuz's). This "substitution" is difficult to conceive, however, the libretto of *Histoire du Soldat* having undergone as great a degree of transformation and rearrangement as that of *Les Noces.*

1973). The book includes sixty-two letters from Stravinsky to Russian addressees.

6. A collection of over 300 pages of Stravinsky's letters, including a newly discovered cache of twenty from the composer to Vladimir Rimsky-Korsakov.

7. *Dialogues*, an omnibus of volumes 1–4 of the Stravinsky-Craft conversation books, edited and annotated by I. Beletsky and I. Blazhkov (Muzyka, Leningrad, 1971).

8. A monograph, *Igor Stravinsky*, by Michael Druskin, has been announced for publication in 1974.

The subject matter of No. 7 being the most familiar to me, I will confine my discussion to it and to the letters, but to the letters in general, rather than to these Russian collections, for the composer's correspondence forms a truer autobiography than the one which he published in 1935.

First a word must be said regarding No. 4, the book about Stravinsky's father. A booklet on the composer's parent appeared in 1951, and was read by Stravinsky without comment, probably because it consisted of little more than an outline of the eminent bass's career, a listing of his sixty-six roles at the Maryinsky Theater, and a garland of quotations from Tchaikovsky and others on the elder Stravinsky's remarkable artistic and intellectual qualities. But, unlike the earlier publication, the new book looks at him as the father of the composer, though without slighting the achievements of the parent in his own right.

One of the outstanding opera singers and actors of his time, Feodor Ignatievich Stravinsky was also renowned as a gifted graphic artist and a *littérateur* and bibliophile. I have often heard Stravinsky refer to his father's talents as a painter and watercolorist but had seen no example of his work until a few months ago when George Balanchine acquired some color photographs of it in a Leningrad library. The most striking of these are self-portraits in the costumes of various operatic roles, of which the new biography reproduces thirty-two, but unfortunately not in color. Feodor's library was among the largest privately owned ones in all Russia, of such importance that in January 1919 the Ispolkom of the Union of Communes of the Northern Territory passed a resolution placing his apartment under protective guard. Three years later his widow bequeathed the music section to the Petrograd Conservatory, and in 1941–42, during the siege of Leningrad, most of the remaining books[7] were destroyed.

The biography of Feodor Ignatievich Stravinsky—bookish singer, actor in public, and introvert in private—is indispensable to anyone interested in the son, for the composer inherited not only his father's musical gifts but his complex character as well. And Feodor Ignatievich endowed Igor Feodorovich with other talents, too: histrionic (the composer's early letters describe his acting in amateur theatricals, and C. F. Ramuz's correspondence reveals that Stravinsky entertained the idea of playing the part of the Devil in the premiere of *Histoire du Soldat*); graphic and calligraphic (as a young man Stravinsky painted in oils, and throughout his life did sketches and drawings); literary and bibliophilic (Stravinsky had a fanatical respect for learning, and he bound in leather many of the books that had influenced his thinking).

Before examining the Soviet edition of the Stravinsky-Craft *Dialogues*, I must explain that the junior partner in this collaboration always regarded the senior's recollections, with their exaggerations, distortions, and other nuances of memory, as more important than the encyclopedia facts. Junior thought that "anyone" could dig out the dates and places, and though

7. Among the few volumes in the composer's possession was a copy of the original edition of the plays of Catherine the Great, stamped with the imperial seal of Tsarskoe Seloe.

"anyone" could not, Soviet musicologists could and did. I am grateful to them for their paralipomena, and I am certain that Stravinsky would have been too.

Apart from the data on the composer's early years, the *Dialogues* offer several glimpses concerning the state of the arts in the Soviet Union in the all-too-recent past. Some of the cultural blind spots are familiar, and when the Soviet editors chide Stravinsky for his partiality to Kandinsky, Larionov, Malevich, and other émigrés, while ignoring the Socialist Realist School, the reader feels that Zhdanovism is not altogether dead. But when the editors identify Lourdes (which Stravinsky mentions in connection with Werfel's *Bernadette*) by referring to Emile Zola's writings on the subject, the effect is bizarre. Readers should be advised, too, that the Soviet text is not always reliable on Stravinsky's non-Russian music. Thus the Ugly Duchess, in Auden's first draft of *The Rake's Progress*, was not, as the Soviet editors suppose, based on Marguerite, Duchess of Tyrol (1318–69), the protagonist of Feuchtwanger's *The Ugly Duchess*. Stravinsky knew Feuchtwanger in California but had not read this novel; furthermore, the conception and the name originated with Auden.

The book's scholarship on the Russian works is more sound. *The Saucers*, Stravinsky's songs of Yuletide divination, for female chorus, are traced to Afanasiev's *The Slav's Poetic Attitudes Toward Nature* (Vol. II, Moscow, 1868, p. 194), and the texts are analyzed both linguistically and in terms of their symbolism; by means of the former, one of them, *Chigisy Across Yauza*, is identified as Central rather than, as Stravinsky mistakenly thought, Northern Russian. This may be run-of-the-mill research, yet it is a run that no one else had taken. More legwork of this kind provides information concerning the concerts and operas the composer attended in his youth, his studies with Rimsky-Korsakov, and the discrepancies between Stravinsky's accounts of the stagings of his Russian theater pieces and those of his collaborators.

These new corrections and amplifications do not alter our picture of Stravinsky in any fundamental, but they help to complete it, and they modify the colors of some of its details. The composer's birthplace, which he was unable to find when he went in search of it, October 5, 1962, because of a change in street names, has now been established as Khudyntzev Cottage, 137 Shveitzarsky Street (now Uprising Street), in Oranienbaum (now Lomonosov). Corrective surgery has also been performed on Stravinsky's version of his family tree, its two oldest branches now having been regrafted. The great-grandfather who lived to 111 was not Ignace Ignatievich Stravinsky, as the greatest of his great-grandsons wrote, but I. I. Skhorokhodov, the composer's maternal great-grandfather. Furthermore, this Methuselah reached the age of 112 (1767–1879). Stravinsky's error probably occurred while identifying a medallion portrait of the centenarian on its reverse; he appears inadvertently to have switched the family names, both ancestors having the same initials. As for Ignace Ignatievich, he died in Tiflis, May 29, 1893, a stripling of the age of eighty-four.

Stravinsky's memory of distances and dates has provoked extensive correction but seldom in a subject of much consequence. And in at least one instance the Soviet editors base their rectification on a dubious premise. Stravinsky recalled that in his youth he had admired Tanaev's *Mobile Counterpoint of the Strict School*, but this treatise appears not to have been published until 1909, by which date, the editors reason, the composer would have been beyond consulting a textbook. Yet Stravinsky was never above studying even the most elementary theoretical writings, and this was true throughout his life; at the age of seventy, for example, he was deeply influenced by Křenek's *Studies in Counterpoint*. Whatever Stravinsky's opinion of didactic music, he did not despise didactic books.

—

The addressees of Stravinsky's Russian letters include members of the Rimsky-Korsakov family, musicians, publishers, editors, artists of the Diaghilev circle, even government officials. To one of the latter, Commissar Arthur Lourié, Stravinsky wrote on September 9, 1920, asking for assistance in obtaining a visa for his mother to leave the U.S.S.R. and move to France; in later years Lourié became the composer's musical secretary and philosopher *éminence grise*. Here is another note to an official, this one the Commissariat of Education, which I quote because it reveals the composer trying to keep the door open and adds to the background of his return to Russia thirty-seven years later:

. . .

Owing to numerous prior engagements abroad, extending into the foreseeable future, I am unhappily obliged to decline your kind invitation to undertake a concert tour of Moscow, Leningrad, Kiev, and Odessa.

I thank you very much for your kind words, in any event, and I hope that in the future it will be possible personally to acquaint my countrymen with my art.

Pray accept, Madame, assurances of my utmost respect.

Igor Stravinsky
Paris, August 18, 1925

P.S.: Forgive me, Madame, for not answering you in Russian, but I do not have a typewriter with Russian letters.[8]

8. Diaghilev found one in London in August 1928, and made a gift of it to Stravinsky, who typed all of his own Russian letters thereafter, and who appears never to have made a typographical mistake.

Stravinsky's correspondence grew with his fame, of course, and by the twenties had reached unmanageable proportions. French superseded Russian as the language of the larger part of it, though important French letters were usually drafted in Russian. Moreover, most letters from the beginning of the French years until the end of his life were written with secretarial assistance, from which point they decline in interest. This is partly because the letters of the Russian years were not concerned with posterity, and because, as he grew older, his disputes with publishers, conductors, and critics consumed time that formerly might have been spent sharing artistic conceptions with friends.

The following pair of letters to C. F. Ramuz was written directly in French. I have chosen these two from the composer's vast correspondence because they show contradictory sides of his character as well as reveal the profound change in that character which took place when Russian influences began to give way to French. (Note that the letters are dated eight years apart.) In the first, he writes with gusto about his ill health, as he continued to do up to his eighty-eighth year. But he states his grievance immediately, whereas in the second letter his true feelings can be found only between the lines. The second letter is as circumspect and stingy with words, I might add, as the first was generous with them, but I offer only extracts from the first:

Carantec, Brittany
August 23, 1920

My dear Ramuz,

. . .

After my return to Carantec I had an attack of indigestion and it is only now that I feel well enough to write to you—on a disagreeable subject.

My role in *Histoire du Soldat* was not limited to composing music for a play that already existed. And yet one would deduce from the credits page that the *Soldier* could be played with other music, just as it could be acted (which goes without saying) in front of other decors. Is this how you now feel about it, Ramuz? I don't think it is, for you know only too well the part that I played in the development of the scenario; and that if a genuine collaboration had not existed between us, the "story" of the *Soldier* would be completely different. Do not construe this as a desire on my part to have my name placed next to yours when the text is published separately. As I wrote on my card, I merely suggest that this faulty first page be replaced with the page from the premiere program . . . This would be enough to suggest to the reader an intimate collaboration between *us* for *our Soldier*. I stand firm about this, my dear Ramuz, and it pains me a great deal, this unfortunate single page, which you have composed quite consciously and for your own reasons . . .

I await your prompt response . . .

Enough of this! I am sick of it all! How are you? Myself, I have felt rather poorly of late, and only sporadically normal. I don't know why, but I do know that the number of days when I feel well is regrettably small. People here (some acquaintances from Paris) bore me to death. Then, too, I can't say that I'm particularly fond of Brittany (in the way that I loved the Vaudois countryside!). The weather is always bad, and, so far as I'm concerned, bad weather is not French but English. Some of the peasants are good people, but peasants are good everywhere—even in Bochie! Why not, after all? The picturesque fatigues me, as do the races in the seaside village. The vacationing bourgeois come here because they can't afford Deauville. Not at all amusing, these people who promenade in the street and sing songs under our windows when we are resting—much louder than necessary; they think that being on vacation justifies their lack of restraint. I don't sleep much and I compose music.

Your Stravinsky

In the next letter Stravinsky acknowledges Ramuz's *Souvenirs sur Igor Stravinsky,* the contents of which have clearly surprised the composer, and not altogether agreeably. Perhaps I am reading too much into his answer because I know that he disliked the book and that he felt a private relationship had been exploited. But observe the adroitness with which he avoids the larger questions, while meeting the request for criticism with only two insignificant details:

December 16, 1928

Dear Ramuz,

I thank you with all my heart for your *Souvenirs,* of which volume three is as fine as the preceding ones.

These *Souvenirs* have touched me deeply: the *marc* of the past, once deposited, begins its geological life carefully covered over by new layers, and this *marc,* no less potent than those we have often drunk together in three quick swallows (your three volumes), has gone to my head—which is spinning, and which turns to you in gratitude for having kept these memories, dear to both of us, in so safe a place.* I am therefore astonished by your proposal that I add some "notes" to your text expressing my personal reactions.

Of course I have reactions, dear Ramuz; but when someone asks me, as you have just done, to write them down, I recoil like a snail into its shell, apprehensive that I will reveal too much. Let me explain: in this instance it is a question, you will agree, of making intelligent statements. Now everyone (myself included) can make intelligent statements; but if I am asked to write them down, to fix them, I am quickly overcome by anxiety. It takes skill to write, as you know very well, and I must admit to you that I have never trained myself to do it. Then, too, I confess that I am slightly lazy.

* Your bottle, which still seems to bear the label of the three bells, was delivered to me and was uncorked, as you predicted, by my *grand fils.*

But I will gladly satisfy you with a few remarks which you will find in the Post Script. Here they are:

1) It was not by "direct order from God" that Gogol wrote the second part of *Dead Souls,* but following the advice of his religious mentor, Father Rjevaki, a man of great spiritual qualities.

2) I have never lived in Candebec-sur-mer and, consequently, could never have written to you from there—a place not even mentioned in Larousse. Carantec does exist, however, and I wonder if you could have received my letter from there (in 1920, not 1921)?

3) Some other small errors are hardly worth mentioning.

Hoping that you will not be too angry by this somewhat evasive response, I humbly restrain myself from sending you any but the very best of *my "souvenirs."*

P.S. See my remarks above.

The letters from the American period contain no example comparable to the first of this pair addressed to Ramuz. Furthermore, the editorial difficulties presented by the American letters, because of the farrago of styles in both English and French and the ever-varying Americanisms, are almost insuperable. Stravinsky's principal scribe before 1947 was Mrs. Adolph Bolm, from which date and until 1969 the position was assumed by his son-in-law, an example of whose collaboration is apparent in a letter about Dylan Thomas published in the magazine *Adam* in 1954. Other letters of these years were written with my help, which is apparent in a note concerning Artur Schnabel written in 1961 and published in the *Observer.* Both missives say neither more nor less than what Stravinsky wanted them to say, but they lack the true mark of personality which can be given only by one's own writing and which *is* found in these letters to Ramuz, namely style.

—

The word "problems" in my title refers in part to certain perplexing areas in Stravinsky's life and work. Too many even to be enumerated here, they range from such large questions as his religious beliefs to a host of relatively minor ones. Among the latter, for instance, I would classify the gaps in our understanding of Stravinsky's musical origins, for the leap from academic anonymity into *The Firebird* is extraordinarily sudden. No doubt the Soviet publications, above all of the *Chant Funèbre* for Rimsky-Korsakov, if it is ever found, will be helpful. One would also like to know more about *Zvezdoliki*, that work so rich in possibilities which the composer did *not* develop, and so startlingly unlike any other, though its intervalic motto (a major second up, then a downward fourth) lies at the center of Stravinsky's music.

Still another area to be explored is that of the genesis of Stravinsky's subject matter. Andrey Rimsky-Korsakov broached this in the Russian magazine *Apollo*, No. I, 1915, remarking that Stravinsky had begun with the fairy tale and "progressed" to primitivism. But fairy tales were to remain a part of Stravinsky's imaginative world (in *Le Baiser de la Fée*), as was primitivism, though under the larger concept of ritual, both secular (*Les Noces*) and sacred (the *Mass*). To these he was to add morality plays (*Histoire du Soldat*, *The Rake's Progress*), myths (*Oedipus Rex*, *Perséphone*), and, finally, biblical drama (*The Flood*, *Abraham and Isaac*).

Stravinsky's obsession with the player piano is an enigma of a different kind, important only because the transcribing of virtually all of his music for this instrument, up to the mid-1920s, occupied such a disproportionate amount of his time and energy. But what continues to be enigmatic in these labors is his failure to exploit the machine's mechanical advantages, the composer never venturing to devise complex rhythms for it (by subdividing the beat beyond the possibilities of human performers, for instance) or even to employ such an effect as a *glissando* of the entire keyboard in the fraction of a second. His *Etude for Pianola* (1917) and the pianola part in the penultimate version of *Les Noces* (1919) use the contraption only to the extent of assuring a rigid rendition and of economizing on live pianists.

Stravinsky's "creative processes" are no less mysterious than those of any other great artist, but their patterns, when analyzed, often upset claims put forth by the composer himself. For example, he has said that as a rule his music was composed straight through, but his sketchbooks show that this was seldom the case and that he rarely began at the actual beginning. Thus the waltz variation in the Octet, which occurs midpoint in the piece (and is itself an unused episode from the *Symphonies of Wind Instruments*), was composed before the theme.

Stravinsky also stated that musical ideas always came to him in the timbres of particular instruments or voices, which he seldom changed in later stages. Yet his sketchbooks again contradict him. Thus, the String Concerto included winds in the original drafts, while the *Symphonies of Wind Instruments* actually featured violin and viola, in what later became the duos for flute and clarinet. This string duet was obviously a continuing idea from the Concertino for String Quartet (composed just before the *Symphonies*), with its violin and cello obbligati, and an idea—two solo string instruments in relief to a wind ensemble—to which he was to return when he arranged the Concertino for twelve instruments in 1952. For yet another example, the second section of the first movement of the four-hand Sonata was conceived, and even scored, as an orchestra piece, in which form it has nothing pianistic or percussive about it but might be an offshoot of the second movement of the Symphony in C.

A larger and more puzzling question than any of these is this: Why, at the end of 1944, did Stravinsky, a communicant of the Russian Orthodox Church, compose a Kyrie and a Gloria for a Roman Catholic Mass? It was not in fulfillment of a commission and had not been proposed to him. His avowed reason, that he was inspired to write a more liturgical kind of music than he found in Mozart's Masses, is hardly a complete answer. So far as musical influences enter into the question, he was engrossed at the time in all the music he could find by Jacopo da Bologna and Machaut. Yet this *Mass* is no mere exercise in musical style but a work born of religious faith.

Having lived close to Stravinsky for nearly a quarter of a century, and much of that time in the same house with him, I knew him to be, as the expression goes, "profoundly religious." What this means in his case, however, I am unable to say. He believed in the Devil Incarnate, and in a literal, Dantesque Hell, Purgatory, Paradise. And he was deeply superstitious, forever crossing himself and those around him, wearing sacred medals,[9] and performing compulsive acts without which the auguries for the day were certain to be unfavorable. Furthermore, he believed in miracles, both large and of the Houdini sort, and never questioned the provenance of any sacred relic. Dogmatism was another part of his religion, as it was of Stravinsky himself. (It is ironic that the opinions of this least syllogistic and, in method, least Socratic of men have appeared in the form of dialogues, yet that form is artificial, of course, and, even so, was closer to Hebrew versicle and response, in Stravinsky's mind, than to Platonic question and "answer.")

That Stravinsky had reached a spiritual crisis in 1944 is evident in his reading, which consisted of parts of the

9. An image of "La Vierge de Perpétuel Secours," with votary candle, stood in his home at 25 rue du Faubourg St-Honoré.

Summa, Bossuet's *Lettres sur l'Evangile,* Bloy, Bernanos, and T. S. Eliot.[10] In that year, too, Stravinsky visited Santa Clara, the Convent of Dominican Sisters in Sinsinawa, Wisconsin, and he was often with Jacques Maritain. At about the same time, the composer filled the margins of Ramuz's *Questions* with criticisms of its Protestantism, while endorsing the Roman Catholic views of C. A. Cingria in the margins of *his* books. Yet none of this accounts for the creation of that *Mass* for a church which Stravinsky never joined and which disappointed him by failing to use the work in its services.

But a more powerful force than dogma in Stravinsky was an abiding intellectual curiosity—an openness to ideas, an irresistible attraction to new ones, and a limitlessly receptive mind. Finally, the genius of his artistic instinct overrode all else.

10. He has underscored approvingly two passages in the essay "Catholicism and International Order," in his copy of *For Lancelot Andrewes.* Incidentally, he credited his reading of Eliot to Nadia Boulanger.

INDEX OF NAMES

A NOTE ON THE TYPE

This book was set on the Linotype in Bodoni Book, so called after Giambattista Bodoni (1740–1813), son of a printer of Piedmont. After gaining experience and fame as superintendent of the Press of the Propaganda in Rome, Bodoni became in 1768 the head of the ducal printing house at Parma, which he soon made the foremost of its kind in Europe. His *Manuale Tipografico*, completed by his widow in 1818, contains 279 pages of specimens of types, including alphabets of about thirty languages. His editions of Greek, Latin, Italian, and French classics are celebrated for their typography. In type designing he was an innovator, making his new faces rounder, wider, and lighter, with greater openness and delicacy.

Composed, printed, and bound by
The Book Press, Brattleboro, Vermont.
Typography and binding design by Clint Anglin.